The Financial Times Guide
Inheritance Tax, Probate
nd Estate Planning

FT Prentice Hall
FINANCIAL TIMES

In an increasingly competitive world, we believe it's quality of thinking that will give you the edge – an idea that opens new doors, a technique that solves a problem, or an insight that simply makes sense of it all. The more you know, the smarter and faster you can go.

That's why we work with the best minds in business and finance to bring cutting-edge thinking and best learning practice to a global market.

Under a range of leading imprints, including *Financial Times Prentice Hall*, we create world-class print publications and electronic products bringing our readers knowledge, skills and understanding, which can be applied whether studying or at work.

To find out more about Pearson Education publications, or tell us about the books you'd like to find, you can visit us at
www.pearsoned.co.uk

The Financial Times Guide to Inheritance Tax, Probate and Estate Planning

Amanda Fisher

**Financial Times
Prentice Hall**
is an imprint of

Harlow, England • London • New York • Boston • San Francisco • Toronto • Sydney • Singapore • Hong Kong
Tokyo • Seoul • Taipei • New Delhi • Cape Town • Madrid • Mexico City • Amsterdam • Munich • Paris • Milan

PEARSON EDUCATION LIMITED

Edinburgh Gate
Harlow CM20 2JE
Tel: +44 (0)1279 623623
Fax: +44 (0)1279 431059
Website: www.pearsoned.co.uk

First published in Great Britain in 2010

© Pearson Education Limited 2010

The right of Amanda Fisher to be identified as author of this work has been asserted by her in accordance with the Copyright, Designs and Patents Act 1988.

Pearson Education is not responsible for the content of third party internet sites.

ISBN: 978-0-273-72996-9

Crown Copyright material is reproduced with the permission of the Controller of HMSO and the Queen's Printer for Scotland under the terms of the Click-Use Licence.

British Library Cataloguing-in-Publication Data
A catalogue record for this book is available from the British Library

Library of Congress Cataloging-in-Publication Data
Fisher, Amanda.
   The financial times guide to inheritance tax, probate and estate planning / Amanda Fisher.
      p. cm.
   Includes bibliographical references and index.
   ISBN 978-0-273-72996-9 (pbk. : alk. paper)
   1. Probate law and practice--Great Britain--Popular works. 2. Estate planning--Great Britain--Popular works. I. Title.
   KD1518.F57 2010
   346.4105'6--dc22
                                        2010025976

10 9 8 7 6 5 4 3 2 1
14 13 12 11 10

Typeset in 9pt Stone Serif by 3
Printed and bound in Great Britain by Ashford Colour Press Ltd, Gosport

Contents

Preface

This book will guide you through all aspects of inheritance tax, the organisation of financial affairs, tax-efficient estate planning and will offer help to people who are faced with managing the events following the death of someone. Its aim is also to inspire and encourage people to put their own financial affairs in order and at least make a will so that, in the event of their own death, life will be easier for those left to manage events.

Dealing with the death of a friend or a relative can be a traumatic time and it is not unusual to be in a situation where you are not only coming to terms with the event, but finding there is a lot to sort out such as the property and the paperwork of the person who has died. There is also a perception that dealing with the paperwork and administration surrounding someone's death can be very difficult, not just in terms of the legalities that must be dealt with, but also knowing even where to start.

This book has been written with the intention of easing that situation by helping those left to deal with the death, the funeral and the administration of the estate. It takes you through the stages of what needs to be done when someone has died, ranging from registering the death in the first instance, to applying for probate and finally completing all the administration of the estate, passing on the property of the deceased to those that are to benefit.

The book also gives an insight into the advantages of making a will. Most people haven't made a will, so that if they should die, the rules of intestacy would apply, which can be very different to the intended wishes. On reading this book, it will become apparent that drawing up a will not only leaves clear instructions on who should benefit, but will leave guidance and wishes on how children should be cared for and how the funeral should be conducted. A will can provide vital support to those left after a death, just in the knowledge that matters are being taken care of in the way the deceased would have wished.

The final part offers some guidance on lifetime planning and how to save inheritance tax, which can be significant in some cases. Simply by reviewing your assets and drawing up a will that ensures your estate is left in a tax-efficient manner can save a huge amount of potential inheritance tax on death.

A note on jurisdiction

This guide aims to cover the inheritance tax, probate and estate planning matters across the UK. However, it should be noted that there are sometimes differences in the laws and procedures in England and Wales, Scotland and Northern Ireland. Therefore, to provide a concise and informative guide and accommodate these differences, the book has been written in accordance with the laws and procedures for England and Wales, which very often include Scotland and Northern Ireland, but has mentioned any variations for Scotland and Northern Ireland, mainly at the end of each chapter, where relevant.

If a reader is in any doubt about the law and procedures for Scotland and Northern Ireland, there are helpful links to further information that will assist the reader to obtain the relevant knowledge.

It has not been possible to stretch the guide to cover the laws and procedures for the Channel Islands or Isle of Man.

The application for probate

1

Registering a death

This chapter will guide the reader on how to formally register a death

- When and where to register a death
- If the death is referred to a coroner
- Who can register a death?
- Documents and information you will need to register a death
- Documents you will receive once the death has been registered
- Removing a body from England or Wales
- When someone dies abroad
- Registering a death for Scottish residents
- Registering a death for residents of Northern Ireland

When someone dies, it can be a daunting and devastating time for the friends and family of the individual, yet despite this there are matters that must be taken care of almost immediately. Registering the death is one of those matters that has to be done as soon as possible, and usually within five days.

The Directgov website has a link which you can use to help register a death, depending on the circumstances. The interactive tool gives instructions on how to register the death, tailored to the situation: www.direct.gov.uk/bereavement_radio.dsb?pro=BDT

When and where to register a death

In England and Wales, a death must normally be registered with a register office within five days.

The death must be registered in the district where the person died. It is best to go to the register office in the area, because if the death is registered in another district it may take longer to obtain the necessary documents, which can delay the funeral arrangements. Registering the death will usually only take about thirty minutes, however it is necessary to make an appointment in advance of visiting the register office.

The local register office can be found in the telephone book, or you can use the following link via the government website:
http://maps/direct.gov.uk/LDGRedirect/MapAction.do?ref=grolight

A death can only be registered once you have the following:

■ Medical Cause of Death Certificate from the doctor;

■ or, in the case of a death reported to the **coroner** as detailed below, confirmation from the coroner's office that the relevant paperwork has been issued to the register office. If there is an inquest, or the death has to be referred to the coroner, the coroner's officer or registrar will advise you.

If the death is referred to a coroner

There are sometimes instances where the cause of a death may be unclear, sudden or suspicious such as:

■ an accident or injury;

■ an industrial disease;

■ during a surgical operation;

■ if the cause of death is unknown;

■ if the death is sudden or unexpected.

In these cases, the emergency staff, doctor or hospital registrar will report the death to the coroner, who is the person who must then decide whether any further investigation, an inquest, is necessary. The relatives are notified by the coroner that an inquest is taking place.

Sometimes, a **post-mortem** is carried out at this time, which is a medical examination of the body to find out the cause of death. This can be done without the permission of the relatives.

If referral to a coroner has been necessary, the death cannot be registered at the register office until the coroner's decision has been made and, because this can sometimes take some time, the death may not be able to be registered until after the five days. However, the responsibility for registering the death is usually then taken on by the coroner and once a decision has been made as to the cause of death, the death certificate is often issued directly by the coroner to allow the funeral to take place. If there is likely to be a delay in determining the cause of death, perhaps because the inquest has been adjourned, a temporary death certificate stating the fact of death will be issued to enable the funeral to take place and for steps to be taken to administer the estate.

Who can register a death?

If the person died in a house or hospital, the death can be registered by:

- a relative;
- someone present at the death;
- an occupant of the house;
- an official from the hospital – the hospital staff would normally contact the person named by the deceased as the next of kin. The body is kept in the hospital mortuary until the **executor** arranges for it to be taken away;
- the person making the arrangements with the funeral directors. Most funeral directors have a chapel of rest in which the deceased will be held, pending the funeral.

If the death occurred anywhere else, it can be registered by:

- a relative;
- someone present at the death;
- the person who found the body;
- the person in charge of the body;
- the person making the arrangements with the funeral directors.

Most deaths are registered by a relative. The registrar would normally only allow other people to register a death if there are no relatives available.

Stillbirths

A stillbirth is different in that it normally needs to be registered within forty-two days, and at the latest within three months. In most cases this is done either at the hospital or at the local register office. Advice on registering a stillbirth can be found on the government website, using the following link: www.direct.gov.uk/en/Governmentcitizensandrights/Registeringlifeevents/ Birthandadoptionrecords/Registeringorchangingabirthrecord/DG_175614

Documents and information you will need to register a death

When registering a death with the register office, you'll need to take the following:

- the medical certificate showing the cause of death (signed by a doctor);
- or, in the case of a death reported to the coroner, confirmation from the coroner's office that the relevant paperwork has been issued to the register office.

Other helpful documents of the deceased person to take with you will include:

- birth certificate;
- passport;
- marriage/civil partnership certificates;
- NHS Medical Card, if available.

The registrar will also need the following information:

- the person's full name at time of death;
- any names previously used, including their maiden surname, if applicable;
- the person's date and place of birth (town and county if born in the UK and country if born abroad);
- their last address;
- their occupation;
- the full name, date of birth and occupation of a surviving spouse or civil partner;
- whether they were receiving a state pension or any other state benefit.

The registrar will enter all these details into a register and it is important that you check the information very carefully before signing, as any mistakes are difficult to alter later. If there is an error made in making the entry into the register, details can be changed or added. Ideally the person who registered the death should arrange this with the office where the death was registered. You may be asked to provide documentary evidence to prove an error was made.

Documents you will receive once the death has been registered

If a post-mortem is not being carried out, after the relevant information has been written into the death register, the registrar will issue the necessary forms and certificates:

- a 'green form'. This is a Certificate for Burial or Cremation, giving permission for the body to be buried, or permission for an application for cremation to be made.
- a form BD8 – this is a certificate for the Benefits Agency. This should be completed, if any benefits or state pensions were received by the deceased, and sent to the Benefits Agency as soon as possible so that any payments can be cancelled.
- A Death Certificate. Additional copies can be obtained for an additional small charge.

The death certificates are needed by the personal representatives dealing with the deceased's estate. For example, they are sent to all the financial institutions that hold any of the deceased's assets, so that details of the assets can be provided to the personal representatives administering the estate.

It is recommended that a number of death certificates are purchased from the register office at this time so that a certificate can be sent to more than one financial institution at the same time, rather than wait for the one death certificate to be dealt with several times. This would help to speed up the administration considerably.

If a post-mortem is needed, the coroner will issue any necessary documents as quickly as possible afterwards.

Removing a body from England or Wales

There is no restriction on moving a body within England and Wales. However, if you need to move a body to Scotland, Northern Ireland, the Isle of Man, the Channel Islands or overseas, then the coroner for the district from which the body is being moved needs to be notified. To do this, you will need a form, which can be obtained from the coroner or registrar. You will then need to give the completed form to the coroner, and enclose any certificate for burial or cremation that has been issued to you. The coroner will acknowledge receiving that notice, and will let you know when the body can be moved. This is usually four clear days from when the notice was received. However, in urgent situations, the process can usually be speeded up.

When someone dies abroad

When an individual dies abroad, the death may seem more complicated and distressing because of being away from the UK and dealing with unfamiliar procedures, but you can get help from the British authorities in the UK and overseas. The death will need to be registered according to the local regulations in the country where the individual has died, and a death certificate will need to be obtained. The local police, British consulate (or tour guide, if applicable) will be able to advise on this. They can also help with arranging a funeral overseas, and offer support and guidance if there is to be an inquest. For guidance on deaths that have occurred overseas, the usual link is:

www.direct.gov.uk/en/Governmentcitizensandrights/Death/
WhatToDoAfterADeath/DG_10029476

Bringing the body home to the UK

If the body of the deceased is to be brought back to the UK, you can find help and guidance from staff at the British consulate, who will be able to put you in touch with an international funeral director. The body will need to be embalmed and placed in a zinc-lined coffin before it can be removed from the country. This may take some time, especially if a post-mortem examination is held.

To bring the body back home to the UK, several documents will be needed, and this depends on whether or not a post-mortem has taken place.

If no post-mortem has taken place:

- a certified English translation of the foreign death certificate from the country in which the person died. This will need to be taken to the register office in the UK where the funeral is to take place. The register office will then give the authority for the funeral to go ahead;
- authorisation to remove the deceased's body from the country;
- a certificate of embalming.

The British consulate can help to arrange the above documentation.

If a post-mortem has taken place, the coroner will issue either a Certificate E for Cremation, if a cremation will take place, or an Order for Burial.

Travel insurance

It would be worth checking the individual's travel insurance, if there was some in place, to see if any of the costs of the funeral or any additional expenses caused by the death taking place abroad are covered. If there is no insurance cover, these costs will need to be paid, including hospital bills and repatriation (bringing home) of the body and possessions.

Registering a death for Scottish residents

The following link for the General Register Office for Scotland can provide advice:
www.gro-scotland.gov.uk/regscot/registering-a-death.html

A death that occurs in Scotland must be registered within eight days, and can be registered in any registration district in Scotland. An appointments system is operated and it is recommended that you contact the register office before arrival so that an appointment can be made. You can obtain the address of the local registrar from the local telephone book, or using the following link:
www.gro-scotland.gov.uk/regscot/groslocate/index.html

Who can register a death in Scotland?

The death can be registered by any of the following:

- any relative of the deceased;
- any person present when the person died;

■ the deceased's executor or other legal representative;

■ the occupier of the property where the person died;

■ anyone else who knows the information to be registered.

The documents that should be taken to the registrar are no different to those needed for deaths in England or Wales, detailed above.

When the registration is complete, the registrar will give you:

■ a certificate of registration of death for production to the person in charge of the burial ground or crematorium;

■ a Social Security registration or notification of death certificate for use in obtaining or adjusting benefits;

■ an abbreviated extract (i.e. excluding cause of death and parentage details) of the death entry. You can obtain a full extract of the death entry for a fee.

For further advice, there is a booklet published by the Scottish Government that can be obtained from:
www.scotland.gov.uk/Resource/Doc/213661/0056769.pdf

The booklet can also be obtained from the Scottish register offices on 0131 244 2193.

Registering a death for residents of Northern Ireland

The following link is for the General Register Office for Northern Ireland and can provide useful advice:
www.groni.gov.uk/

A death that occurs in Northern Ireland must be registered within five days, except where the matter has been referred to the coroner, and can be registered with:

■ the registrar in the district where the individual died; or

■ the registrar in the district where the individual usually lived.

You can obtain the address of the local registrar from the local telephone book, or using the following link:
www.groni.gov.uk/index/district-registrars-offices.htm

Who can register a death in Northern Ireland?

In Northern Ireland, the death can be registered by:

■ Any relative of the deceased who has knowledge of the details required to be registered (this includes a relative by marriage).

■ A person present at the death.

■ A person taking care of the funeral arrangements.

■ The executor or **administrator** of the deceased's estate.

■ The occupier, at the time of death, of the premises in which the death occurred.

■ A person finding the body.

■ A person taking charge of the body.

To register the death in Northern Ireland, a medical certificate of cause of death will be needed, which is issued by a doctor who has treated the deceased within twenty-eight days before the date of death. If the deceased had not been seen by a doctor within that period or where the death was not caused by natural illness the case would have to be referred to the coroner – the registrar or funeral director will advise you.

When the registration is complete, the registrar will give you two documents:

■ A form GRO 21 which permits the burial or cremation to take place.

■ A form 36 for production to the Social Security offices regarding benefits.

As usual, if a death has been referred to the coroner, funeral arrangements should not be made before the consent of the coroner has been obtained. The death can be registered and a Death Certificate issued only after the registrar has received the necessary certificate from the coroner.

Once the registrar's office receives the appropriate form they will contact a relative of the deceased and ask them to call and register the death in the usual way. It is wise to apply for additional death certificates so that the administration can be dealt with more easily and it is considerably cheaper to apply for them at this stage of the process than at a later date.

2

Other matters to address when someone has died

This chapter covers matters to be taken care of in addition to registering the death

- Arranging to see the deceased's solicitor or other professional adviser and the reading of any will
- Arranging a funeral
- Making sure that everyone who needs to know is informed
- Checking whether all benefits are being claimed
- Starting to collect information and documents

Arranging to see the deceased's solicitor or other professional adviser and the reading of any will

This is an important task in the days following a death because, if there is a **will**, it is likely to say if there are any special funeral wishes. It is vital to know the requests of the deceased so that these can be taken into account. The will also states who the executors are. It is essential to know this so that attempts can be made to deal with the estate as soon as possible.

If no will is in place, then executors will not have been appointed. **Personal representatives** will then be nominated to take on the role of dealing with the estate. There is more about personal representatives in Chapter 3.

Arranging a funeral

If the individual has left a will, it is likely that instructions or special wishes are detailed, about how they would like their funeral carried out, or what should happen to their body. If there are no clear wishes it is generally up to the executor or the personal representatives to make these decisions.

The date for a funeral cannot be determined until after the death has been registered. If the death has to be reported to the coroner, for reasons discussed in Chapter 1, then this could take a little longer and this should be taken into account.

The legal requirements regarding funerals in the UK are:

■ The death has to have been certified and registered.

■ The body has to be properly taken care of, either by burial or cremation.

Many people choose to use a professional funeral director and they will be able to help with the arrangements. Families and friends may know of a firm of funeral directors that they could recommend, perhaps if they have used one in the past. Otherwise, most local funeral directors would be listed in the telephone directory or online. It would be a good idea to contact a few firms before a decision is made, unless of course the deceased has indicated who they would like the funeral to be carried out by.

Most funeral directors are members of one of two trade associations, either the National Association of Funeral Directors (www.nafd.org.uk) or the National Society of Allied and Independent Funeral Directors (www.saif. org.uk). It is recommended that you check that the funeral director of your choice is registered with one of these professional bodies. Members of these organisations must provide you with a quote and are not permitted to exceed the fees quoted, without permission or agreement.

There are a number of things to consider when planning the funeral. There may also be other wishes of the individual and there may be contributions that the members of the family may want to add. The funeral director can help with these matters, but you will need to consider:

■ Where the body should rest before the funeral.

■ The time and the place of the funeral.

■ The type of service required and arranging for this to be carried out.

■ How much to spend on the funeral.

- Whether to have flowers at the funeral.
- How to donate money to a chosen charity.
- Notice in the newspapers.
- Notifying those who may wish to attend the funeral.

Provided there are no special requests in the individual's will, it is possible to arrange a funeral without the help of a funeral director. If you wish to do this, you would need to contact the cemeteries and crematorium department of your local authority for advice and guidance. You can also get help and information from the Natural Death Centre (www.naturaldeath.org.uk).

Funerals outside England and Wales

You will need permission from the coroner in the local district before a body can be moved out of England and Wales, including abroad. In such cases, the coroner would require at least four working days before the body of the deceased is to be moved. The coroner would issue a removal notice (form 104), part of which is sent to the Registrar of Births, Deaths and Marriages. The rules are complicated but the coroner's office will be able to provide help and information in this situation.

If the funeral costs cannot be paid

When a funeral director is instructed to take care of some or all of the funeral arrangements, this would be a contract, or legally binding agreement to pay for the services provided. If you are the executor or personal representative of the estate, you should do this only if there are sufficient funds in the estate to pay for the funeral. If you fail to do this you will be liable for any of the balance of the fees that are not covered by the estate of the deceased. However, if there is not enough money in the estate to pay for the funeral and you are receiving a means-tested benefit, you may be eligible for a Funeral Payment grant.

If you are arranging a funeral, you may be eligible for a Funeral Payment from the Social Fund if you or your partner are getting any of the following benefits or tax credits:

- Income Support;
- Income-based Jobseeker's Allowance;
- Income-related Employment and Support Allowance;

▪ Pension Credit;

▪ Housing Benefit;

▪ Council Tax Benefits;

▪ Working Tax Credit (which includes a disability or severe disability element);

▪ Child Tax Credit at a rate higher than the family element.

The amount of assistance depends on the benefits you are receiving and the relationship with the person who has died. In addition, consideration is given to any other money, other than your personal savings, that may be available to help with the cost of the funeral. You might have to repay some or all of it from the estate of the person who died. The following link will take you to the brochure and application form that you will need to complete for financial assistance:
www.dwp.gov.uk/advisers/claimforms/sf200_print.pdf

Making sure that everyone who needs to know is informed

As well as informing people who are close to the person, there may be others who would benefit from knowing about the death of the individual. These may include relatives, friends, employers, school, solicitor, accountant and doctor.

If the individual was self-employed, it would be important to notify the relevant offices:

▪ The tax office that dealt with the deceased's tax affairs.

▪ The national insurance contributions office to cancel Class 2 NIC payments.

If the individual was in receipt of child benefits or tax credits you will need to notify the child benefit office (within eight weeks of the death) and the child tax credits office.

Other government offices to notify include:

▪ local authority, council tax department;

▪ local authority if they rented a property;

▪ UK Identity and Passport Service;

■ DVLA – to return any driving licence;

■ DVLA – to change ownership of a car, or cancel car tax.

Utilities, household contacts and financial organisations that need to be informed include:

■ gas and electricity providers;

■ water utilities;

■ Royal Mail, if post needs re-directing;

■ TV licensing;

■ telephone and internet companies;

■ house insurance company. Be careful that you don't cancel any insurance that is still required, but it is advisable to inform the insurance company of the death. The insurer may impose special terms if the house is unoccupied;

■ car insurance company. Again, be careful that you don't cancel any insurance that is still required, but it is advisable to inform the insurance company of the death;

■ travel insurance;

■ medical insurance;

■ any company that was providing a loan or credit cards to the deceased;

■ pension providers;

■ life insurance companies;

■ banks and building societies;

■ mortgage provider.

Note that there may be direct debits paid to organisations by the individual that has died, or there may be subscriptions or insurances that may need to be cancelled.

Checking whether all benefits are being claimed

When a husband, wife or civil partner has died, the remaining partner may be entitled to benefits:

■ Bereavement Payment;

■ Bereavement Allowance;

■ Widowed Parent's Allowance (form BB1).

The entitlement to these benefits will depend on the national insurance contributions paid by the deceased before they died and these benefits are available in England, Scotland and Wales only. If you believe you may be entitled, you should visit your nearest Jobcentre Plus office and complete the relevant application forms. The following link will take you to the full guidance brochure and application form for either of the above benefits: www.dwp.gov.uk/advisers/claimforms/bb1_print.pdf

The **Bereavement Payment** is a lump sum of £2,000. It is based on your late husband, wife or civil partner's national insurance contributions record. You may be able to claim this payment if your husband, wife or civil partner had paid their national insurance contributions (NICs) or their death was caused by their job and either:

■ you were under state pension age (60 for women and 65 for men) when they died; or

■ your husband, wife or civil partner was not entitled to Category A state retirement benefit when they died.

When you fill in the claim form you'll be asked to give your late husband, wife or **civil partner**'s national insurance number and details of their recent employment history. This will allow the office that deals with your claim to look into their national insurance record and to work out if you qualify for the Bereavement Payment. The time limit for claiming the payment is now twelve months following the death of the spouse or civil partner.

The **Bereavement Allowance** (which used to be call the Widow's Pension) is a regular payment, paid for fifty-two weeks from the bereavement, and is based on your late husband or wife's national insurance contributions. Bereavement Allowance (standard rate) is £97.65 a week for 2010–11 and changes each year. It is important to check your availability to this benefit as soon as possible because claims can only be backdated for three months. The applications are dated when the office gets them.

The **Widowed Parent's Allowance** may be available if you are a parent and your husband, wife or civil partner has died and you have a dependent child or a young person for whom you receive Child Benefit. The allowance is £97.65 a week for 2010–11 and changes each year. Again, claims for this benefit can only be backdated for three months. The applications are dated when the office gets them.

State pension

If both you and your husband, wife or civil partner were getting the basic state pension when they died, you may be able to use their national insurance contributions to get extra basic pension.

Starting to collect information and documents

If there is a will, the executor will be named in the will as the person to deal with the estate.

If there is no will, then an executor will not have been appointed and it will need to be decided who will apply to sort out the deceased's estate. The person that this role is likely to be carried out by is detailed further in Chapter 3. It will be necessary to contact the **Probate Registry** to apply for **letters of administration**.

In either case, the executors or personal representatives will need to start dealing with the estate and there will inevitably be a considerable amount of information that they will require. It is therefore useful to make a start on collecting the information that will be required. Some of the personal information will include:

- National Insurance number;
- NHS number;
- date and place of birth;
- date of marriage or civil partnership (if appropriate);
- tax reference number.

Chapter 6 covers obtaining the details of the **assets** and **liabilities** of the estate and how to take this forward through the probate application.

3

The duties of executors and administrators

This chapter covers the legal rights and responsibilities in dealing with an estate

- If a will was left by the deceased
- If no will was left by the deceased
- Duties of the personal representatives
- Getting professional help
- Duties under Scottish law

The person or persons who deal with the deceased's **estate** will depend on whether a will was made or not. They have a legal right and responsibility to deal with the estate.

If a will was left by the deceased

If a will was left, then executors will be named in the will. The **testator** (person) who made the will would have given thought as to whom they would like to take responsibility for their estate on their death and nominated these persons in their will. If they are nominated as executors, it is their responsibility to start dealing with the estate.

Normally, the testator would ask these named individuals at the time of making the will, but this is not always the case. If the named executor is not aware of this responsibility and/or decides that they are not able to do this, then they are under no obligation. They can step down. However, testators cannot step down once they have committed themselves by starting to deal with the estate.

The executors act in a fiduciary relationship and therefore are not able to make a profit out of this role. However, sometimes professional individuals are appointed and in this case, a charging clause must be included in the will. A beneficiary of a will can act as an executor. However, a witness to a will cannot be a beneficiary.

If nominated executors die before the testator or are unable or unwilling to act, the nearest surviving relative of the testator can apply for letters of administration, but the will remains valid. There are commonly two executors who will act together, but there may only be one and there can be as many as four. You may also hear the term executrix which is the female equivalent of executor.

If no will was left by the deceased

If no will was left by the deceased, then no individuals have been nominated to take the responsibility of dealing with the estate. These individuals therefore have to be appointed and agreed; they are not called executors, but they are the **administrators** of the estate. The law specifies who is entitled to be an administrator and this is covered by the Administration of Estates Act 1925.

The person who will administer the estate is the closest living relative to the deceased person, chosen in the following order:

1 The husband, wife or civil partner of the person who has died.
2 The deceased's children (aged over 18) or their children's descendants (for example, grandchildren, if they are over 18).
3 The deceased's parents.
4 The deceased's brothers or sisters with the same mother and father, or descendants of the brothers or sisters.
5 The deceased's half-brothers or half-sisters or their descendants.
6 The deceased's grandparents.
7 The deceased's uncles and aunts 'of the whole blood' (this means brothers and sisters of their parents, as long as they had the same mother and father themselves) or their descendants.
8 The deceased's uncles and aunts 'of the half blood' (this means

brothers and sisters of their parents who had only the same mother or father) or their descendants.

9 The Crown (the state) if there are no relatives.

Note that there may still be decisions to make. For example, if more than one person has an equal right to deal with the estate (such as brothers and sisters), the letters of administration would normally be given to the first of these people who applies. More than one person can be appointed as an administrator. If the deceased individual has several brothers or sisters who all want to be in charge of the funeral or administration and they cannot agree about this themselves, they must apply to the Probate Registry, which will decide who will take responsibility. This process can be complex and it is advisable to seek help from a solicitor. Any legal dispute costs a lot of money and takes time to resolve. The costs will probably be taken out of the estate, if the court agrees to this. You may hear the term administratrix and this is female equivalent of administrator.

Anyone that has the right to act as an administrator can apply to the Probate Registry for a grant of letters of administration, which allows the person to deal with the estate. You will find the local office of the Probate Registry in the local telephone directory, or using this website: www.hmcourts-service.gov.uk/infoabout/civil/probate/registries.htm

Duties of the personal representatives

The term personal representative refers to both executors and administrators. They are responsible for the affairs of the deceased after his or her death. To carry out these duties it will usually be necessary to obtain a document known as a **grant of representation**. The representatives must administer and wind up the deceased's estate, which includes several duties.

The first task is to determine the assets and liabilities of the estate. This would include arranging for the estate to be valued and obtaining details of all the debts of the estate.

Next, comes obtaining probate or letters of administration. In all but the most straightforward estates it is necessary for the personal representatives to apply to the Probate Registry for the grant of representation. When there is a will, this is usually described as the **grant of probate**. Probate is the final proof of the validity of the will which then gives authority (essentially from the will) to the executors, to deal with the distribution of the property. When there are no executors, it is a grant of letters of administration.

Administrators gain their authority from the court and the letters of admin-istration give them the permission they need to deal with the property.

Another task is to collect in the assets of the estate and pay the liabilities of the deceased. The personal representatives can take charge of the house and possessions of the person who has died, unless it passes automatically to a joint owner, thus protecting the estate before this is distributed. Where the deceased lived alone in his or her own house, the representatives should ensure it is secure and consider moving any valuable contents into safe-keeping. They should also check that insurance is in place.

Then, there may be tax liabilities to settle. The estate is subject to income tax and capital gains tax as a separate entity and the representatives must make appropriate tax returns. The personal representatives are responsible for calculating any inheritance tax and ensuring this is paid to HM Revenue and Customs. However, the administration of most estates in the UK does not result in the payment of any inheritance tax, for reasons that will be covered in later chapters.

Once these tasks are complete, the distribution of the estate to the benefi-ciaries in accordance with the terms of the will or the intestacy rules can begin. The personal representatives must administer the estate's assets with due care and for the benefit of the estate's beneficiaries.

As well as the duties and responsibilities of managing the estate, there may be practical matters for the personal representatives to deal with in the days following the death:

■ The deceased's personal representatives are responsible for arranging the funeral. This is often done in consultation with the deceased's family.

■ If a person has died leaving a valid will, the executors can normally arrange the funeral straight away.

■ The personal representatives should also check the deceased's will to see if the deceased left any special wishes or any funeral directions.

■ They should notify the deceased's bank of his death and cancel any standing orders and direct debits.

Getting professional help

If you are a personal representative acting for an estate, you are either a nominated executor or an administrator instructed by a probate registry.

Either way, you will be personally liable if you do not manage the estate correctly and responsibly, for instance, if you distributed the assets of the estate incorrectly, or underestimated the amount of inheritance tax payable to HM Revenue and Customs.

If the estate is complex it may be preferable to use a solicitor or other professional experienced in estate matters to help deal with the responsibilities. Help in finding professional help can be found in various ways. If you do not have a solicitor, the local phone directory may be a good place to start. Another source is websites; try search terms such as 'probate solicitor' and the town where you live. This should produce a good range of options.

Recommendation may be a better option – perhaps there is a solicitor or other professional that you know of, who has assisted someone you know. There is also the Law Society on 0870 606 6575 (www.lawsociety.org.uk) or the Society of Trust and Estate Practitioners on 020 7340 0500 (www.step. org). Costs may vary, so it is recommended that a few firms are consulted and quotes obtained.

Duties under Scottish law

Different rules apply to the administration of an estate in Scotland.

If a will was left by the deceased, then an executor named in the will is described as the executor-nominative.

If no will was left then an administrator will still have to be appointed, and they are described as an executor-dative.

In both cases, the personal representative above must be approved by the court under a process called **confirmation**, which is the Scottish equivalent of applying for probate or letters of administration. Until confirmation, the powers of the personal representatives are limited – and confirmation is only available once any inheritance tax is paid.

Executors appointed by the court are normally required to provide a bond of caution that guarantees they will carry out their duties and responsibilities. This usually means that a solicitor or other professional will be involved as insurers will not provide the necessary cover unless such professionals are involved.

Otherwise, all duties and responsibilities are the same as in England and Wales, such as determining the assets and liabilities, paying all tax liabilities and distributing the estate to the correct beneficiaries.

4

Consideration of the validity of a will

This chapter details the conditions that must be met for a will to be valid

- The conditions for a will to be valid
- The testator
- Witnesses to a will
- Revocation of a will
- Codicils
- Other matters
- What to do if a will is thought to be invalid
- What to do if a will is thought to be unfair
- Wills under Scottish law

The administration and distribution of an estate depends upon whether or not there is a valid will. If anyone believes that an individual who has died has left a will, but no one can find it, you can take steps to find out if they made one, such as:

- Searching the property and belongings of the person who has died for any evidence that they made a will.
- Contacting solicitors or other professionals the person might have used to check whether they are aware of a will being made.

■ Applying to the Principal Probate Registry to see if a will has been registered.

If there is a valid will, the executors, as the personal representatives, must follow the directions it contains, once probate has been granted. If no will exists, the deceased is said to have died intestate and the requirements of the Administration of Estates Act 1925 apply. In this case, the estate will be dealt with and distributed under the rules of intestacy.

The conditions for a will to be valid

A will is a legal declaration of how you wish to dispose of your property on your death and there are conditions that must be met for a will to be valid:

■ The document must be in writing, either handwritten or typed.

■ The will must be made by an individual (testator) who is capable of making a will.

■ The will must be signed by the testator.

■ The will must be dated when it is signed.

■ The signing of the will must be witnessed by two witnesses.

■ The will must not have been revoked.

The testator

The testator must be at least 18 years old. The only exception to this is if they have privileged status, such as those who are in the armed forces.

Furthermore, the testator must be mentally capable of making a will. This means:

■ The testator must have sound mind and understand the nature of the act of making a will.

■ The testator must have knowledge, at least in general terms, of what is in their estate.

■ There must also have been sound understanding of the content of the will. For instance, the testator must be fully aware of how the estate would be distributed and any consequences this would entail.

If a will is being drawn up and the mental capacity of the testator is under any doubt whatsoever, it is always recommended to obtain a doctor's opinion or testimonial. Under the provisions of the Mental Health Act 1983, the Court of Protection may approve the making of a will, or a **codicil** to a will for someone who is mentally incapable of doing so themselves. It is always recommended to seek professional or legal advice in these cases.

If a blind or illiterate person wants to make a will, further advice should also be sought from professionals who are experienced in these cases to ensure the will is valid. This is to avoid the risk that some of the conditions may be questioned, such as the testator understanding what is actually in the will they are signing. The following is a link to the website for Action for the Blind, where special guidance is given to blind people wanting to make a will: www.actionforblindpeople.org.uk

It is important that the will has not been written or signed under undue influence, or pressure from another individual. If it is suspected that a testator made a will under pressure, or threat, from another, it is rendered invalid.

Witnesses to a will

For a will to be valid, the testator's signature must have been witnessed by two people. The testator should sign the will in the presence of the two witnesses.

Any person who is over eighteen can act as a witness to the signing of a will, provided:

▦ they are not blind;

▦ they are mentally capable and understand their role as a witness, though it is not necessary for them to read the will or know its terms;

▦ are not the testator's spouse, civil partner or anyone who is a beneficiary of executor under the will.

If the testator's spouse or civil partner or a beneficiary witnessed the signing of the will, this wouldn't invalidate the will, but they would lose their legacies.

Revocation of a will

Revocation of a will can happen in the following ways:

▦ A will may be revoked by a later will. This is not automatic but a well worded will should usually begin with a clause revoking all previous wills.

▥ A will may have been deliberately destroyed. For instance, the testator may choose to burn or rip up the will.

▥ A will can be revoked by marriage. The exception is if a will is made in contemplation of the testator's marriage. This includes the registration of a civil partnership.

▥ Divorce does not revoke a will. However, the former spouse can no longer benefit as a beneficiary to the estate following the divorce. If the will also nominates the former spouse as an executor, this will no longer apply. The dissolution of a civil partnership is also treated as divorce.

Codicils

Changes and additions should not be made to the will once it has been signed and witnessed, unless these are done by a separate document that is itself, signed and witnessed. This would then act as a supplement to your will. If the changes or additions are significant or numerous, it may be advisable to make a new will to avoid confusion.

Other matters

A will may be valid but may not include the whole estate of the deceased. For example, it might not effectively dispose of all or part of residue, that is, anything not specifically mentioned in the will. If this is the case, then the part of the estate that is covered by the will is dealt with in accordance with the instructions laid out. The rest is covered by the rules of intestacy.

There may be some assets that cannot be given away by way of the will, such as property held under joint ownership using 'joint tenancy'. This type of property will pass to the other joint owner automatically, and is outside the terms of the will.

What to do if a will is thought to be invalid

A will may be thought to be invalid, which may be due to the following reasons:

▥ It wasn't signed.

▥ It wasn't witnessed, or witnessed correctly.

▥ It wasn't dated.

◼ It has been revoked in some way.

◼ The testator may have got married or divorced since making or signing the will.

◼ The testator wasn't mentally capable of making the will.

◼ The will was made or signed under threat or undue pressure.

It would be advisable to seek legal or professional advice as it is likely to involve a dispute. Medical advice or a medical opinion of the capacity of the testator is also likely to be required.

What to do if a will is thought to be unfair

The testator has the choice to leave their property to anyone they wish and most people would include their family and friends amongst the beneficiaries, together with other legacies. In practice, this is not always the case and there may be members of the deceased's family who are left out of the will. However, if an individual excluded from a will is a dependant of the deceased, they may be able to make a claim under the Inheritance (Provision for Family and Dependants) Act 1975.

The most likely claimants would be:

◼ The husband, wife or civil partner of the person who has died.

◼ The former husband or wife of the person who has died, if they have not remarried or given up their claim when they got divorced.

◼ A partner who lived with the deceased for at least two years immediately before the death.

◼ A child of the deceased.

◼ Someone who was treated as a child of the deceased.

◼ Someone who was totally or partly supported by the deceased.

If an individual believes they may be able to claim against the estate because they fall into one of the above categories, then legal advice should be sought as the process can involve the courts and making a case for provision from the estate. Claiming against an estate can be complex, expensive and there are no guarantees. A claim must be made within six months of the grant of probate or letters of administration.

The equivalent legislation in Northern Ireland is the Inheritance (Provision for Family and Dependants) (Northern Ireland) Order 1979.

Wills under Scottish law

The law governing the signing requirements of a valid will is contained in the Requirements of Writing (Scotland) Act 1995. This states:

■ The will has to be a written document.

■ The will would be described (signed) by the testator and witnessed by one witness.

■ If the will is more than one page in length, each page must be signed by the testator.

■ The testator must have the legal capacity to make a will which includes the understanding of making a will.

■ A testator may be anyone over the age of 12.

The law governing the distribution of estates (both testate and intestate) in Scotland is the Succession (Scotland) Act 1964. The estate of a deceased person under Scottish law is regulated by four sets of rules, as follows:

1 **Legal rights**: common law gives the surviving spouse and children of the deceased fixed 'legal rights', regardless of whether a will has been made. Claims for their legal rights, or legitim, can only be made against the **moveable property** of the deceased's estate and not the **heritable property**.

2 **Prior rights**: statutory provisions to protect the spouse. These prior rights apply on intestacy only and do not apply if there is a valid will.

3 Statutory provisions on intestacy: these regulate the division of an estate on intestacy, in the event that the legal rights and prior rights are not met.

4 Where a valid will exists: the estate is divided in accordance with the will, once the legal rights have been dealt with.

Changing or revoking a will under Scottish law

In general, a testator can revoke a will at any time even though the will states that it is 'irrevocable'. Revocation of a previous will takes place if a testator clearly expresses in a new will that the previous will is revoked, or if a new will is inconsistent with the previous will.

Under Scottish law, marriage does not revoke an existing will. Therefore, when a testator gets married, it is important to realise that an existing will still stands and making a new one is recommended. The new spouse may be entitled to benefit from the estate under the 'legal rights' described above but any remaining estate will be distributed in accordance with the Scottish intestacy rules.

Cohabitees of the deceased have no statutory rights under Scottish law so it is essential that proper provision is made for them, if so wished.

In Scotland, it is essential that fresh wills are made after divorce, as the existing ones are not automatically revoked.

The birth of a child is an occasion when it is recommended to revise a will as the introduction of the 'legal rights' of a child can conflict with the content of an existing will. There is also a presumption, which can be invoked under Scottish law, that the birth of a child can revoke an earlier will if it does not provide for the child.

5

Intestacy and partial intestacy

This chapter explains how an estate should be distributed when an individual dies without leaving a will

- The rules of intestacy in England and Wales
- Cohabitees
- Other dependants and the Inheritance (Provision for Family and Dependants) Act 1975
- Assets held in joint names
- The rules of intestacy in Northern Ireland
- The rules of intestacy under Scottish law

If someone dies without making a will, they are said to have died **intestate**. If this happens, it is the law under the Administration of Estates Act 1925 that sets out who should deal with the deceased's affairs and who should inherit the property in their estate. This act covers England and Wales only.

If an individual dies leaving a will, but this is invalid, it is disregarded and the deceased person's property is distributed in accordance with the **intestacy** rules.

The rules of intestacy in England and Wales

There is a hierarchy of payments. First, any **inheritance tax** must be paid. After that, all debts (including mortgages and other loans) must be repaid to creditors, whether the deceased left a will or not. Following this, there is a strict order that states who the **beneficiaries** are, detailed in the Administration of Estates Act 1925. This can vary in each case and depends on the remaining family of the deceased:

■ If the deceased was married or in a **civil partnership**, the first person entitled to the estate under the intestacy rules is the remaining spouse or civil partner, but they may not be entitled to everything.

■ The Civil Partnership Act 2004 came into effect on 5 December 2005 and gave same-sex couples the right to register their partnerships, giving them broadly the same legal rights as married couples.

■ The property of a man or woman who is divorced or legally separated does not go to the ex-spouse under the intestacy rules.

■ If property is held in joint names this could have special treatment, described later in this chapter.

Intestacy in England and Wales: order of beneficiaries

If there is a spouse but no other relatives

■ The husband, wife or registered civil partner of the deceased is entitled to the whole estate.

■ The spouse must survive for 28 days after the death of the deceased individual.

■ Cohabitees of the deceased are not entitled to any part of the estate under the intestacy rules.

If there is a spouse or civil partner, and children

In this case, the husband, wife or civil partner of the deceased is entitled to the following:

■ The 'personal chattels'. These include items such as a car, pictures and clothing.

■ The first £250,000 of the estate (£125,000 before 1 February 2009).

■ A 'life interest' in one half of the residue (the remainder) of the estate. This gives the right to receive the income or benefit from a property or capital sum (but not to get the capital sum itself) for life. The capital (the original amount) passes to their children when the surviving husband, wife or civil partner dies.

The children of the deceased, including illegitimate and adopted children, share between them:

■ One half of the residue. If they are 18 or over, they will receive this absolutely. If the children are minors, the property is put into trust until they are 18.

■ The remaining half of the residue when the surviving spouse dies and the life interest ends.

Stepchildren get nothing (unless they are named in a will).

If one of the children has already died, leaving children of their own, their share will pass to those children.

If there is a spouse or civil partner and relatives (but no children)

In this case, the husband, wife or civil partner is entitled to the following:

- The 'personal chattels'. These include items such as a car, pictures, clothing etc.
- The first £450,000 of the estate (£200,000 before 1 February 2009).
- One half of the residue, absolutely.

The parents of the deceased are entitled to the remaining half of the residue, absolutely. If the parents of the deceased have died, the brothers and sisters or their descendants will take their place.

If there are children, but no living spouse or civil partner

The children share everything equally. If one of the children has already died, leaving children of their own, their children will take their place and benefit from the property that their parent would have inherited if the parent had been alive. If the children are under 18, their entitlement will be put into trust until they reach 18.

If there is no spouse, civil partner or children

In this case, everything will pass to other relatives, as follows:

1 The parents of the deceased.
2 Brothers or sisters of the deceased who have the same mother and father. (If they are no longer alive, then their own children, the nieces and nephews of the deceased will take their place.)
3 Half-brothers or half-sisters, or their descendants if they are no longer alive.
4 Grandparents.
5 Uncles and aunts 'of the whole blood' (this means brothers and sisters of the parents of the dead person, as long as they had the same mother and father themselves), or their descendants.
6 Uncles and aunts 'of the half blood' (this means brothers and sisters of the parents of the dead person who had only the same mother or father).
7 The Crown (the state).

Adopted children

An adopted or illegitimate child is treated the same as a legitimate child of the deceased.

Cohabitees

If the deceased was living with someone, but was not married, they will not automatically be entitled to any property from the estate. The only option to benefit from the estate is to make a claim under the Inheritance (Provision for Family and Dependants) Act 1975.

Other dependants and the Inheritance (Provision for Family and Dependants) Act 1975

If any other individual was being supported financially by the deceased, and they are not able to benefit under the intestacy rules, then they can only benefit from the estate by making a claim under the Inheritance (Provision for Family and Dependants) Act 1975.

To make a claim, you must have a particular type of relationship with the deceased, such as child, spouse, civil partner, dependant or **cohabitee**, as described above. However, claiming against an estate can be complex, expensive and there are no guarantees. A claim must be made within six months of the grant of probate or letters of administration.

The equivalent legislation in Northern Ireland is the Inheritance (Provision for Family and Dependants) (Northern Ireland) Order 1979.

There are special rules under Scottish law and these are covered later in this chapter.

Assets held in joint names

Assets held in joint names can be held in two ways: either as tenants in common, or joint tenants. The treatment of a jointly-owned asset differs, depending on the way it is owned and it is therefore necessary to check this during the administration of the estate. If there is any doubt about the way joint property is held, legal advice should be sought.

Tenants in common

In this instance, the property is owned by two or more persons, each owning their own part of the property:

■ The co-owners each own a defined share in the property.

■ This form of ownership enables the owners to dispose of their share as they wish. There is no need to obtain permission or agreement from the co-owner(s).

■ On the death of one of the owners, the value of the deceased's share is added into the estate and if there is no valid will, it is distributed in accordance with the intestacy rules along with the rest of the estate.

Joint tenants

In this instance, the property is owned by two or more persons, each owning a share in the whole asset:

▦ If the co-owners wish to dispose of all or part of the property in their lifetime, they all have to agree to do so.

▦ On the death of one of the owners, the property usually passes automatically to the other joint owner, or owners, and does not form part of the deceased's estate.

▦ If joint ownership was held by way of joint tenancy, this therefore means that the property would not pass in accordance with the rules of intestacy.

The rules of intestacy in Northern Ireland

The rules in Northern Ireland are similar to those in England and Wales. However, no **life interests** or trusts are created on intestacy.

Intestacy in Northern Ireland: order of beneficiaries

If there is a spouse but no other relatives

The husband, wife or registered civil partner of the deceased is entitled to the whole estate.

If there is a spouse or civil partner, and children

The husband, wife or civil partner of the deceased is entitled to the following:

▦ The personal chattels.

▦ The first £250,000 of the estate (£125,000 before 1 January 2008)

▦ Where there is only one child, an absolute share in one half of the residue (the remainder) of the estate.

▦ Where there is more than one child, an absolute share in one third of the residue of the estate.

Notice that the difference here is that there is no life interest trust created.

If there is a spouse or civil partner and relatives (but no children)

The husband, wife or civil partner is entitled to the following:

▦ The personal chattels.

▦ The first £450,000 of the estate (£200,000 before 1 January 2008).

▦ One half of the residue, absolutely.

The parents of the deceased are entitled to the remainder. If there are no parents, the brothers and sisters take the residue.

If there are children, but no living spouse or civil partner

The children share everything equally.

If there is no spouse, civil partner or children

Everything will pass to other relatives, as follows:

1 The parents of the deceased.
2 Brothers or sisters of the deceased who have the same mother and father. (If they are no longer alive, then their own children, the nieces and nephews will take their place.)
3 Half-brothers or half-sisters, or their descendants if they are no longer alive.
4 More remote relatives.
5 If no relatives, the Crown (the state).

The rules of intestacy under Scottish law

As mentioned in Chapter 4, the law governing the distribution of estates (both testate and intestate) in Scotland is the Succession (Scotland) Act 1964. The estate of a deceased person under Scottish law is regulated by four sets of rules, as follows:

1 Legal rights: The common law gives the surviving spouse or civil partner and children of the deceased fixed 'legal rights', regardless of whether a will has been made. Claims for their legal rights, or legitim, can only be made against the moveable property of the deceased's estate and not the heritable property.

2 Prior rights: These are statutory provisions put in place to protect the spouse or civil partner. Such rights apply on intestacy only and do not apply if there is a valid will.

3 Statutory provisions on intestacy: Statutory provisions are also in place to regulate the division of an estate on intestacy, in the event that the legal rights and prior rights are not met.

4 Where a valid will exists: The estate is divided in accordance with the will, once the legal rights have been dealt with.

First, any inheritance tax must be paid. After that, all debts (including mortgages and other loans) must be repaid to creditors, whether the deceased left a will or not. The strict order that follows is given in the box opposite.

Intestacy in Scotland: order of inheritance

Prior rights

The prior rights of a surviving spouse or civil partner are:

■ A right to a house in which the surviving spouse resided before death and which was owned by the deceased, provided the value of the property does not exceed £300,000. If the house is worth more than this, the spouse is not entitled to the house itself, but entitled to £300,000 in cash. In some circumstances, the spouse can choose to take the value of the house as a cash sum, instead of the property itself, up to a maximum of £300,000.

■ The contents of the house, up to the value of £24,000.

■ The sum of £75,000 if there are no children of the deceased, or the sum of £42,000, if the deceased is survived by issue.

If there is property remaining in the estate after the prior rights, above, then this is distributed as below.

Legal rights

These rights apply to the deceased's moveable property only, and are as follows:

If there is only a spouse and no children

■ Jus relictae: the right of a widow to one-half of her late husband's moveable estate.

■ Jus relict: the equivalent right of a widower in his deceased wife's moveable estate.

■ The remaining half is available to legatees and those entitled on intestacy.

If there is a spouse and children

■ Jus relictae: the right of a widow to one-third of her late husband's moveable estate.

■ Jus relict: the equivalent right of a widower to one-third in his deceased wife's movable estate.

■ Legitim: the right of children to one-third of the net movable estate if there is a surviving spouse claiming legal rights. (This would be the surviving children of deceased children who would have held a claim had they survived.)

If there is no spouse, but children

Legitim: the right of children to one-half if there is no surviving spouse or if the surviving spouse's claim has been discharged. (This would be the surviving children of deceased children who would have held a claim had they survived.)

Devolution of estate

Statutory prior rights take precedence over legal rights and after all these rights have been satisfied, the intestate's estate is distributed in the following order:

1 Issue; but if none:

2 Parents and brothers or sisters:

- one-half to parents;
- one-half to brothers and sisters;
- if there are no parents, the brothers and sisters take the whole amount;
- if there are no brothers and sisters then the parents take the whole amount.

3 The surviving spouse.

4 Uncles and aunts.

5 Grandparents.

6 Brothers and sisters of grandparents.

7 Remoter ancestors of the intestate, generation by generation successively.

Cohabitees

Cohabitees of the deceased have no statutory rights under Scottish law so it is essential that proper provision is made for them, if so wished.

Divorce

In Scotland, it is essential that new wills are made after divorce, as the existing wills are not automatically revoked.

6

Obtaining details of assets and liabilities

This chapter details the types of assets and liabilities that might be in the estate

- Beginning to deal with assets and liabilities
- Valuing the property in the estate
- Types of assets in the estate
- Types of liabilities in the estate
- Finding unknown creditors or beneficiaries
- Information required to administer the estate
- Starting to value the estate
- If the valuation of the estate results in a loss

Beginning to deal with assets and liabilities

One of the duties of the personal representatives is to obtain details of the assets and liabilities of the person who has died, so that they can deal with the administration of the estate. This will involve sorting through the individual's papers, documents and belongings to begin to compile a catalogue of assets and liabilities. Sometimes this work is dealt with by the solicitors instructed but it is important that it is carried out by a person who is experienced enough to know what documents might be important or not.

Once the assets and liabilities have been established, valuations can be obtained from which it will then be possible to value the estate of the deceased. One of the responsibilities of the personal representatives is to protect the belongings of the deceased, especially if they are to be left unattended during the period of the administration. The personal representatives can also take charge of the house and possessions of the person who has died, unless it passes automatically to a joint owner, thus protecting the estate before this is distributed.

Valuing the property in the estate

Valuing the estate of someone who has died is one of the first things to do if you are acting as the executor or personal representative for that estate.

Inheritance tax may be payable on the total value of the estate, and valuations are necessary for the appropriate forms to be completed correctly. You normally can't get access to the assets in the estate until you've received a grant of probate (or confirmation in Scotland). You need to know the estate's worth to fill in the probate application forms and show whether or not inheritance tax is due.

When valuing a deceased person's estate you must include property, possessions and money they owned at the time of their death, as well as certain gifts they may have made up to seven years before they died. Your valuation must reflect the current market value of the assets.

Types of assets in the estate

Personal possessions and chattels are the personal belongings of the deceased. Such items would still need to be valued because they form part of the estate and may be items that have been gifted in the will to others. It is important that they are safeguarded for this reason and valued if it is thought they may have any value at all. Examples of chattels would be:

■ jewellery;

■ cars;

■ clothing;

■ paintings (valuations are often needed).

If the deceased held investments such as money invested in a bank or building society account, this would be evidenced by written documents. It is advisable to obtain confirmation of the balances from the relevant bank or savings institution and they should be asked to advise on the amount of any interest accrued but unpaid at the date of death. Things the deceased may have had are:

■ bank and building society accounts;

■ stocks and shares (there is a special way of valuing these for inheritance tax purposes and this is detailed in Chapter 13);

■ personal or company pension account statements.

Insurance policies may be held in the form of life assurance (including mortgage cover) and general insurance policies (home, car, travel, medical, etc).

Information about state pension/benefits can be found from relevant correspondence or statements from Jobcentre Plus (for benefits) and/or The Pension Service.

All land and property that was owned by the deceased is part of the estate. Land and property forms the largest part of most estates and the valuation of this is necessary for the calculation of inheritance tax. It is often necessary to obtain a professional valuation of the property, especially to calculate any inheritance tax due, which is covered in Chapter 13. Examples of land and property:

■ houses;

■ buy-to-let property;

■ land;

■ commercial buildings;

■ leasehold property/leases.

Trust property

If the deceased was a beneficiary of a trust, then it is possible that some value will need to be included in the estate. The type of trust and the powers of the trustees will determine whether the deceased is liable to any inheritance tax relating to their entitlement to the trust property on their death.

If the deceased person had been living rent-free in a house that had been left in trust of which they were a life tenant, then the value of this property may need to be included in the estate for inheritance tax purposes.

If the deceased was a beneficiary of a discretionary trust, then there is unlikely to be any value that would be included in the estate.

Finally, if the deceased had shares or other investments that were listed on a recognised stock exchange or they held shares in a private company, you'll need to use their value on the day the deceased person died.

Business interests

If the deceased owned a business, or part of a business, this would also need to be valued. Often, the value of the business is not just the assets or the equipment but may include goodwill. Goodwill is the difference of the total value of the business, less all the assets and equipment at that time. But essentially it is the 'extra' that someone would pay for the business being set up already, the client base perhaps, future earnings that are expected, or the brand name.

There are many different aspects that need to have careful consideration, particularly if the business will continue after the death of an individual and sometimes professional valuation is needed.

Amounts owed to the deceased

When a person dies, any money owed to them is included in their estate. Examples include:

■ Debts owed to the deceased, such as outstanding invoices if the deceased ran a business.

■ Outstanding money owed to the deceased for something that was sold before death but not paid for.

■ Personal debts owed to the deceased.

If the deceased lent money to someone else, it may have been a formal or informal arrangement. In the latter case, there may not be any documentation to support this. If there is no formal agreement, as in most cases, then the person who borrowed the money is under no obligation to pay it back.

Foreign assets

The person that has died may have property that is abroad, such as a holiday home, or foreign bank accounts with funds in them. If this is the case, they are still within the estate and will be distributed in accordance with the will or intestacy. Sometimes, the tax rules in the country where the foreign property is situated may be such that some tax must be paid abroad. If this is the case, the personal representatives may have to deal with the payment of the foreign tax and then deal with claiming some credit for this if there is a UK inheritance tax liability. If the property needs to be valued or sold, then expenses may need to be incurred and these may be deductible from the estate, as a liability.

Types of liabilities in the estate

Liabilities and debts of the estate are anything the deceased person owed at the time they died. Sometimes liabilities also need a valuation for the correct amount to be obtained. The personal representatives should find details of the liabilities when sorting through the deceased's paperwork, but they may also need to contact relevant organisations such as utility companies to ascertain the amount owed to the date of death.

Mortgages

The personal representatives should review any mortgage statements to ascertain the relevant information needed. Types of mortgage include:

- Endowment mortgages, where only the interest on the loan is paid to the mortgage provider each year. In addition to having the mortgage, it is likely that an endowment policy, which is a form of life insurance and investment policy, was taken out to pay off the mortgage at the end of the term. If this is the case, then the value paid out by the endowment policy will be included in the estate.

- Capital repayment mortgages are those where some of the capital of the mortgage (some of the outstanding balance) is paid in addition to the accrued interest each year. In this case, the outstanding balance will not automatically be paid off on death. The outstanding balance can be deducted from the estate as this will need to be paid back to the mortgage provider. Sometimes the mortgagee (person taking out the loan) takes out an insurance policy to provide funds to pay off the mortgage. For instance, to avoid the sale of a property if this is still required to provide for family etc. If a life insurance policy was taken out, this should be included in the estate.

- Joint mortgages: Many couples own a property jointly and have a mortgage in both of their names. If this is the case, only deduct the deceased person's share of the mortgage.

If the deceased person had a mortgage or secured loan on a property, you need to deduct the amount of the mortgage from the property's value. If the mortgage or loan is for more than the property is worth, you can deduct the excess amount from the rest of the estate.

If there is a payout from a mortgage protection policy, you need to add that amount to the value of the estate.

Tax liabilities

There are many types of tax that could have accrued to the date of death. If the deceased was employed, it is likely that there is no income tax due as tax is deducted during the year by the employer under the PAYE scheme. It is possible, however, that a tax repayment can be due for any unused personal allowances. If the deceased was self-employed, it is likely that some tax will be payable. Self-employed people pay their tax liabilities either once and twice a year and if the deceased worked up to the date of death, then there is likely to be further tax due in relation to accounts not yet prepared. It is advisable for the personal representatives to check the matter with any professional adviser that was acting for the deceased and this will become apparent when going through the belongings.

If the deceased disposed of any assets before they died, then there could be a liability to **capital gains tax (CGT)**.

If the deceased was in business and was VAT registered, then it is likely there will be some VAT returns that will require completion and VAT could be payable, or refundable.

The personal representatives are responsible for calculating any inheritance tax payable and this will be a liability of the estate. This is covered in depth, in later chapters.

Loans and credit card debts

If the deceased person had any loans and credit card balances, then these are liabilities of the estate. The balance of the loan together with any accrued interest to the date of death would be deducted from the value of the estate. It is advisable to check whether any insurance cover was taken out on these liabilities. For instance, life cover or payment protection insurance may have been taken out by the deceased, with the loan provider. Other examples would include leases, and hire-purchase agreements. It is also advisable to check the terms of the agreements to see whether any special action is necessary.

Uncashed cheques

There may be cheques that the deceased person had written before their death that have not been cashed or presented to the bank yet. The value of these cheques can be deducted from the estate. If the deceased person had written a cheque as a gift, this type of gift is treated as though it hadn't been made. The amount cannot be deducted from the estate and shouldn't be taken into account when calculating the inheritance tax liability.

Household bills and utilities

Check for any services that the deceased person had used but not yet paid for. There may be invoices among the personal and business papers of the deceased which show amounts due or unpaid. Examples might include invoices from builders and decorators; or from solicitors and accountants; or for goods or services the deceased had received, but not yet paid for.

Debts owed to friends or family

Debts can only be deducted from the estate if they are legally enforceable. A debt owed to a close friend or family member is usually accepted as being legally enforceable if one or more of the following applies:

- the loan was documented in writing;
- a verbal agreement when the loan was made, providing there is evidence;
- there is evidence that the deceased person was making repayments.

The rules are different in Scotland. A statement from a third party is sufficient to make a loan legally enforceable.

Guarantee debts

A 'guarantee' debt is a promise to pay someone else's debt if they can't pay it themselves. The deceased person might have acted as a 'guarantor' for someone else to help them get a loan, for example. If the loan hadn't been repaid at the time the deceased person died, you may be able to make a deduction from the value of the estate. It is necessary to check the terms of the agreement to see whether a deduction can be made. If you do make a deduction, you'll have to value it as a cash payment.

Funeral expenses

Funeral expenses can be deducted from the value of the estate, together with a reasonable amount for mourning expenses. Expenses can include a reasonable amount to cover the cost of:

■ flowers;

■ refreshments for mourners;

■ necessary expenses incurred by the executor or administrator when arranging the funeral;

■ the cost of a headstone.

Finding unknown creditors or beneficiaries

As we have discussed before, the personal representatives have a responsibility to administer the deceased's estate correctly and failure to do this will mean they are personally liable if a creditor or unknown beneficiary is found to be a genuine one. When carrying out their duties, the personal representatives sometimes have the problem of not being able to trace the named beneficiaries of the deceased's will. However, they have a responsibility to do everything they can to trace them. There are specialist firms that can help make this possible if initial enquiries are not fruitful.

The personal representatives can protect themselves from personal liability by placing an official notice of the death in the local papers in the area where the land is owned and the *London Gazette* (the *Edinburgh Gazette* or the *Belfast Gazette* for deaths of Scottish residents or residents of Northern Ireland) as a way of notifying anyone who may have a claim on the estate. The personal representatives should then wait two months and one day from the date of the advertisements before distributing the estate.

If there is any doubt of additional creditors, or any named beneficiaries cannot be traced, it is possible for the personal representatives to protect themselves further against personal liability by taking out insurance and this is wise if there are any doubts of additional creditors, unknown beneficiaries or untraceable beneficiaries.

Information required to administer the estate

The following documents and information will be required by the personal representative or close relative to contact relatives and friends or to return documents to relevant organisations:

▩ The death certificate. It is advisable to obtain more than one copy of the death certificate at the time of registering the death, as it is more expensive and time consuming to obtain copies at a later date. If a few copies are held, one can each be sent to each relevant organisation to access funds.

▩ The will, if there is one. The personal representatives should review the will to identify the beneficiaries. It is possible at an early stage in the administration to contact the beneficiaries to inform them that they are named as a beneficiary in the will and will be contacted once the administration has taken place with confirmation of how much they have inherited.

▩ The personal address book of the deceased. This information will help in the job of informing those that need to be told of the death.

▩ Passport.

▩ Vehicle registration documents in relation to the ownership of a car.

▩ Driving licence to notify DVLA of the death.

▩ Membership cards, etc.

If the deceased was employed, documentation that is likely to be relevant and necessary includes a PAYE form P60 and latest payslips, and copies of tax returns and tax calculation statements.

If the deceased was in business as an incorporated business (company) or unincorporated business (such as a sole trader or partnership), then the documentation that is likely to be relevant includes company registration documents; accounts; and tax and VAT returns.

If the deceased's business is a going concern, and one that will continue after the death, then the personal representatives should ensure that any provisions for the continuance of the business is carried out with the least disruption. For instance, if there are employees that are affected by the death, they may need support and reassurance. There may be other business partners who would ensure it continues. Alternatively, owners of a business can arrange for cover or insurance to ensure that the business can continue in the event of death.

The paperwork must be reviewed to see whether any gifts were made before the death of the individual. Any gift made in the seven years before the person died could have an inheritance tax liability to pay on it. Note, however, that some gifts are exempt. A gift that the deceased gave away at any time, but which they still use, needs to be ascertained and included in any inheritance tax liability calculation, even if it is no longer available to distribute as part of the estate.

You will also need to find out how the deceased person owned any property or assets to work out the value of their share. There are two ways of owning property jointly (see Chapter 5).

Starting to value the estate

As mentioned at the beginning of this chapter, valuing the estate of someone who has died is one of the first things to do if you're acting as the executor or personal representative for that estate. Note that:

■ Inheritance tax may be payable on the total value of the estate, and valuations are necessary for the appropriate forms to be completed correctly. Chapter 13 discusses the rules on how to value property for the purposes of inheritance tax.

■ You normally can't get access to the assets in the estate until you've received a grant of probate (or confirmation in Scotland).

■ You need to know the estate's worth to fill in the probate application forms and show whether or not inheritance tax is due.

■ It is advisable to keep a catalogue or list of all the assets and liabilities. This will be needed to fill in any return forms and if there are any queries from HM Revenue and Customs.

The value of the estate is, basically, the total value of the assets with the value of the liabilities deducted from the total assets.

Total value of the estate = Total assets − total liabilities

If the valuation of the estate results in a loss

When the personal representatives have valued the assets and the liabilities to calculate the overall result of the value of the total estate, this can sometimes result in a loss. Whoever is administering the estate must make sure all the debts are paid before any beneficiaries. If the beneficiaries are paid before any outstanding debts, and these are then left unpaid, the personal representatives are personally liable for the debts.

If there are insufficient funds in the estate to pay all debts, then they must be paid in a strict order. This is as follows:

1 The funeral expenses and expenses relating to the administration of the will.

2 Any mortgage debt secured on a property.

3 Tax liabilities to HM Revenue and Customs.

4 Repayment of any benefits overpaid to the Department of Work and Pensions.

5 Unpaid pension contributions or wages.

7

The need for a grant

This chapter explains the need to apply for probate and the process of probate being granted once inheritance tax has been paid

- Probate
- The grant of probate
- Applying for a grant
- When a grant may not be needed
- Once the grant of probate has been received
- Different terms associated with probate
- Scottish variations

The rules on probate are common for England, Wales and Northern Ireland. The variations for Scotland are covered in the final section.

Probate

Probate is the term that describes the process of applying for the right to deal with a deceased person's affairs. Essentially it is the 'administration of the estate'.

This process is called 'confirmation' in Scotland.

Note that the personal representatives won't be granted probate until some or all of the inheritance tax that is due on the estate has been paid.

The grant of probate

The personal representatives of someone's estate may need the legal document called a 'grant of probate' to enable them to deal with the administration of the estate. This is obtained from the High Court. Basically, it is the official approval for the executor (if there is a will) or the personal administrator (if there is no will) to deal with the estate.

In Scotland, the administrators would apply for a 'grant of confirmation'.

Applying for a grant

If the person who has died left a will, it is likely that one or more 'executors' are nominated to deal with the person's affairs after their death. The executor applies for a 'grant of probate' from the probate registry.

If the person who has died didn't leave a will, a person will be nominated to deal with the estate by the probate registry, as detailed in Chapter 3. This is likely to be the deceased's next of kin.

The nominated individual will apply for a 'grant of letters of administration'. If the grant is given, they are known as 'administrators' of the estate. This serves the same purpose as probate, and the grant of letters of administration are applied for in the same way as for the grant of probate. Like the grant of probate, the grant of letters of administration is a legal document which confirms the administrator's authority to deal with the deceased person's assets.

When applying for probate, the personal representatives are promising the probate court that they will administer the estate as set out in the will and according to law. If they don't carry out this role, they will be accountable to the court and the beneficiaries, so probate ensures that they take on this responsibility and carry out the role.

Many personal representatives instruct a solicitor to handle the application on their behalf, however they may apply personally. An application is made to:

▪ the Principal Registry (in London); or

▪ a district probate registry office (in other cities and many large towns).

The registry can send you information packs. These include probate application forms and information on how to fill them in. You can also talk to registry staff if you are having difficulty filling in a probate application.

When a grant may not be needed

Sometimes it is not necessary to apply for a grant of probate. In these cases, it is possible to deal with the estate without obtaining a grant.

A grant is not usually needed if the deceased's estate is below £5,000, and:

▦ the estate doesn't contain any land, property or shares;

▦ the deceased individual owned everything jointly with someone else and everything passes automatically to the surviving joint owner (joint tenancy);

▦ any bank or building society accounts that the person had contain less than £5,000 each (although banks and building societies do have the right to insist on probate if the total value of the estate exceeds £5,000).

However, a grant of probate will need to be applied for if the person that has died:

▦ had a bank, building society or National Savings account with more than £5,000 in it;

▦ stocks or shares;

▦ owned property or land (unless it is owned as a joint tenancy and so passes automatically to the other owner);

▦ had life insurance or term insurance policies that are paid to the estate, rather than straight out to the nominated beneficiaries.

In these situations, the bank or relevant organisation, holding the asset for the deceased, will need to see the grant before transferring control of the assets.

Once the grant of probate has been received

When the personal representatives have received the official go-ahead, the grant of probate, they can start to collect in the assets and distribute them to the debtors and beneficiaries. When they produce evidence that the grant has been issued, they can produce the certificate to a bank, for example, so they know the personal representative has the right to administer the estate, and the bank will be able to release the funds, such as the money in the bank account.

Different terms associated with probate

Most terms used in this book are defined in the glossary. However, it may be useful to define some terms relating to probate at this stage.

If the deceased left a will, the person that the testator has nominated in the will to deal with the estate is an executor. The executor then applies for a 'grant of probate'.

If the deceased did not leave a will, then an individual will be nominated as the administrator and they then apply for the grant of letters of administration.

Personal representative is a general term which means executor or administrator.

Grant of representation is a general term which includes grants of probate and grants of letters of administration.

Scottish variations

The process of obtaining probate is generally the same as England and Wales. However, there are a few differences with the terminology in Scotland:

■ The process of probate is called confirmation in Scotland and the administrators would apply for a grant of confirmation.

■ An executor appointed in a will is described as an executor-nominate.

■ If no will was left, someone nominated by the court to act as the administrator is described as an executor-dative.

■ Letters of administration are called by the same name but are issued by the commissionary department of the sheriff court.

8

Applying for probate and letters of administration

This chapter will explain the application for the grant of representation

When a grant may not be required

A grant of representation (which is another term to describe either the grant of probate or the grant of letters of administration) may not be needed where the individual that died left less than £5,000, and:

- left an estate that doesn't contain any land, property or shares;
- owned everything jointly with someone else and everything passes automatically to the surviving joint owner (under the joint tenancy rules).

If there are small amounts contained in a bank or building society, the financial institution will not always insist on seeing sight of a grant and may be happy to release the funds without this. To establish whether assets can be obtained without a grant, the executor or administrator would need to write to each institution informing them of the death and enclosing a photocopy of the death certificate (and will if there is one).

Applying for the grant in England and Wales

If a grant of probate or grant of letters of administration is required, the next step is to apply for the grant. A named executor would apply to the Probate Registry for this. If there is no valid will, then the application is for the Probate Registry to grant letters of administration, which is essentially the same.

To be able to administer someone's estate, the administrators normally need to apply to the probate registry for the grant. They can ask a solicitor to help with applying for a grant or make a personal application.

Where to apply for the grant

The probate service is part of Her Majesty's Courts Service (HMCS) and it administers the system of probate, the administration of a deceased's estate, in England and Wales. The personal representatives apply to a probate registry for the grant. Use the following website to locate the directory of probate registries and interview venues:
www.hmcourts-service.gov.uk/HMCSCourtFinder/GetLeaflet.do?
court_leaflets_id=744

All registries are open Monday to Friday. Most are open 9.30am to 4.00pm, but there may be some minor local variations (e.g. in London, the hours are 10.00am to 4.30pm), so you are recommended to check before attending. This is the link to use to locate your local probate registry:
www.hmcourts-service.gov.uk/infoabout/civil/probate/registries.htm

There are three types of registry but all do the same work:

▓ The London Probate Registry

▓ District probate registries in Birmingham, Brighton, Bristol, Cardiff (Probate Registry of Wales), Ipswich, Leeds, Liverpool, Manchester, Newcastle, Oxford and Winchester.

▓ Probate sub-registries in: Bodmin, Caernarfon, Carlisle, Carmarthen, Chester, Exeter, Gloucester, Lancaster, Leicester, Lincoln, Maidstone, Middlesbrough, Norwich, Nottingham, Peterborough, Sheffield, Stoke-on-Trent and York.

The personal representatives can ask a solicitor to apply for the grant. There is likely to be a charge for this work. The solicitor will take care of the completion of the probate application forms and ask for the personal representatives to swear an oath before a different solicitor.

If the personal representatives require assistance with the probate application process and any of the return forms that require completion, the following website will enable the reader to locate a solicitor in their area:
www.lawsociety.org.uk/choosingandusing/findasolicitor.law

Alternatively, you could use the local telephone book to find some local firms, with whom you can make some enquiries. Always obtain an idea of the cost of fees before engaging the solicitor or firm.

The personal representatives can undertake to complete the probate application forms without a solicitor but need to be aware of the correct forms that should be completed. There are different forms, depending on where the deceased individual lived and the size of the estate and whether any inheritance tax is payable.

The personal representatives will need to establish whether the estate is an excepted estate first.

Excepted estates

Excepted estates are discussed further in Chapter 18, but generally, for an estate to be excepted, one of the following applies:

▓ It's a low-value estate, valued at under the inheritance tax (IHT) threshold (£325,000 in 2009–10 and 2010–11).

▓ It's an exempt estate: the deceased person left everything (or everything over and above the inheritance tax threshold) to a spouse or civil partner living in the UK or to a registered UK charity (and the estate is valued at under £1 million).

■ The deceased person was a 'foreign domiciliary': they lived permanently abroad and died abroad and the value of their UK assets is under £150,000.

If an estate is an excepted estate, this means the personal representatives will file a brief return of information about the estate as a whole, form IHT205 Return of Estate Information (or form C5 in Scotland) as part of the probate process. An example of these two forms are in Chapter 18.

However, the personal representatives must first be sure that the estate doesn't meet any of the conditions that disqualify it from being excepted (see Chapter 18), in which case the full inheritance tax return form IHT400 would need to be completed (Table 8.1).

Table 8.1 Forms needed for excepted and non-excepted estates in England and Wales

Required IHT forms if the estate is likely to be an excepted estate	*Required IHT forms if the estate is unlikely to be an excepted estate*
PA1 (Figure 8.1)	PA1 (Figure 8.1)
IHT205 (Figure 18.1)	IHT400 (Figure 12.1)
	Form IHT421 (Figure 8.2)

Required forms and returns for excepted estates

The executors will need to complete a Probate Application Form PA1 shown in Figure 8.1 on page 71. In addition to this, they will need to complete the Revenue tax form IHT205 (instead of the full inheritance tax return form IHT400). An example of the IHT205 form is shown in Chapter 18.

To obtain probate, one of the personal representatives will need to attend an interview to confirm the details in the application. To do this, first decide which venue you'd like to be interviewed at from those listed above under the heading 'Where to apply for the grant'. Then, send all your forms, and the additional documents and probate fee requested on the PA1 checklist, to the appropriate controlling probate registry office for that venue. You'll receive an appointment for an interview within about ten days of sending in your application. If everything is satisfactory, you should receive the grant of probate by post soon after the interview.

A copy of form PA1 can be printed out for completion from the HM Courts Service website:
www.hmcourts-service.gov.uk/HMCSCourtFinder/GetForm.do?
court_forms_id=735

There are also some notes to assist with the completion of the application form at:
www.hmcourts-service.gov.uk/courtfinder/forms/pa1_e.pdf

You can print out a copy of form IHT421 for completion from the Directgov website:
www.hmrc.gov.uk/inheritancetax/iht421.pdf

Required forms and returns for non-excepted estates

If the estate does not meet the conditions for being an excepted estate, the forms that will require completion are as follows:

- PA1: probate application form (Figure 8.1).
- IHT421: probate summary (Figure 8.2).
- In addition, inheritance tax return form IHT400 will need to be filled in and sent to HMRC together with the payment for inheritance tax.

To obtain probate, one of the personal representatives will need to attend an interview to confirm the details in the application. To do this, decide which venue you'd like to be interviewed at from the list above under the heading 'Where to apply for the grant'. Send the forms PA1 and IHT421, and the additional documents and fee requested on the PA1 checklist to the appropriate controlling probate registry office for that venue. The Probate Registry will return form IHT421 with their address filled in, with your interview appointment letter within about ten days of sending in your application.

The tax element is dealt with separately. Send form IHT421 and form IHT400 (together with any payment of inheritance tax if you've already worked this out) to HMRC (you'll find the relevant address in the IHT400 notes). If you've indicated that you'd like HMRC to work out the tax for you, they will do this and tell you what is due. Once any tax due has been paid, or if there's no tax to pay, HMRC will stamp and return form IHT421 to the probate registry office confirming this.

Once this has been done, the probate registry office will issue the grant.

The interview with the probate registry

When attending an interview at one of the probate offices, the personal representative will need to take the following documents:

- proof of identity;
- a certified death certificate, or coroner's certificate;
- the original will if there is one, together with any codicils;
- marriage certificate or decree absolute if the individual was divorced.

The interview is informal and is simply to confirm the details on the probate application form. The personal representative will also sign a form of oath which confirms that the information given is to the best of their knowledge.

Note that if inheritance tax is due on the estate, some or all of this must be paid before a grant will be issued.

The cost of applying for the grant

There is no fee to pay if the amount left in the deceased person's sole name after funeral expenses and debt payment is £5,000 or less, because it is not necessary to apply for a grant. However, if the net estate is over £5,000, an application must be made and the current fee is £90. Extra copies of the grant cost £1 each if ordered at the time of application.

Obtaining the grant

On receipt of the grant of probate or grant of letters of administration, the personal representatives become authorised to administer the estate. The grant provides proof to banks, building societies and other organisations that they have authority to access and distribute funds that were held in the deceased's name.

Additional copies of the grant should be ordered at the time of the application because the cost of these additional copies is very much less than the cost of additional copies requested at a later date. A number of copies are likely to be required by the personal representatives to send out to the various financial institutions when calling in the assets for distribution, and it will save time at this stage.

Further information

For further information, you may find the link to the Directgov website helpful:
www.direct.gov.uk/en/Governmentcitizensandrights/Death/Preparation/
DG_10029716

Alternatively, if you have any queries about applying for probate, call the Probate and Inheritance Tax helpline on 0845 302 0900. Lines are open Monday to Friday, 9am to 5pm.

The equivalent for Northern Ireland: applying for probate

The process for the application of the grant of probate in Northern Ireland is mainly the same as England and Wales, including the rules for excepted estates, detailed above or in Chapter 18. There are just a few differences.

A grant of representation (which is another term to describe either the grant of probate or the grant of letters of administration) may not be needed where:

■ The person who died left less than £10,000 (£5,000 for England and Wales) and doesn't contain any land, property or shares.
■ They owned everything jointly with a spouse or civil partner and everything passes automatically to them.

To establish whether the assets can be obtained without a grant, the executor or administrator would need to write to each institution informing them of the death and enclosing a photocopy of the death certificate (and will if there is one).

One of the differences is that the personal representatives will need to apply to the probate offices in Northern Ireland:

The Principal Probate Registry
Probate Office
Royal Courts of Justice
Chichester Street
Belfast
BT1 3JF

The District Probate Registry
The Courthouse
Bishop Street
Londonderry
BT48 6PQ

If the deceased lived in County Fermanagh, Londonderry or Tyrone, you may apply for a grant at either of the registries.

If the deceased lived in County Antrim, Armagh or Down, you may only apply for a grant at the registry in Belfast.

The required forms depend also on whether the estate is an excepted estate, as in Table 8.2.

Table 8.2 Forms for applying for the grant in Northern Ireland

Required IHT forms if the estate is likely to be an excepted estate	Required IHT forms if the estate is unlikely to be an excepted estate
IHT205 (Figure 18.1)	IHT400 (Figure 12.1)
	IHT421 (Figure 8.2)

When requesting an interview, the personal representatives do not have to complete and submit the probate application form PA1. Instead, they just request an interview and the probate officer will take the details and complete the forms on their behalf. However, when attending an interview at one of the offices in Northern Ireland, the executor or personal administrator will still need to take the following documentation:

■ proof of identity;

■ a certified death certificate, or coroner's certificate;

■ the original will, if there is one;

■ marriage certificate or decree absolute if the individual was divorced;

■ form IHT205 Return of Estate Income if the estate is an excepted estate, or a stamped IHT421 Inheritance Tax Account Probate Summary, which confirms the amount of inheritance tax payable.

There is no fee to pay if the amount left in the deceased person's sole name after funeral expenses and debt payment is £10,000 or less, as it is not necessary to apply for a grant.

If the net estate is over £10,000, an application must be made. The fee in 2010–11 is £200 plus a personal application fee of £50. Extra copies of the grant cost £10 each if ordered at the time of application.

Probate in Northern Ireland

There is a useful booklet on how to deal with the probate process for deaths in Northern Ireland at:

www.courtsni.gov.uk/NR/rdonlyres/3F5B0018-B401-4ABA-9656-57D120ED7040/0/p_ul_Deceasedpersonsestate.pdf

The Scottish variant: applying for confirmation

Instead of obtaining a grant of probate or letters of administration, in Scotland the process is called applying for a grant of confirmation. However, it is still the same process of giving the executors the authority to administer the estate.

As with any death in the UK, the deceased's assets, such as bank and building society accounts, are automatically frozen when the individual dies. The administrators of the estate, whether a will was left by the deceased or not, may need to apply for confirmation.

The executors of the estate will not need to apply for a grant of confirmation if:

■ Everything the deceased owned was held in joint names with their spouse, or

■ If the estate only consists of accounts with a bank or building society and these are willing to pay out the capital funds to the beneficiaries without seeing the grant of confirmation – usually if the estate has a value of £30,000 or less.

If this is the case, no application need be made and the estate can be distributed immediately, once the executors are happy that all liabilities, such as funeral expenses and mortgages, have been settled.

If it has been established that a grant of confirmation is required, the executor-nominative, if a will was left, or the executor-dative if no will was left, needs to apply to the Commissary Department of the Sheriff Court serving the area in which the deceased was domiciled at the time of death. As part of the application, any inheritance tax needs to be paid, as with the applications in the rest of the UK.

Once confirmation is received, all the assets can be released and the executors have the right to distribute the assets in accordance with the will or Scottish intestacy rules.

> **Finding a Scottish solicitor**
>
> If the executors decide to use a solicitor to assist with the administration of the estate and apply for the grant of confirmation, the following link may be useful. It will assist you in finding a solicitor in Scotland who specialises in confirmation work at: www.lawscot.org.uk

Applying for the grant of confirmation in Scotland

When the valuation of all assets has been completed, the executors must then apply for the grant of confirmation. The procedure will vary, depending on whether a solicitor is used to assist the executors, or not.

If a solicitor is used, the executors must swear an affidavit or oath. In making this oath, they confirm:

■ That they are appointed by the will.

■ They must give details of the value of the estate.

■ They will distribute the estate in accordance with the terms of the will, and/or in accordance with the law.

It is then likely that the solicitor will assist the executors by completing the application form C1, which is the form used to apply for the grant and provides an inventory of the deceased's estate. This completed form is then sent to the sheriff court.

The executors can apply directly to the sheriff court and make an appointment to swear an affidavit or oath at the court. The procedure is the same as that for using a solicitor, it is just that they will be applying in person, rather than through a solicitor. The executors will need to complete a form C1 to make their application to the sheriff court. An example of this is shown in Figure 8.3 on page 77.

Excepted estates in Scotland

If the estate is an excepted estate, then a form C5 would be used instead. An example of the form C5 is in Chapter 18. Excepted estates are discussed further in Chapter 18, but generally, an excepted estate might be if one of the following applies:

▪ It's an estate valued at under the inheritance tax threshold (£325,000 in 2009–10 and 2010–11).

▪ It's an exempt estate: the deceased person left everything (or everything over and above the inheritance tax threshold) to a spouse or civil partner living in the UK or to a registered UK charity (and the estate is valued at under £1 million).

▪ The deceased person was a foreign domiciliary: they lived permanently abroad and died abroad and the value of their UK assets is under £150,000.

This means you'll probably need to fill in form C5 as part of the probate process. However, you must first be sure that the estate doesn't meet any of the conditions that disqualify it from being excepted (see Chapter 18).

The required forms depend also on whether the estate is an excepted estate, as in Table 8.3.

Table 8.3 Required forms in Scotland

Required IHT forms if the estate is likely to be an excepted estate	Required IHT forms if the estate is unlikely to be an excepted estate
Form C1 (Figure 8.3)	Form C1 (Figure 8.3)
Form C5 (Figure 18.3)	IHT400 (Figure 12.1)

There is help and guidance to help you complete these forms on the HMRC website:
www.hmrc.gov.uk/cto/forms/c3-2006-2.pdf

The executors will then also have to complete an inheritance tax return and pay over any inheritance tax. Sometimes, only a reduced account (on form C5) is necessary which shows an overall picture of the estate rather than the full inheritance tax return form (IHT400), particularly where there is no inheritance tax liability and the estate is an excepted estate, as discussed in Chapter 18.

Obtaining the grant of confirmation

The sheriff court will send confirmation to the executors along with any additional certificates if they have been requested. Once the grant has been received by the executors, they can set about completing the administration

of the estate, calling in all the assets and funds of the deceased. The financial institutions such as banks and building societies, stockbrokers and life insurance companies will release the assets and funds once they have seen · the certificate of confirmation. The executors can then set about distributing these out to the beneficiaries. For further information on obtaining confirmation in Scotland, see:
www.scotland.gov.uk/Publications/2008/02/26152921/2

Form C1 can be downloaded from:
www.hmrc.gov.uk/cto/forms/c1_2_lined.pdf

Summary

As we have seen, there are various forms to be completed and the correct form depends largely on where the deceased lived and the reason for the estate to be an excepted estate. Table 8.4 gives a summary.

Table 8.4 Summary of UK forms

Country where the deceased lived	Required IHT forms if the estate is likely to be an excepted estate	Required IHT forms if the estate is unlikely to be an excepted estate
England and Wales	Probate application PA1 (Figure 8.1)	Probate application PA1 (Figure 8.1)
	IHT205 estate information (Figure 18.1)	IHT400 inheritance tax account (Figure 12.1)
		IHT421 probate summary (Figure 8.2)
Northern Ireland	IHT205 estate information (Figure 18.1)	IHT400 inheritance tax account (Figure 12.1)
		IHT421 probate summary (Figure 8.2)
Scotland	C1 confirmation (Figure 8.3)	C1 confirmation (Figure 8.3)
	C5 information return (Figure 18.3)	IHT400 inheritance tax account (Figure 12.1)

Probate Application Form - PA1

Click here to reset form

Please use **BLOCK CAPITALS**

Name of deceased

Interview venue

Dates to avoid

Please read the following questions and PA2 booklet 'How to obtain probate' carefully before filling in this form. Please also refer to the Guidance Notes enclosed where an item is marked *.

PLEASE COMPLETE ALL SECTIONS.

Section A: The Will / Codicil

This column is for official use

*A1 Did the deceased leave a will/codicil?
*(Note: These may not necessarily be formal documents. If the answer to question 1 is Yes, you must enclose the **original** document(s) with your application.)*

Will		Codicil	
Yes ☐	No ☐	Yes ☐	No ☐

If **No** to both questions, please go to Section B

Date of will

A2 Did the deceased marry or enter into a Civil Partnership after the date of the will/codicil?
Yes ☐ Date: No ☐

Date of codicil

A3 Is there anyone under 18 years old who receives anything in the will/codicil?
Yes ☐ No ☐

A4 Did any of the witnesses to the will or codicil or the spouse/civil partner of any witness receive a gift under the will/codicil? If Yes, state name of witness.
Yes ☐ No ☐

A5 Are there any executors named in the will/codicil?
Yes ☐ No ☐

*A6 Give the names of those executors who are **not** applying and the reasons why. **Note:** All executors **must** be accounted for.

Full names	Reason A,B,C,D,E

A = Pre-deceased
B = Died after the deceased
C = Power Reserved
D = Renunciation
E = Power of Attorney

Section B: Relatives of the deceased

*B1 - B6

Please refer to the Guidance Notes.

Sections B1 - B4 must be completed in all cases.

Please state the **number** of relatives of the deceased in categories B1 - B4.

If there are no relatives in a particular category, write 'nil' in each box and move onto the next category.

Note: Sections B5 and B6 only need to be completed if the deceased had no relatives in Section B1 - B4.

Number of relatives (if none, write nil)	Under 18	Over 18
B1 Surviving **lawful** husband or wife or surviving **lawful** civil partner		
B2a Sons or daughters who survived the deceased		
b Sons or daughters who did **not** survive the deceased		
c Children of person(s) indicated at '2b' **only**, who survived the deceased *		
B3 Parents who survived the deceased		
B4a Brothers or sisters who survived the deceased		
b Brothers or sisters who did **not** survive the deceased		
c Children of person(s) indicated at '4b' **only**, who survived the deceased *		
B5 Grandparents who survived the deceased		
B6a Uncles or aunts who survived the deceased		
b Uncles or aunts who did **not** survive the deceased		
c Children of person(s) indicated at '6b' **only**, who survived the deceased *		

PA1 - Probate Application Form (11.08)   © Crown Copyright 2008

Figure 8.1 Form PA1: application for a grant of probate for England and Wales

Please note that the grant will normally be sent to the first applicant. Any applicant named will be required to attend an interview. It is, however, usually only necessary for one person to apply (please see PA2 booklet, page 3).

Section C: Details of applicant(s)

This column is for official use

C1	Title	Mr ☐ Mrs ☐ Miss ☐ Ms ☐ Other ☐
C2	Forenames	
C3	Surname	
C4	Address	

I.T.W.C

Postcode: _____

C5	Telephone number	Home _____
		Work _____
	E-mail address (optional)	
C6	Occupation	

C7   Are you related to the deceased?   Yes ☐   No ☐

If Yes, what is your relationship?   Relationship:

C8   If there are any other applicants, up to a maximum of three, give their details. (Note: **All** applicants named in Sections C1 and C8 must attend an interview.)

Details of other applicants who wish to be named in the grant of representation. (Please give details as C1 to C7 including relationship to deceased.)

C9   Name and address of any surviving lawful husband or wife/civil partner of the deceased, unless stated above.

Postcode:

*C10   If you are applying as an attorney on behalf of the person entitled to the grant, please state their name, address and capacity in which they are entitled (e.g. relationship to the deceased).

Postcode:

Relationship:

*C10a   Have you been appointed by the person entitled as their attorney under an Enduring Power of Attorney (EPA) or a Property and financial affairs Lasting Power of Attorney (LPA)?

EPA ☐   LPA ☐   No ☐

*C10b   If Yes, has it been registered with the Office of the Public Guardian?

Yes ☐   No ☐

*C10c   Does the donor of the EPA/LPA lack mental capacity within the meaning of the Mental Capacity Act 2005? *(see PA1a)*

Yes ☐   No ☐

Section D: Details of the deceased	This column is for official use

*D1	Forenames			
*D2	Surname			True name
*D3	Did the deceased hold any assets **(excluding joint assets)** in another name?	Yes ☐	No ☐	Alias
*D4a	If Yes, what are the assets?			
	And in what name(s) are they held?			
D4b	Was the deceased known by any other name in which he/she made a will? If so, what name was it made in?	Yes ☐	No ☐	Address
D5	Last permanent address of the deceased.			
				D/C district and No.
		Postcode:		
D6	Date of birth			
D7	Date of death	Age:		L.S.A.
	Domicile			D.B.F.
*D8	Was England and Wales the domicile/permanent home of the deceased at the date of death? If No, please specify the deceased's permanent home or domicile.	Yes ☐	No ☐	
*D9	Tick the last **legal** marital or civil partnership status of the deceased, and give dates where appropriate.	Bachelor/Spinster ☐ Widow/Widower/Surviving Civil Partner ☐ Married/Civil Partnership ☐ Date: Divorced/Civil Partnership dissolved ☐ Date: Judicially separated ☐ Date:		
	Note: These documents (✦) may usually be obtained from the Court which processed the divorce/dissolution of civil partnership/separation.	*(If the deceased did not leave a will, please enclose official copy✦ of the Decree Absolute/Decree of Dissolution of Civil Partnership/Decree of Judicial Separation (as applicable))*		
*D10	Was the deceased legally adopted?	Yes ☐	No ☐	
*D11	Has any relative of the deceased been legally adopted? (If Yes, give name and relationship to deceased.)	Yes ☐ Name: Relationship:	No ☐	
D12	*Answer this section **only** if the deceased died **before 4th April 1988 or left a will or codicil dated before that date**.*			
D12a	Was the deceased illegitimate?	Yes ☐	No ☐	
D12b	Did the deceased leave any illegitimate sons or daughters?	Yes ☐	No ☐	
D12c	Did the deceased have any illegitimate sons or daughters who died leaving children of their own?	Yes ☐	No ☐	

Important - please complete the checklist overleaf before submitting your application

Important

Checklist

Please return your forms to the probate registry which controls the interview venue at which you wish to be interviewed (see PA4) otherwise your application may be delayed.

Before sending your application, please complete this checklist to confirm that you have enclosed the following items:

1   PA1 (Probate Application Form)   ☐

2   Either IHT205 (signed by all applicants)   ☐
     or IHT421   ☐
     Note: Do not enclose IHT Form 400 – **this must be sent to HMRC (Inheritance Tax)** (see PA2)

3   Original will and codicil(s), **not a photocopy**   ☐
     Note: Do **not** remove or attach anything to the will/codicil

4   Official copy of death certificate or coroner's letter, **not a photocopy**   ☐

5   Other documents as requested on PA1 – please specify

6   Please state number of official copy grants required for use in England and Wales (see PA3)   ☐

7   Please state number of official copy grants required for use **outside** England and Wales (see PA3)   ☐   **For official use only (sealed and certified)**

8   Please state total amount of cheque enclosed for fee (made payable to HMCS) including cost for the number of official copy grants stated in 6 and 7 above.   £

Note: If you do not enclose all the relevant items, your application may be delayed.

PLEASE ENSURE THAT ALL INFORMATION GIVEN IS ACCURATE AND THAT YOU KEEP COPIES OF ALL DOCUMENTS SENT

Official Use Only

Type of grant:

Power reserved to _____ [Name of executor/s]

Will message: with a codicil / and _____ codicils (delete as appropriate)

Limitation _____

Min interest   Yes / No

Life interest   Yes / No

Figures:- DNE / amounts to   Gross: £
                         Net: £   Fee paid: £

Clearing:-

Title:-

Footnote:-

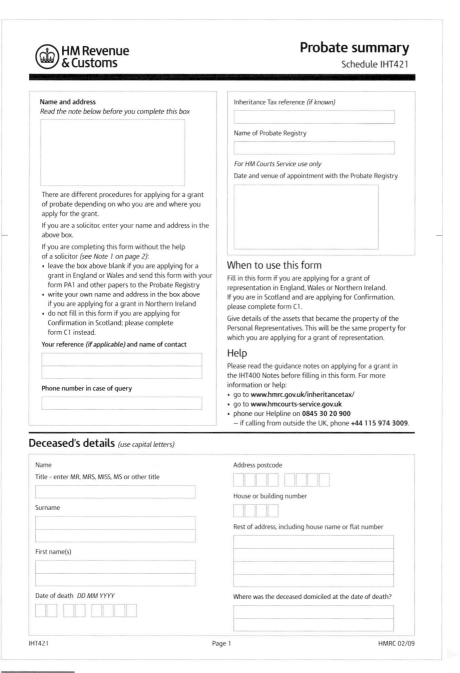

Figure 8.2 Form IHT421: probate summary for England and Wales

Summary

This is a summary for probate purposes only and will not necessarily include all the assets you have listed in the form IHT400 for Inheritance Tax purposes. It will not include:

- lifetime gifts
- foreign assets
- assets held in trust
- nominated assets
- gifts with reservation and pre-owned assets.

Estate in the UK before deductions
IHT400, box 79 + IHT404, box 13

1 £ _____

Joint assets passing by survivorship
Copy amount from IHT404, box 11, total of column A

2 £ _____

Gross value of assets for probate (box 1 *minus* box 2)

3 £ _____   *See Note 2 below*

Liabilities
IHT400, box 83 + box 84 + IHT404, box 12

4 £ _____

Net value (box 3 *minus* box 4)

5 £ _____   *See Note 2 below*

Tax and interest paid on this account
If you want us to work out this amount, leave this box
blank. Otherwise, copy amount from form IHT400,
box 117 or IHT400 calculation box 64 as appropriate.
If there is no tax to pay, write '0'.

6 £ _____

Signature of person or name of firm calculating the amount due

[   ]

Date *DD MM YYYY*

[ ] [ ] [   ]

Notes

1 If the deceased was domiciled outside the UK at the date of
death you should send this form to HMRC Inheritance Tax
with form IHT400, all the completed schedules and any
supporting documents before you go any further.

2 **HM Courts Service and Solicitors' only**
Copy the amounts in boxes 3 and 5 to the oath.

For HM Revenue & Customs use only

Inheritance Tax stamp

[   ]

Confirmation

Your name and address

Your reference

HMRC reference

About the person who has died

Surname

Title

Forenames

Occupation

Date of birth

Date of death

Place of death

Address

Postcode

Testate
(delete as appropriate)

Total estate for
Confirmation   £

Executors

Full name(s) and address(es). If nominate, list in order shown in the Will, etc.

20

Recorded in the Court Books of the

along with relative Deeds

C1   1   HMRC 10/08

Figure 8.3 Form C1: application for a grant of confirmation in Scotland

Declaration by

1. who declares that the deceased (full name)

died on the date and at the place shown on page 1

domiciled in

2. That I am

3. That I/ _____ have entered or am   about to enter, upon possession and management of the deceased's estate as Executor   foresaid along with the said

4. That I do not know of any testamentary settlement or writing relating to the disposal of the deceased's estate or any part of the deceased's estate other than that mentioned in paragraph 2.

5. That the Inventory (on pages 3 - ☐) is a full and complete Inventory of the:
   • heritable estate in Scotland belonging to the deceased or the destination of which (s)he had the power to and did evacuate
   • moveable estate of the deceased in Scotland
   • real and personal estate of the deceased in England and Wales and in Northern Ireland
   • estate of the deceased situated elsewhere
   including property, other than settled property, over which (s)he had and exercised an absolute power of disposal.

6. That confirmation of the estate in Scotland, England and Wales and Northern Ireland amounting in
   value to   £ _____   is required.

To the best of my knowledge and belief the information I have given in this form is correct and complete.

Signature   Date

Warning to Executors

You may be liable to penalties or prosecution if you fail to make full enquiries and to include all property on which Inheritance Tax is payable.

2

Inventory

Inventory of:

- the heritable estate in Scotland belonging to the deceased or the destination of which (s)he had power to and did evacuate
- the moveable estate of the deceased in Scotland
- the real and personal estate of the deceased in England, Wales and Northern Ireland
- the estate of the deceased situated elsewhere.

Include property, other than settled property, over which the deceased had and exercised an absolute power of disposal.

List the estate under these headings and in this order

Estate in Scotland (heritable property first)
Estate in England and Wales
Estate in Northern Ireland
Summary for confirmation
Estate elsewhere (say in which country).

Item No	Description	Price of shares	£
		Carried forward	

3

1. Value of estate for Confirmation

Gross value of estate	1.1	£
Less: funeral expenses	1.2	£
standard security/mortgage	1.3	£
other debts and liabilities	1.4	£
Net value of estate	1.5	£

2. About the deceased (if you have completed a form IHT400 do not complete sections 2 and 3; go to section 4)

At the time of death was the deceased
a   married or in a civil partnership
b   single
c   divorced or former civil partner
d   widowed or surviving civil partner   a, b, c or d ☐

Surviving relatives   Spouse or civil partner ✓ ☐   Parent ✓ ☐   Sister(s)/brother(s) ✓ ☐

Number of children/grandchildren who survived the deceased   Children ☐   Grandchildren ☐

Tax district and reference for the deceased

District ☐   UTR ☐   NINO ☐☐☐☐☐☐

3. Gross value of estate for Inheritance Tax (see page 21 of C3)

Gross value of estate for Inheritance Tax (see page 21 of C3)	A	£
Net value of estate for Inheritance Tax	B	£
Net qualifying value of estate	C	£

4. For Inheritance Tax, is the estate

- an excepted estate   D ✓☐ or
- an exempt and excepted estate   E ☐

Or has form IHT400 been submitted to HMRC?   F ☐

5. Summary of amounts to be paid before Confirmation

Tax and interest now being paid which may not be paid by instalments
(box 117 on form IHT400, or box 63 on form IHT400 Calculation)

Tax and interest now being paid which may be paid by instalments
(box 62 on form IHT400 Calculation)

Total tax and interest now being paid

For HMRC use only

Received this day the sum of

£ _____

For Inheritance Tax and interest thereon

HMRC Cashiers

For Commissioners of
HM Revenue & Customs

The stamp and receipt are provisional. The Inventory will be examined after it has been recorded and the amount of tax will
then be adjusted if appropriate.

Income tax and
capital gains tax

9

Treatment of income before and after the death

This chapter gives an overview of how income and gains should be treated before and after the date of death

- Tax liabilities of the deceased to the date of death
- Tax liabilities at the date of death
- Tax liabilities of the estate following death
- Tax liabilities following the administration period

When a person dies, their personal tax liabilities will only apply up to the date that they died. From that moment on, their wealth and property (estate) is no longer deemed to be that of the deceased. It actually belongs to the beneficiaries named in the will, or beneficiaries that will benefit as a result of the intestacy laws. Therefore, the income and capital gains of the estate during the administration period when the personal representatives are dealing with the estate, must be treated as a separate matter from those of the deceased. To summarise, there are a number of stages in the process, as follows:

- The tax liabilities of the deceased to the date of death.
- The tax liabilities arising as a result of the death, namely inheritance tax.
- The tax liabilities arising on the income and gains of the estate administration period.
- The tax liabilities once the property and wealth have been distributed to the beneficiaries.

Figure 9.1 gives a time line and helps show this more clearly.

	Date of death		End of administration

- All tax liabilities to this date relate to the deceased
- Paid out of the estate to HMRC by the personal representatives

Period of administration

Personal representatives are liable to income tax and capital gains tax during this period

Assets are distributed to the beneficiaries who become responsible for any tax on income and gains

An IHT return may be prepared for the IHT liability on the estate

Figure 9.1   Tax position of events up to and following a person's death

Tax liabilities of the deceased to the date of death

The income tax and the capital gains tax liabilities of the deceased must be computed and paid for by the personal representatives. Any tax liabilities that still need to be paid would act as a liability of the estate and would need to be deducted from the residue that is finally distributed to the relevant beneficiaries. Alternatively, any repayment of tax due to the deceased would be collected from HM Revenue and Customs and added to the estate. To arrange for this to take place, the personal representatives would need to contact the office within HMRC that dealt with the tax affairs of the individual and notify them of the individual's death. The office would inform the personal representatives of the information that is required.

The personal representatives must ensure that the individual's tax affairs are up to date, to the date of death. This might include arranging for tax returns to be completed for the period that runs from the previous 6 April to the date of the death. They may also need to complete a return for the previous tax year if one was required, but not yet submitted.

The tax liabilities of the deceased to the date of death are covered fully in Chapter 10.

Tax liabilities at the date of death

At the time of death, the wealth and property (estate) of the person who has died is valued and the total value is subject to inheritance tax (IHT). An inheritance tax return form IHT400 is often required to be completed and this is covered in detail in Chapter 12. The personal representatives have the duty of completing the inheritance tax return and paying over any IHT to HMRC.

Tax liabilities of the estate following death

The personal representatives would notify HMRC that the person has died and they would arrange for a record to be set up for the administration period, if this is likely to be some time. Tax returns for the administration period would then need to be completed. There is an example of the tax return form SA900 in Appendix A.

The income tax liabilities and the capital gains tax liabilities that arise need to be computed and reported to HMRC. This is usually done using the self assessment form SA900. This is covered in detail in Chapter 11.

Tax liabilities following the administration period

Once the estate administration has been completed, the personal representatives can submit a clearance application form IHT30 to HMRC for confirmation that inheritance tax liabilities are satisfied, the estate can come to an end and the assets distributed to the beneficiaries (Figure 9.2 overleaf).

For clearance on other tax liabilities, it is sufficient to write to the relevant tax office. Once the assets, or the funds from the sale of the assets, have been distributed to the beneficiaries of the estate, the ownership is now that of the beneficiary or beneficiaries. From this point on, any income and gains arising from these assets or capital funds will be assessable on the beneficiary and the responsibility for reporting the income and gains is thus with the beneficiary.

Application for a clearance certificate

Inland **Revenue** Capital Taxes

Inheritance Tax Act 1984 s239(2) or Finance Act 1975 sch.4 para.25(2) or Finance Act 1894 s11(2)

Name and address of the person to whom IR Capital Taxes should send the certificate.

IR CT reference *(if known)*

Your reference

Telephone number

- Send this form to us only when you believe that all the inheritance tax due has been paid.
- Fill in **one section only** of sections A, B or C.
- Section B is for a liability arising on death in respect of a lifetime transfer. Section A is for any other liability arising on death, most commonly in respect of the deceased's own estate or the coming to an end on death of an interest in possession in settled property.
- Fill in section D by entering the relevant date(s) **and** tick either the 'Yes' or 'No' box as appropriate.

IR Capital Taxes, P.O. Box 38, Ferrers House, Castle Meadow Road, Nottingham, NG2 1BB, (DX 701201 Nottingham 4).   **Tel: 0115 974 2400.**

IR Capital Taxes, Meldrum House, 15 Drumsheugh Gardens, Edinburgh EH3 7UG (DX ED 542001 Edinburgh 14).   **Tel: 0131 777 4050/4060.**

IR Capital Taxes, Level 3, Dorchester House, 52-58 Great Victoria Street, Belfast, BT2 7QL. (DX 2001 NR Belfast 2).   **Tel: 028 9050 5353.**

Please send the completed form in duplicate to the IR Capital Taxes office dealing with the estate.

Section A   Liability arising on a death

Full name of the person who has died.

Date of death.

Title under which the property is taxable (e.g. 'Will of the deceased' or 'Settlement dated...').

Section B   Liability in respect of a lifetime transfer

Full name of the person who **made** the transfer.

Date of death.

Please give details of the transfer, including the date on which it was made.

Section C   Liability in respect of a settlement without an interest in possession

Full title and date of the settlement.

Please give brief details, including the date of the chargeable event.

Section D   Application in respect of property or transfers of value included in:

Original account(s) or inventory(ies) dated

Corrective account(s) or inventory(ies) dated

Calculation(s) of tax from IR Capital Taxes dated

Have there been changes to the value since the above? *If you have answered 'Yes', please give details on a separate sheet.*   Yes ☐ No ☐

IHT30 (PDF) Version 2.0.0.2

Figure 9.2   Form IHT30 to apply for a clearance certificate from HMRC

Section E   Repayment

A repayment cheque can only be paid into the account of the person(s) to whom the cheque is made payable. If you believe that a repayment of tax may be due, please state the name(s) of the person(s) to whom any repayment cheque should be made payable. This information is only required if a repayment of tax is claimed.

Section F   Declaration by the appropriate person(s)

To the best of my/our knowledge and belief, the information given above is correct. I am/We are not aware of any other information which I/we should disclose. I/We apply for a statutory certificate of discharge.

	Name	
	Signature	
	Capacity*	
	Date	
	Name	
	Signature	
	Capacity*	
	Date	

Capacity i.e. Executor, Administrator, Transferee, Trustee. Professional agents must not sign this form on behalf of the appropriate person(s).

Section G   Certificate (for official use only)

The Commissioners of Inland Revenue discharge the above named applicant(s) from any (further) claim for tax or duty on the value attributable to the property at section D, on the occasion specified at section A, B, or C **except for any tax which is being paid by instalments.**

The certificate is not valid unless IR CT stamp this box.

Signed by _____
(name stamp or block capitals)

Signature _____
for and on behalf of the Commissioners.

Date _____

This certificate does not itself constitute a determination of values of individual items for any other Revenue purpose. In particular, the issue of the certificate does not necessarily mean that values have been "ascertained" or that values may be taken as market values for capital gains tax within the provisions of section 274 and paragraph 9, schedule 11, Taxation of Chargeable Gains Act 1992. This certificate is not valid in certain circumstances, such as in the case of fraud or failure to disclose material facts or if further tax becomes payable as a result of an instrument of variation - see section 239 (4) Inheritance Tax Act 1984.

113507062000DTP

10

Tax liabilities and obligations to the date of death

This chapter details why and how a tax return may be completed to the date of death

- Income tax
- National insurance
- Capital gains tax
- Dates for submitting tax returns

During our lifetimes, we often have a tax liability on income that we receive each tax year. When someone dies, that income can very often continue, especially if it is generated from assets, such as investment property. These tax liabilities still need to be dealt with, despite the fact that an individual may have died during the tax year.

The income tax and the capital gains tax liabilities of the deceased must be computed and paid for by the personal representatives. Any tax liabilities that still need to be paid would act as a liability of the estate and would need to be deducted from the residue that is finally distributed to the relevant beneficiaries. Alternatively, any repayment of tax due to the deceased would be collected from HM Revenue and Customs (HMRC) and added to the estate. For this to take place, the personal representatives would need to contact the office within HMRC that dealt with the tax affairs of the individual and notify them of the individual's death. The office can then inform the personal representatives of the information that is required and guide them through bringing the deceased's tax affairs up to date.

Income tax

Tax returns up to the date of death may need to be completed, in accordance with the usual self assessment rules. The personal representatives must ensure that the individual's tax affairs are up to date, to the date of death. This is so that they can take into account any tax that needs to be paid to HMRC as a liability of the estate. This might include arranging for tax returns to be completed for the period that runs from the previous 6 April to the date of the death. They may also need to complete a return for the previous tax year if one was required, but not yet submitted. To locate the appropriate office that deals with the individual's tax affairs, use the following website:
www.hmrc.gov.uk/enq

The person who has died will still be entitled to their personal allowances, in full, for the year in which they died. This could mean that their income during the year of death is fully covered by their allowance which means that if any tax has been deducted during the tax year before the death, there could be a repayment of tax due to the estate.

National insurance

Liability to national insurance stops when someone dies. If someone was employed, then the liability to Class 1 NIC was taken through the Pay As You Earn system (PAYE) and therefore it is unlikely that any further NIC will be collected. However, if the deceased was self employed, it is likely they will have been paying Class 2 NICs. It is important therefore that the personal representatives contact the National Insurance Contributions Office so that they can ensure that direct debit or other payment arrangements are cancelled. They can call the NIC helpline on 0845 915 4655 (Monday to Friday, 8.00 am to 5.00 pm).

Class 4 contributions, which is the additional NIC for self-employed individuals, will be dealt with automatically through their self-assessment tax return.

Capital gains tax

As a general rule, no CGT arises on the assets that an individual held at the date of their death. Assets held by the individual, at the time of their death, are revalued to the market value of that asset for probate purposes. This means that any gains that have arisen on those assets during the person's lifetime are free of capital gains tax.

However, there may be a capital gains tax liability on any gains realised by the individual before they died, which would need to be reported to HMRC on the tax returns to the date of death. Any capital gains tax payable would be a liability that would be treated as a debt and must be paid out of the estate funds by the personal representatives.

For the year of death, the deceased is entitled to the whole of their annual exemption. The annual exempt amounts are:

2008–9	£9,600
2009–10	£10,100
2010–11	£10,100

Any chargeable gains above these levels are charged to tax at 18 per cent (increased to 28 per cent for higher rate tax payers from 23 June 2010).

Capital losses

Normally, when an individual makes a loss on the disposal of an asset, this is called a capital loss. The tax treatment of this is that the capital loss is carried forward to future tax years so that the individual can then set the loss against a future capital gain. However, if an individual dies, this is no longer possible as there will be no future capital gains on assets. The assets are now owned by someone else. There are then two matters that might need to be considered. First, if the deceased made capital losses during the tax year in which they died, then these losses can be set against any capital gains they also made before they died, in the tax year. Second, if there are no, or insufficient, capital gains to set the capital losses against in the year of death which leaves a balance of capital losses available, there is a special claim that can be made by the personal representatives to carry these capital losses back three tax years, to try and use the losses in some way. See the example below.

Example

Income tax and capital gains tax to the date of death

Jo died on 1 April 2010, so this was in the 2009/10 tax year. During the year, she was self-employed and received rental income from an investment property. Her profits amounted to £20,000 for the period 6 April 2009 to 1 April 2010 and she received rental income of £1,200 per month.

In December 2009, she sold some shares in ABC plc and realised a capital gain of £30,000.

At her death, she had the following assets:

- car worth £10,000;
- home worth £300,000;
- investment property worth £250,000.

The tax obligations are:

- The personal representatives of Jo's estate will be responsible for ensuring the self-employed accounts are prepared to the date of Jo's death.
- They will then be responsible for ensuring the tax returns are completed to the date of death and for any tax and Class 4 NIC to be paid over to HMRC, as a liability of the estate.
- As a capital gain was made by Jo before her death, this will be added to the tax return and any capital gains tax due will be a liability of the estate and also paid over to HMRC by the personal representatives.

Dates for submitting tax returns

The personal representatives must submit all tax returns to HMRC by the later of:

- 31 January after the end of the tax year to which it relates. So, for example, 31 January 2011 for the tax return 6 April 2009 to 5 April 2010.
- Three months and seven days after the tax return is issued.

Tax liabilities during the estate administration period

This chapter details the tax liabilities and obligations of the personal representatives during the period of administration

- Income tax
- Capital gains tax
- Assets sold during the administration period before distributions
- Assets not sold but transferred to the beneficiaries
- Tax planning
- Distributions of income during administration
- Dates for submitting tax returns

The personal representatives would notify HMRC that the person has died and they would arrange for a record to be set up for the administration period, if this is likely to be some time. Tax returns for the administration period would then need to be completed.

Income tax

The income tax that arises on any income still being received from the deceased's assets also needs to be computed and reported to HMRC. This is usually done using the self assessment form SA900. There is an example of form SA900, in Appendix A.

The personal representatives are not entitled to any personal allowances or reliefs and the income they receive is taxed only at the rate of 10 per cent for dividends, 20 per cent for all other income. Administration expenses are not an allowable deduction when calculating the income tax for this period, although it is possible that any expenses may be an allowable capital gains tax or inheritance tax deduction. However, if a loan has been taken out to pay for any inheritance tax and obtain the grant of probate, the interest paid on the loan for the first year is a deductible expense in determining the income tax liability of the personal representatives during the administration period.

Capital gains tax

The assets of the estate are dealt with in one of two ways when dealing with the administration of the estate and ultimately distributing the estate to the beneficiaries:

1 Assets may be sold during the administration period before any distributions being made to beneficiaries. If this is the case, the cash funds that are produced by the sale of the assets are usually then collected, and it is those liquid funds that are distributed to the beneficiaries, and not the original assets.

2 The assets are not sold during the administration period, but are actually transferred to the beneficiaries.

The capital gains tax treatment in each case is different.

Assets sold during the administration period before distributions

It is likely that the personal representatives will collect in the assets of the estate and sell some or all of these. When this occurs, there could be a liability to capital gains tax on the sale of any chargeable assets. If this is the case, these gains need to be reported to **HMRC** on the tax return, and the personal representatives then have the duty of paying the capital gains tax out of the estate funds.

The personal administrators are treated as acquiring all assets at their market value at the date of death and so capital gains tax will only be payable on any chargeable assets if they are disposed of for more than the value at death. Personal representatives then have an annual exempt amount that is available for set off against the gains for the year of death and then for the next two tax years. The annual exempt amounts are:

2008–09   £9,600
2009–10   £10,100
2010–11   £10,100

Any chargeable gains above these levels are charged to tax at 18 per cent (increased to 28 per cent from 23 June 2010).

Example

Assets sold during the administration period

Annie died on 14 October 2009. At her death she had the following assets:

- A car worth £4,500, which cost £18,000 when she bought it.
- A home worth £300,000 which she had lived in since the purchase, three years earlier. The home had cost £150,000 when she bought it.
- A holiday home in Kent which was worth £250,000 at the date of death, which had cost her £175,000 two years previously.

The personal representatives of Annie's estate called in all the assets and sold these during the tax year 2009–10, so they then had the cash funds to pay out to the beneficiaries. They sold the assets for the following amounts:

Car	£4,400
Annie's home	£310,000
Holiday home	£270,000

The capital gains tax position of the personal representatives will therefore be:

	£
Car: this is an exempt asset for capital gains tax	0
Annie's home (£310,000 less the probate value of £300,000)	10,000
The holiday home (£270,000 less the probate value of £250,000)	20,000
Chargeable gains	30,000
Less annual exemption for 2009–10	(10,100)
Taxable gains	19,900

Tax due £19,900 at 18 per cent = **£3,582**

The personal representatives have the role of declaring the gains on to the tax return for the administration period and paying the capital gains tax over to HMRC.

In computing the taxable gain, the expenses of selling an asset may be deducted from the gain. In some cases that can result in a loss, especially if the proceeds of the asset before deducting expenses are the same as its probate value. It is also possible to claim a deduction for a proportion of the general costs of probate. HMRC publishes a scale that is used for calculating this deduction.

If the administration period is likely to continue beyond the two years when the personal representatives have the annual exemptions, it is important to consider whether all of the assets should be sold during the tax years when the relief is available.

Assets not sold but transferred to the beneficiaries

The personal representatives may transfer an asset to a beneficiary in a number of ways, including:

■ under the terms of the deceased's will;

■ under the rules of intestacy (where there is no will).

When this transfer takes place, the beneficiary is treated as having acquired the asset at its market value at the date of death. This transfer does not count as a disposal for capital gains tax purposes and no CGT is payable on it by the personal representatives.

Example

Assets transferred to a beneficiary

Using the same facts as in the earlier example, Annie died on 14 October 2009. At her death she had the following assets:

■ A car worth £4,500 which cost £18,000 when she bought it

■ A home worth £300,000 which she'd lived in since the purchase, three years earlier. The home had cost £150,000 when she bought it.

■ A holiday home in Kent which was worth £250,000 at the date of death, which had cost her £175,000 two years previously.

The personal representatives of Annie's estate transferred the assets to the two named beneficiaries, Bertie and Carlie, who then sold the assets themselves during the tax year 2009–10. Bertie and Carlie sold the assets for the following amounts:

Bertie

| The car | £4,400 |
| Annie's home | £310,000 |

Carlie

| The holiday home | £270,000 |

Firstly, the personal representatives have no liability to capital gains tax as the assets are treated as being made at the probate values, the market value at the date of death.

The capital gains tax position of the two beneficiaries will therefore be as follows:

Bertie	£
Car: exempt for capital gains tax	0
The home (£310,000 less the probate value of £300,000)	10,000
Chargeable gains	10,000
Less annual exemption for 2009–10	(10,100)
Taxable gains	Nil

Carlie	
The holiday home (£270,000 less the probate value of £250,000)	20,000
Chargeable gains	20,000
Less annual exemption for 2009–10	(10,100)
Taxable gains	9,900

Tax due £9,900 at 18% = **£1,782**

Bertie and Carlie will have the obligations of entering the gains on to their tax returns and paying any capital gains tax liability under the self-assessment system.

Tax planning

Using the examples above, it is important to decide whether the personal representatives themselves should realise any capital gains or whether the transfer of assets should be made to the beneficiaries who will then realise the gains. Overall, and as can be seen in the above examples, the beneficiaries, especially if there are more than one, may have a lower tax liability than the personal representatives. The decision depends on the tax positions of both options, together with the wishes or requirements of the deceased's will (especially now with the proposal from the Summer Budget 2010 to increase the rate of capital gains tax to 28 per cent from 23 June 2010 for trustees, personal representatives and individuals who are higher rate tax payers). Specialist advice taken on this matter is likely to be worthwhile.

Distributions of income during administration

The personal representatives will usually pay out legacies (gifts) as directed by the deceased's will. Interest on a legacy that is paid more than one year after the death is also paid out with the legacy to cover the length of time it has taken to distribute the gift. The interest is usually calculated from the first anniversary of the date of death to the date of payment, and this is paid gross, without deduction of tax. During the administration period, any payment of income from an asset, to a residuary beneficiary that is ultimately entitled to that asset, is made with deduction of tax.

Example

A payment of rental income to a beneficiary

Georgie was the named beneficiary in a will, whereby she is to receive an investment property. The administration of the estate is being dealt with but the transfer of the property cannot yet officially take place until the grant of probate is received by the personal representatives. Meanwhile, however, the personal representatives have received rental income from the investment property amounting to £10,000 and they pay this to Georgie, since she is entitled to the asset from the date of death.

The personal representatives have an income tax liability themselves of 20 per cent on this income, amounting to £2,000 and will pay this to HMRC via the self assessment tax returns. Georgie will then have received net income of £8,000 with a tax credit of £2,000 to enter on her self-assessment tax return. She should also receive a form R185 that is completed by the personal representatives to vouch for the tax deducted.

A form R185 needs to be completed when an income distribution is made to a beneficiary (Figure 11.1 on page 100). Personal representatives should complete the relevant boxes and give the form to the beneficiary. In the case of Georgie, above, the details of her name and address would be entered on the form. The net rental income of £8,000 would be entered in box number 7.13, the tax of £2,000 would be entered in box number 7.14 and the total amount taxable on Georgie would be £10,000 entered in box number 7.15.

An example of the form R185 is also shown in Appendix A, together with some useful notes.

The beneficiaries will have then received income, that has been subject to tax, and they may need to report this income to their own tax office and complete a self-assessment tax return. They may need to contact their own tax office to check whether this is necessary as it can depend on their tax position.

If a beneficiary is a basic rate taxpayer, the income from the administration period may not be subject to any additional tax in his or her hands, but it is wise to check that the level of income distribution has not taken the beneficiary into paying a higher rate of tax. The tax office will be able to advise whether this is the case.

If a beneficiary is already a higher rate taxpayer, the income will be chargeable at the higher rates of tax and therefore the completion of a tax return is likely. The income distribution must be reported to the tax office dealing with the beneficiary so that the additional higher rate tax can be calculated and paid to HMRC. If the beneficiary is not a taxpayer, for example, because they have no other income, it is likely that there will be a repayment of tax available in relation to the tax that has been deducted by the personal representatives. A claim can be made to HMRC.

Dates for submitting tax returns

The personal representatives must submit all tax returns to HMRC by the later of:

- 31 January after the end of the tax year to which it relates. So for example, 31 January 2011 for the tax return 6 April 2009 to 5 April 2010.

- Three months and seven days after the tax return has been issued by HM Revenue and Customs.

Statement of income from estates

Personal representatives (who can be either executors or administrators) may use this form to advise beneficiaries about income from the residue (see note below) of the estate of a deceased person:
• for each year during the administration of the estate if a 'sum' (see note below) is paid to the beneficiary in that year, and
• for the year in which the administration of the estate is completed.

The beneficiary's estate income for the year ended 5 April `2` `0` is the deemed income shown on page 2 of this form.

The beneficiary
Full name of beneficiary

Address

Postcode

The deceased person
Full name of deceased person

Date of death *DD MM YYYY*

Notes for personal representatives

Personal representatives may complete the relevant boxes on page 2 and give the form to the beneficiary.

For the purpose of this form, a 'sum' includes cash, assets transferred or appropriated, and debts set off or released. The **residue** is what is left in the estate after you have paid all debts, legacies and taxes.

If the administration period has been ongoing for more than a year, the following example shows how to work out the income which each beneficiary should show in their tax return/repayment form.

Step 1
Add the net amount (the amount **after tax taken off**) of the beneficiary's share of the income from the residue for the tax year to any net amount brought forward.

Step 2
Compare the figure in Step 1 with the sum paid to the beneficiary in the tax year.
• If the sum paid is greater than or equal to the result of Step 1, the beneficiary's share of the income from the residue for the tax year is the amount at Step 1.
• If the sum paid is less than the result of Step 1, the beneficiary's share is the sum actually paid in the tax year. The balance of the beneficiary's entitlement is carried forward to the next tax year, and will then be their income entitlement in the next year if no distributions are made.

For the final tax year of the administration period, the beneficiary's share of the income from the residue will be treated as having been fully paid.

Notes for beneficiaries

Keep this form and refer to it if making a tax return or claiming a tax repayment.

If you need to complete a tax return the box numbers on page 2 match those on the SA107 *Trusts etc.* pages of the tax return. Transfer the amounts of income after tax taken off from those boxes to the corresponding boxes on the SA107 (for more information see SA107 Notes *Trusts etc. notes* - go to **www.hmrc.gov.uk**).

If you need to claim a tax repayment transfer the figures to the relevant boxes in the R40 *Claim for repayment of tax deducted from savings and investments*, as follows:
• income and tax paid or tax credit at box 16 to boxes 4.3 and 4.4 on the R40
• income and tax paid or tax credit at box 17 to boxes 4.5 and 4.6 on the R40
• income and tax paid or tax credit at box 18 to boxes 6.1 to 6.4 (as appropriate) on the R40
• income at box 20 to box 4.10 on the R40
• income and tax paid or tax credit at box 21 to boxes 4.7 and 4.8 on the R40
(for more information see R40 Notes *Notes for completing form R40* - go to **www.hmrc.gov.uk**).

Please note that the tax described as 'non-repayable' or 'non-payable' cannot be repaid.

R185(Estate Income)   Page 1   HMRC 03/10

Figure 11.1 Form R185 for statement of income from estates

Income from the estates of deceased persons

Income from United Kingdom (UK) estates

If the beneficiary was in receipt of income from a UK estate only, enter the net income and tax paid or tax credit in boxes 16 to 21.

16 Non-savings income - **after tax taken off**
This includes rental income and profits from a trade

£ [   ] . [   ]

Tax paid or tax credit on box 16 income

£ [   ] . [   ]

17 Savings income - **after tax taken off**
This includes bank or building society interest

£ [   ] . [   ]

Tax paid or tax credit on box 17 income

£ [   ] . [   ]

18 Dividend income - **after tax taken off**
This includes dividends from foreign companies that do not qualify for UK tax credit

£ [   ] . [   ]

Tax paid or tax credit on box 18 income

£ [   ] . [   ]

19 Non-savings income taxed at non-repayable basic rate - **after tax taken off**. *This includes gains realised on certain life insurance policies, and any undistributed estate income carried forward from 1998–99 or earlier years*

£ [   ] . [   ]

Tax paid or tax credit on box 19 income

£ [   ] . [   ]

20 Income taxed at 22% – **after tax taken off**
This includes any income that has had tax taken off at 22% when this was the basic rate of tax, but is not passed over to the beneficiaries until after the reduction in the basic rate to 20%

£ [   ] . [   ]

Tax paid or tax credit on box 20 income

£ [   ] . [   ]

21 Dividend income taxed at non-payable dividend rate – **after tax taken off**. *This includes dividends from UK companies and dividends from foreign companies that qualify for UK tax credit*

£ [   ] . [   ]

Tax paid or tax credit on box 21 income

£ [   ] . [   ]

Income from foreign estates

If the beneficiary was in receipt of income from a foreign estate, do not complete boxes 16 to 21.
Instead, enter the income in box 22 and any relief for UK tax already accounted for in box 23.

22 Foreign estate income

£ [   ] . [   ]

23 Relief for UK tax already accounted for

£ [   ] . [   ]

Foreign tax paid on estate income

Complete box 24 if any foreign tax credit relief is claimable but has **not** been claimed on foreign income arising to a UK estate or a foreign estate.

24 Foreign tax for which foreign tax credit relief has not been claimed

£ [   ] . [   ]

Signature and date

I confirm that the information given on this form is correct.

Signature of the personal representative

[   ]

Date *DD MM YYYY*

[ ] [ ] [   ]

Inheritance tax

12

Completing the inheritance tax return

This chapter explains how to complete the inheritance tax return form (account) IHT400

- Inheritance tax return form IHT400
- Completing form IHT400
- Calculating the inheritance tax payable
- Delivering the return form to HMRC
- Making amendments or corrections to form IHT400
- Scotland and Northern Ireland

Inheritance tax return form IHT400

The inheritance tax return form IHT400 is the account that must be completed by the personal representatives to show the assets and liabilities in the deceased's estate. It must be completed for all estates that are not excepted estates (as detailed in Chapter 18). To recap, an excepted estate is one that would fall in the following categories:

- Valued at under the inheritance tax threshold (£325,000 in 2009–10 and in 2010–11).

- An exempt estate: the deceased person left everything (or everything over and above the inheritance tax threshold) to a spouse or civil partner living in the UK or to a registered UK charity (and the estate is valued at under £1 million).

▪ The deceased person was a foreign domiciliary who lived permanently abroad and died abroad and the value of their UK assets is under £150,000.

Where all, or a substantial part of an estate, passes to exempt beneficiaries, HMRC may accept a reduced account from the personal representatives. The completion of the return form IHT400 is done on the principle of self-assessment, which means that the executors or administrators must assess the value of the estate, net of any liabilities, and then disclose this on the form to the best of their knowledge. They then calculate any IHT payable.

The following pages tell you more about the account. They provide guidance on how you should deal with the information in each part of the account or tell you where you can find this information in other parts of this book.

Completing form IHT400

Form IHT400 consists of 16 pages and is shown in Figure 12.1 on page 108. It covers the following:

▪ Personal details of the person that has died.

▪ Details of the persons acting as personal representatives and dealing with the estate.

▪ Details of the will, if one was left.

▪ Details of the assets and liabilities of the deceased.

▪ Claims for any exemptions or reliefs.

▪ Details of any additional schedules that are enclosed with the return.

▪ Declarations.

▪ A checklist.

The basic 16-page return would apply to most estates. However, each estate is different and will consist of different assets, liabilities, claims, etc. Therefore, any additional information is reported to HMRC on a supporting schedule that would be enclosed with the main tax return. Only the supporting schedules that are relevant to the person that has died will require completion and submission with the tax return form IHT400. A list of these is given in Table 12.1.

There is further advice and guidance to help the personal representatives complete the return form IHT400 on the HMRC website at: www.hmrc.gov.uk/inheritancetax/iht400-notes.pdf

Table 12.1 List of IHT400 schedules

IHT401   Domicile outside the United Kingdom

IHT402   Claim to transfer unused inheritance tax nil rate band

IHT403   Gifts and other transfers of value

IHT404   Jointly-owned assets

IHT405   Houses, land, buildings and interests in land

IHT406   Bank and building society accounts

IHT407   Household and personal goods

IHT408   Household and personal goods given to charity

IHT409   Pensions

IHT410   Life assurance and annuities

IHT411   Listed stocks and shares

IHT412   Unlisted stocks and shares and control holdings

IHT413   Business or partnership interests and assets

IHT414   Agricultural relief

IHT415   Interest in another estate

IHT416   Debts due to the deceased

IHT417   Foreign assets

IHT418   Assets held in trust

IHT419   Debts owed by the deceased

IHT420   National Heritage assets, conditional exemption and offers in lieu of tax

IHT421   Probate summary

IHT422   Application for an inheritance tax reference

IHT423   Direct payment scheme bank or building society account

Alternatively, the Probate and Inheritance Tax Helpline on 0845 30 20 900 is available to offer guidance.

HM Revenue & Customs

Inheritance Tax account

IHT400

When to use this form

Fill in this form if:
- the deceased died on or after 18 March 1986, and
- there is Inheritance Tax to pay, or
- there is no Inheritance Tax to pay, but the estate does not qualify as an excepted estate.

The IHT400 Notes, page 1, gives details about excepted estates.

Deadline

You must send this form to us within 12 months of the date of death. Interest will be payable after six months.

The Inheritance Tax (IHT) account

The account is made up of this form and separate Schedules. You will have to fill in some of the Schedules.

To help you get started
- Gather the deceased's papers and the information you have about the deceased's estate. Make a list of the deceased's assets, liabilities, investments and other financial interests and any gifts made.
- Fill in boxes 1 to 28 then work through boxes 29 to 48 of this form to identify which Schedules you will need. If you do not have them all:
  – download them from **www.hmrc.gov.uk/inheritancetax/** or
  – phone the helpline to request them.
- Fill in the Schedules before moving on to complete this form.

IHT reference number

If there is any tax to pay, you will need to apply for an IHT reference number and payslip before you send this form to us. You can apply online at **www.hmrc.gov.uk/inheritancetax/** or fill in form IHT422 and send it to us. Apply for a reference at least two weeks before you plan to send us this form.

Filling in this form

- Use the IHT400 Notes to help you fill in this form.
- Fill in the form in black or blue ink.
- Make full enquiries so you can show that the figures you give and the statements you make are correct.
- If an instrument of variation has been signed before applying for a grant, fill in the form to show the effect of the Will/intestacy and instrument together. *See IHT400 Notes.*

Answer all the questions and fill in the boxes to help us process your form.

Help

For more information or help or another copy of this form:
- go to **www.hmrc.gov.uk/inheritancetax/**
- phone our helpline on **0845 30 20 900**
  – if calling from outside the UK, phone **+44 115 974 3009.**

Deceased's details

1 Deceased's name
Title - enter MR, MRS, MISS, MS or other title

Surname

First name(s)

2 Date of death *DD MM YYYY*

3 IHT reference number (if known) *See note at the top of this form*

4 Was the deceased male or female?

Male ☐   Female ☐

5 Deceased's date of birth *DD MM YYYY*

6 Where was the deceased domiciled at the date of death?

- England & Wales ☐
- Scotland ☐
- Northern Ireland ☐
- other country ☐   *specify country in box below.*

See IHT400 Notes for information about domicile.

If the deceased was not domiciled in the UK, fill in
IHT401 now, and then the rest of the form.

Please turn over

Figure 12.1 IHT400: the 16-page inheritance tax return form

If the deceased was domiciled in Scotland at the date of death

7　Has the legitim fund been discharged in **full** *following the death? See IHT400 Notes*

Yes ☐　*Go to box 8*

No ☐　*Please provide a full explanation in the 'Additional information' boxes, pages 15 and 16*

Deceased's details

8　Was the deceased:

- married or in a civil partnership ☐
- single ☐
- widowed or a surviving civil partner ☐
- divorced or a former civil partner? ☐

9　If the deceased was married or in a civil partnership at the time of their death, on what date did the marriage or registration of the civil partnership take place? *DD MM YYYY*

☐☐ ☐☐ ☐☐☐☐

10　Who survived the deceased? *Tick all that apply*

- a spouse or civil partner ☐
- brothers or sisters ☐
- parents ☐
- children ☐　number ☐☐
- grandchildren ☐　number ☐☐

11　Deceased's last known permanent address

Postcode

☐☐☐☐ ☐☐☐☐

House number

☐☐☐☐

Rest of address, including house name or flat number

12　Was the property in box 11 owned or part-owned by the deceased or did the deceased have a right to live in the property?

Yes ☐　*Go to box 13*

No ☐　*Give details below. For example, 'deceased lived with daughter' or 'address was a nursing home'*

13　Deceased's occupation, or former occupation if retired, for example, 'retired doctor'.

14　Deceased's National Insurance number (if known)

☐☐ ☐☐ ☐☐ ☐☐ ☐☐ ☐

15　Deceased's Income Tax or Unique Taxpayer Reference (UTR) (if known)

☐☐☐☐☐ ☐☐☐☐☐

16　Did anyone act under a power of attorney granted by the deceased during their lifetime? This may have been a general, enduring or lasting power of attorney.

No ☐

Yes ☐　*Please enclose a copy of the power of attorney*

Contact details of the person dealing with the estate

For example, a solicitor or executor.

17 Name and address of the firm or person dealing with the estate

Name

Postcode

House or building number

Rest of address, including house name or flat number

18 Contact name *if different from box 17*

19 Phone number

20 DX number and town (if used)

21 Contact's reference

22 Fax number

23 If we have to repay any overpaid Inheritance Tax, we need to know who to make the cheque out to.

Do you want any cheque we send to be made out to the firm or person shown at box 17?

Yes [ ]   *Go to box 24*

No [ ]   *Give the name(s) here, as you would like them to appear on the cheque.*

Deceased's Will

24 Did the deceased leave a Will?

No [ ]   *Go to box 29*

Yes [ ]   *Go to box 25. Please enclose a copy of the Will and any codicils when sending us your account. If an instrument of variation alters the amount of Inheritance Tax payable on this estate, please also send a copy.*

25 Is the address of the deceased as shown in the Will the same as the deceased's last known permanent address (at box 11)?

No [ ]   *Go to box 26*

Yes [ ]   *Go to box 27*

26 What happened to the property given as the deceased's residence in the Will?
If the deceased sold the property but used all the sale proceeds to buy another main residence for themselves and this happened more than once, there is no need to give details of all the events. Simply say that the 'residence was replaced by the current property'. In all other cases give details of exactly what happened to the property, and give the date of the event(s).

Items referred to in the Will but not included in the estate

Only fill in boxes 27 and 28 if the deceased left a Will. If not go to box 29.

27 Are you including on this form all assets specifically referred to in the Will?
(For example, land, buildings, personal possessions, works of art or shares.)

No ☐ *Go to box 28*

Yes ☐ *Go to box 29*

28 Items referred to in the Will and not included on this form (any gifts should be shown on form IHT403)

Items given away as gifts, sold or disposed of before the deceased's death	Who was the item given or sold to, or what happened to it?	Date of gift, sale or disposal	Value of the item at the date of gift, sale or disposal £	If the item was sold, what did the deceased do with the sale proceeds?

What makes up your Inheritance Tax account – Schedules

To make a complete account of the estate you may need to complete some separate Schedules.
Answer the following questions by ticking the 'No' or 'Yes' box.

29 **Transfer of unused nil rate band**

Do you want to transfer any unused nil rate band from the deceased's spouse or civil partner who died before them?

No ☐   Yes ☐   Use Schedule [IHT402]

30 **Gifts and other transfers of value**

Did the deceased make any lifetime gifts or other transfers of value on or after 18 March 1986? *See IHT400 Notes*

No ☐   Yes ☐   Use Schedule [IHT403]

31 **Jointly owned assets**

Did the deceased jointly own any assets (other than business or partnership assets) with any other person(s)?

No ☐   Yes ☐   Use Schedule [IHT404]

32 **Houses, land, buildings and interests in land**

Did the deceased own any house, land or buildings or rights over land in the UK in their sole name?

No ☐   Yes ☐   Use Schedule [IHT405]

33 **Bank and building society accounts**

Did the deceased hold any bank or building society accounts in their sole name, including cash ISAs, National Savings and Premium Bonds?

No ☐   Yes ☐   Use Schedule [IHT406]

34 **Household and personal goods**

Did the deceased own any household goods or personal possessions?

No ☐   Yes ☐   Use Schedule [IHT407]

If the deceased did **not** own any household goods or personal possessions or they do not have any value, please explain the circumstances in the 'Additional information' boxes on pages 15 and 16.

35 **Household and personal goods donated to charity**

Do the people who inherit the deceased's household goods and personal possessions want to donate some or all of them to a UK registered charity and deduct charity exemption from the value of the estate?
For example, they may wish to donate the deceased's furniture to a charity shop.

No ☐   Yes ☐   Use Schedule [IHT408]

What makes up your Inheritance Tax account – Schedules continued

36 Pensions

Did the deceased have any provision for retirement other than the State Pension? *For example, a pension from an employer, a personal pension policy (or an alternatively secured pension)*

No ☐   Yes ☐   Use Schedule IHT409

37 Life assurance and annuities

Did the deceased pay premiums on any life assurance policies, annuities or other products which are payable either to their estate, to another person or which continue after death?

No ☐   Yes ☐   Use Schedule IHT410

38 Listed stocks and shares

Did the deceased own any listed stocks and shares or stocks and shares ISAs (excluding control holdings)?

No ☐   Yes ☐   Use Schedule IHT411

39 Unlisted stocks and shares and control holdings

Did the deceased own any unlisted stocks and shares (including AIM and OFEX), or any control holdings of any listed shares?

No ☐   Yes ☐   Use Schedule IHT412

40 Business relief, business and partnership interests and assets

Do you want to deduct business relief from any business interests and assets owned by the deceased or a partnership in which they were a partner?

No ☐   Yes ☐   Use Schedule IHT413

41 Farms, farmhouses and farmland

Do you want to deduct agricultural relief from any farmhouses, farms or farmland owned by the deceased?

No ☐   Yes ☐   Use Schedule IHT414

42 Interest in another estate

Was the deceased entitled to receive any legacy or assets from the estate of someone who died before them and that they had not received before they died?

No ☐   Yes ☐   Use Schedule IHT415

43 Debts due to the estate

Was the deceased owed any money by way of personal loans or mortgage at the date of death?

No ☐   Yes ☐   Use Schedule IHT416

44 Foreign assets

Did the deceased own any assets outside the UK either in their sole name or jointly with others?

No ☐   Yes ☐   Use Schedule IHT417

45 Assets held in trust

Did the deceased have any right to benefit from any assets held in trust (including the right to receive assets held in a trust at some future date)?

No ☐   Yes ☐   Use Schedule IHT418

46 Debts owed by the deceased

Do you wish to include a deduction from the estate for debts and liabilities of the following types:
- money that was spent on behalf of the deceased and which was not repaid
- loans
- liabilities related to a life assurance policy where the sum assured will not be fully reflected in the estate
- debts that the deceased guaranteed on behalf of another person?

No ☐   Yes ☐   Use Schedule IHT419

47 National Heritage assets

Is any asset already exempt or is exemption now being claimed, on the grounds of national, scientific, historic, artistic, scenic or architectural interest? Or does any such asset benefit from an Approved Maintenance Fund for the upkeep and preservation of national heritage assets?

No ☐   Yes ☐   Use Schedule IHT420

If you answered Yes to any of questions 29 to 47, please fill in the Schedule for that asset. The Schedule number is shown at the end of each question.

48 Do you have all of the Schedules you need?

No ☐
- download the Schedules from www.hmrc.gov.uk/inheritancetax/ or
- phone us on **0845 30 20 900** (**+44 115 974 3009** from outside the UK), or
- ask for them by email hmrc.ihtorderline@btconnect.com

When you have got all the Schedules you need, fill them in before you go to box 49.

Yes ☐   *Fill in the Schedules **now** before going to box 49*

Estate in the UK

Use this section to tell us about assets owned by the deceased in the UK. You should include all assets owned outright by the deceased and the **deceased's share** of **jointly owned** assets. You will need to copy figures from the Schedules you have filled in. Any assets the deceased had outside the UK should be shown on form IHT417 and **not** in boxes 49 to 96.

Jointly owned assets

Enter 'U' in the box if the deceased did not own any of the assets described.

	Column A	Column B
49 Jointly owned assets (form IHT404, box 5)		£
50 Jointly owned assets (form IHT404, box 10)	£	

Assets owned outright by the deceased

Enter the value of the assets owned outright by the deceased in the amount boxes attached to each question. Enter '0' in the box if the deceased did not own any of the assets described.

	Column A	Column B
51 Deceased's residence (except farmhouses and jointly owned houses) (form IHT405, box 7). Include the value of jointly owned houses at box 49 and farmhouses at box 68 instead		£
52 Bank and building society accounts in the deceased's sole name (form IHT406, box 1)	£	
53 Cash (in coins or notes) and uncashed traveller's cheques	£	
54 Premium Bonds and National Savings & Investments products (form IHT406, box 5)	£	
55 Household and personal goods (form IHT407, box 6)	£	
56 Pensions (form IHT409, boxes 7 and 15). Include the value of any pensions arrears due at the date of death	£	
57 Life assurance and mortgage protection policies (form IHT410, box 6)	£	
58 Add up all the figures in **Column A** (boxes 50 to 57)	£	
59 Add up all the figures in **Column B** (boxes 49 + 51)		£

Estate in the UK continued

	Column A	Column B
60 Copy the figure from box 58	£	
61 Copy the figure from box 59		£
62 UK Government and municipal securities (form IHT411, box 1), but include dividends and interest at box 64	£	
63 Listed stocks, shares and investments that did not give the deceased control of the company (form IHT411, box 2)	£	
64 Dividends or interest on stocks, shares and securities	£	
65 Traded unlisted and unlisted shares except control holdings (form IHT412, box 1 + box 2)	£	
66 Traded unlisted and unlisted shares except control holdings (see IHT412 Notes)		£
67 Control holdings of unlisted, traded unlisted and listed shares (form IHT412, box 3 + box 4 + box 5)		£
68 Farms, farmhouses and farmland (give details on forms IHT414 and IHT405)		£
69 Businesses including farm businesses, business assets and timber		£
70 Other land, buildings and rights over land (give details on form IHT405)		£
71 Interest in another estate (form IHT415, box 7)		£
72 Interest in another estate (form IHT415, box 9)	£	
73 Debts due to the estate (form IHT416, box 3 total)	£	
74 Income Tax or Capital Gains Tax repayment	£	
75 Trust income due to the deceased – see IHT400 Notes	£	
76 Other assets and income due to the deceased (enter details in the 'Additional information' boxes on pages 15 and 16 of this form if not given elsewhere)	£	
77 Add up all the figures in **Column A** (boxes 60 to 76)	£	
78 Add up all the figures in **Column B** (boxes 61 to 71)		£
79 Gross total of the estate in the UK (box 77 + box 78)	£	

Deductions from the estate in the UK incurred up to the date of death

80 Mortgages, secured loans and other debts payable out of property or assets owned outright by the deceased and shown in
Column B on pages 6 and 7. For example, a mortgage secured on the deceased's house or a loan secured on a business.
Enter the name of the creditor and say which property or asset the deduction relates to and describe the liability.

Name of creditor	Property or asset and description of liability	Amount £
	Total mortgages and secured loans	£

81 Funeral expenses

Funeral costs	£
Headstone	£

Other costs (please specify)	
Total cost of funeral	£

82 Other liabilities

Enter any other liabilities that have not been shown in boxes 80 or 81. (For example, outstanding
gas and electricity bills, credit card balances or nursing home fees.)

Creditor's name and description of the liability	Amount £
Total other liabilities	

Deductions from the estate in the UK continued

Deductions summary

		Column A	Column B
83	Box 80 figure		£
84	Box 81 + box 82	£	
85	Box 77 *minus* box 84. If the result is a minus figure enter '0' in the box and enter the deficit in box 88	£	
86	Box 78 *minus* box 83. If the result is a minus figure enter '0' in the box and enter the deficit in box 87		£
87	Enter the deficit figure from box 86 (if there is one)	£	
88	Enter the deficit figure from box 85 (if there is one)		£
89	Box 85 *minus* box 87	£	
90	Box 86 *minus* box 88		£
91	Total estate in the UK (box 89 + box 90)	£	

Exemptions and reliefs

92 Exemptions and reliefs deducted from the assets in the deceased's sole name shown in **Column A** on pages 6 and 7
- *see IHT400 Notes.* If you are deducting spouse or civil partner exemption, enter the spouse or civil partner's full name, date and country of birth and their domicile.
Do not include exemptions or reliefs on jointly owned assets, these should be deducted on form IHT404, at box 9.

Describe the exemptions and reliefs you are deducting. For example 'cash gift to charity in the Will' and show how the amount has been calculated – please use the 'Additional information' boxes on pages 15 and 16 of this form if you need more space.	Amount deducted £
Total exemptions and reliefs from assets in **Column A**	£

Exemptions and reliefs continued

| 93 | Exemptions and reliefs deducted from the assets in the deceased's sole name shown in **Column B** on pages 6 and 7 – see *IHT400 Notes*. If you are deducting spouse or civil partner exemption enter the spouse or civil partner's full name, date and country of birth and their domicile (unless already given at box 92). **Do not include exemptions or reliefs on jointly owned assets, these should be deducted on form IHT404, at box 4.** |

Describe the exemptions and reliefs you are deducting. For example, 'agricultural relief on farm' and show how the amount has been calculated - please use the 'Additional information' boxes on pages 15 and 16 if you need more space.	Amount deducted £
Total exemptions and reliefs from assets in **Column B**	£

94	Box 89 *minus* box 92	£
95	Box 90 *minus* box 93	£
96	Total net estate in the UK, after exemptions and reliefs (box 94 + box 95)	£

Other assets taken into account to calculate the tax

		Column A	Column B
97	Foreign houses, land, businesses and control holdings (form IHT417, box 5)		£
98	Other foreign assets (form IHT417, box 10)	£	
99	Assets held in trust on which the trustees would like to pay the tax now (form IHT418, box 12)		£
100	Assets held in trust on which the trustees would like to pay the tax now (form IHT418, box 17)	£	
101	Nominated assets. Include details of the nominated assets in the 'Additional information' boxes on pages 15 and 16 – see *IHT400 Notes*	£	
102	Box 98 + box 100 + box 101	£	
103	Box 97 + box 99		£
104	Gifts with reservation and pre-owned assets (IHT403, box 17)	£	
105	Assets held in trust on which the trustees are not paying the tax now (form IHT418, box 18)	£	
106	Alternatively secured pension fund(s) (form IHT409, boxes 32 and 42 - only where the date of death is between 06/04/06 and 05/04/07 inclusive)	£	
107	Total other assets taken into account to calculate the tax (box 102 + box 103 + box 104 + box 105 + box 106)	£	
108	Total chargeable estate (box 96 + box 107)	£	

Working out the Inheritance Tax

ⓘ If there is no Inheritance Tax to pay, you do not need to fill in this page and should go to box 119 on page 12.

If you are filling in this form yourself without the help of a solicitor or other adviser, you do not have to work out the tax yourself; we can do it for you – but first read the following note about paying Inheritance Tax by instalments.

Paying Inheritance Tax by instalments
Instead of paying all of the Inheritance Tax at once, you may pay some of it in 10 annual instalments (that is, one instalment each year for 10 years). You can pay by instalments on any assets shown in **Column B** on pages 6 and 7 that have not been sold.

Interest will be payable on the instalments.
The total value of the assets on which you may pay the tax by instalments is box 95 + box 97 + box 99 (if any).

109 Are you filling in the form without the help of a solicitor or other adviser and you wish us to work out the tax for you?

No ☐ Go to 'Simple Inheritance Tax calculation'

Yes ☐ Go to box 110

110 Do you wish to pay the tax on the amounts shown in box 95 + box 97 + box 99 by instalments?

No ☐ Go to box 118

Yes ☐ If any of the assets in **Column B** have been **sold**, write the total value of those assets here

£ _____

Now go to box 118

Simple Inheritance Tax calculation

You can use the simple calculation in boxes 111 to 117 to work out the Inheritance Tax on the estate as long as the following apply:
• you are paying the tax on or before the last day of the sixth month after the death occurred so no interest is payable
• you want to pay all of the tax now and not pay by instalments on property in Column B (see note above about paying Inheritance Tax by instalments)
• the total of any lifetime gifts is below the Inheritance Tax nil rate band
• you are not deducting double taxation relief on any foreign assets (see note on IHT400 Calculation)
• you are not deducting successive charges relief on assets inherited by the deceased in the last five years from another estate on which Inheritance Tax was paid (see note on IHT400 Calculation).

If the simple calculation does not apply to you, you will need to use the form IHT400 Calculation to work out the Inheritance Tax due then continue to fill in this form at box 118.

111 Total chargeable value of gifts made by the deceased within the seven years before their death (form IHT403, box 7)	£ _____
112 Aggregate chargeable transfer (box 108 + box 111)	£ _____
113 Inheritance Tax nil rate band at the date of death See IHT400 Rates and Tables	£ _____
114 Transferable nil rate band (form IHT402, box 20)	£ _____
115 Total nil rate band (box 113 + box 114)	£ _____
116 Value chargeable to tax (box 112 minus box 115)	£ _____
117 Inheritance Tax (box 116 x 40%)	£ _____ • ☐ ☐

Direct Payment Scheme

This is a scheme under which participating banks and building societies will release funds from the deceased's accounts directly to HM Revenue & Customs to pay Inheritance Tax. For National Savings & Investments, see the note on page 14.

118 Do you wish to use the Direct Payment Scheme?

No ☐

Yes ☐   *Fill in form IHT423 (you will need a separate form for each bank and building society account concerned)*

Declaration

119 I/We wish to apply for the following type of grant (see note 'Grant of representation' in IHT400 Notes to decide on the type of grant)

- Probate ☐
- Confirmation ☐
- Letters of Administration ☐
- Letters of Administration with Will annexed ☐
- Other (please specify)

To the best of my/our knowledge and belief, the information I/we have given and the statements I/we have made in this account and the Schedules attached (together called 'this account') are correct and complete.
Please tick the Schedules you have filled in.

IHT401 ☐	IHT408 ☐	IHT415 ☐
IHT402 ☐	IHT409 ☐	IHT416 ☐
IHT403 ☐	IHT410 ☐	IHT417 ☐
IHT404 ☐	IHT411 ☐	IHT418 ☐
IHT405 ☐	IHT412 ☐	IHT419 ☐
IHT406 ☐	IHT413 ☐	IHT420 ☐
IHT407 ☐	IHT414 ☐	

I/We have made the fullest enquiries that are reasonably practicable in the circumstances to find out the open market value of all the items shown in this account. The value of items in the box(es) listed below are provisional estimates which are based on all the information available to me/us at this time.

I/We will tell HM Revenue & Customs Inheritance Tax the exact value(s) as soon as I/we know it and I/we will pay any additional tax and interest that may be due.

List the boxes in the account that are provisional here.

Where Schedule IHT402 has been filled in I/we declare that to the best of my/our knowledge and belief:
- the deceased and their spouse or civil partner were married or in a civil partnership at the date the spouse or civil partner died
- where a Deed of Variation has not been provided there has been no change to the people who inherited the estate of the spouse or civil partner.

I/We understand that I/we may be liable to prosecution if I/we deliberately conceal any information that affects the liability to Inheritance Tax arising on the deceased's death, or if I/we deliberately include information in this account which I/we know to be false.

I/We understand that I/we may have to pay financial penalties if this account is delivered late or contains false information, or if I/we fail to remedy anything in this account which is incorrect in any material respect within a reasonable time of it coming to my/our notice.

I/We understand that the issue of the grant does not mean that:
- I/we have paid all the Inheritance Tax and interest that may be due on the estate, or
- the statements made and the values included in this account are accepted by HM Revenue & Customs Inheritance Tax.

I/We understand that HM Revenue & Customs Inheritance Tax:
- will only look at this account in detail after the grant has been issued
- may need to ask further questions and discuss the value of items shown in this account
- may make further calculations of tax and interest payable to help the persons liable for the tax to make provision to meet the tax liability.

I/We understand that I/we may have to pay interest on any unpaid tax according to the law where:
- I/we have elected to pay tax by instalments
- additional tax becomes payable for any reason.

Each person delivering this account, whether as executor, intending administrator or otherwise must sign on page 13 to indicate that they have read and agreed the statements above.

Declaration continued

Surname

First name(s)

Postcode

House number

Rest of address, including house name or flat number

Signature

Date *DD MM YYYY*

Surname

First name(s)

Postcode

House number

Rest of address, including house name or flat number

Signature

Date *DD MM YYYY*

Surname

First name(s)

Postcode

House number

Rest of address, including house name or flat number

Signature

Date *DD MM YYYY*

Surname

First name(s)

Postcode

House number

Rest of address, including house name or flat number

Signature

Date *DD MM YYYY*

Checklist

For more information look at the relevant page in the IHT400 Notes.
Use the checklist to remind you of:

- the actions you should take, and
- the additional information you should include when sending the Inheritance Tax forms to HM Revenue & Customs Inheritance Tax.

- If the deceased died leaving a Will, provide a copy of the Will, and any codicils.

  No ☐   Yes ☐

- If the estate has been varied in any way and the variation results in either an increase or decrease in the amount of tax, provide a copy of the instrument of variation.

  No ☐   Yes ☐

- Any professional valuation of stocks and shares.

  No ☐   Yes ☐

- Any professional valuation of household effects or personal possessions.

  No ☐   Yes ☐

- Any professional valuation of houses, land and buildings.

  No ☐   Yes ☐

- A copy of any insurance policy (and annuity, if appropriate) where the deceased was paying the premiums for the benefit of someone else and any trust documents if the policy has been written in trust.

  No ☐   Yes ☐

- A copy of any trust deed(s), if the trustees are paying tax at the same time as you apply for the grant.

  No ☐   Yes ☐

- Any evidence of money owed to the deceased, including loan agreements and related trusts or policies and any evidence of the debts being released.

  No ☐   Yes ☐

- A copy of any joint life assurance policy or policy on the life of another person.

  No ☐   Yes ☐

- A copy of any structural survey and/or correspondence with the loss adjuster about any structurally damaged property.

  No ☐   Yes ☐

- If you are deducting agricultural relief, a plan of the property and a copy of the lease or agreement for letting (where appropriate).

  No ☐   Yes ☐

- If you are deducting business relief, a copy of the partnership agreement (where appropriate) and the last two years' accounts.

  No ☐   Yes ☐

- If you are deducting double taxation relief or unilateral relief, provide evidence of the foreign tax, in the form of an assessment of the foreign tax, a certificate of the foreign tax paid and (if available) the official receipt.

  No ☐   Yes ☐

- Any written evidence of debts to close friends or family.

  No ☐   Yes ☐

- Have all executors signed page 13 of this form?

  No ☐   Yes ☐

- If you have calculated your own tax, have you enclosed the calculation with this form and arranged to pay the tax?

  No ☐   Yes ☐

- If you are applying for a grant, have you enclosed form IHT421 *Probate summary*?

  No ☐   Yes ☐

Direct Payment Scheme (if used)

- If you are using the Direct Payment Scheme, have you sent a form IHT423 to each organisation from which funds will be provided? *See IHT423*

  No ☐   Yes ☐

- If you want HM Revenue & Customs Inheritance Tax to call for payment from National Savings & Investments, provide a letter detailing the investments to be used, how much of the tax is to be paid by National Savings & Investments and official letters from the relevant National Savings & Investments office stating the value of those investments.

- If you want HM Revenue & Customs Inheritance Tax to call for payment from British Government stock, provide a letter detailing the investments to be used and how much of the tax is to be paid by Government stock.

For more information on paying by National Savings or British Government stock go to **www.hmrc.gov.uk** or phone the helpline for a copy of the IHT11 *Payment of Inheritance Tax from National Savings or from British Government stock.*

Return addresses and contact details

- If you are applying for a grant in England, Wales or Northern Ireland you should send the forms to our Nottingham office (the DX addresses are for solicitors, practitioners and banks)

HM Revenue & Customs
Inheritance Tax
Ferrers House
PO Box 38
Castle Meadow Road
Nottingham
NG2 1BB
DX 701201 NOTTINGHAM 4

Phone **0845 30 20 900**

- If you are applying for Confirmation in Scotland you should send the forms to our Edinburgh office (the DX addresses are for solicitors, practitioners and banks)

HM Revenue & Customs
Inheritance Tax
Meldrum House
15 Drumsheugh Gardens
Edinburgh
EH3 7UG
DX ED 542001 EDINBURGH 14

Phone **0845 30 20 900**

- If you want to know more about any particular aspect of Inheritance Tax or have specific questions about completing the forms go to **www.hmrc.gov.uk/inheritancetax/**

Or phone the Probate and Inheritance Tax Helpline on **0845 30 20 900. (+44 115 974 3009** from outside the UK)

- If you need a copy of any of our forms or leaflets you can download them from our website, phone the Probate and Inheritance Tax Helpline to order them, or email our orderline at **hmrc.ihtorderline@btconnect.com**

Additional information

Use this space:
- to explain the circumstances where the deceased did not own any household effects or personal possessions or they do not have any value (box 34)
- to give us any additional information we ask for, including details of:
  - any claim for discharge of legal rights (box 7)
  - other assets and income due to the deceased (box 76)
  - nominated assets (box 101)
  - successive charges relief (IHT400 Calculation, box 10).

Additional information continued

Additional information continued

If you need more space, please continue on a separate sheet.

IHT400   Page 16

Calculating the inheritance tax payable

Whether the personal representatives will have to pay over any inheritance tax liability on an estate will depend on how much the estate is valued at, and whether this is fully covered by exemptions or business reliefs. The calculation of the inheritance tax liability is covered in Chapter 16. The personal representatives have two choices as to how to calculate the inheritance tax liability of the estate. First, the personal representatives can request that the calculation is performed by the Capital Taxes Office at HM Revenue and Customs. HMRC is always willing to do this calculation and once done will issue an assessment for the amount of tax due. Alternatively, the personal representatives can calculate the inheritance tax liability themselves and submit their calculation with the return form. If this if the preferred action, HMRC will check the calculation and issue an assessment for the amount of tax due. Using this method, the personal representatives would have some idea of the tax due, but they have the reassurance that their calculation will be checked by the Capital Taxes Office.

The following is a link to the inheritance tax account, IHT 400 calculation that takes you through the steps of working out the IHT liability, the tax that may be paid by instalments and the interest that may be due: www.hmrc.gov.uk/inheritancetax/iht400-calc.pdf

An example of this form is in Appendix B.

The calculation of inheritance tax can be complicated, so if the personal representatives are unsure of this, or unable to check any assessment issued by the Capital Taxes Office, they should consider obtaining specialist advice. The costs of such advice are expenses that would be paid out of the estate. If the calculation of inheritance tax is incorrect, and the personal representatives distribute the estate without paying sufficient inheritance tax, they will be personally liable to pay any shortfall out of their own funds.

The date that any inheritance tax must be paid over to HMRC is six months after the end of the month in which the individual died. For example, if Dennis died on 13 September 2009, any inheritance tax will need to be paid by 31 March 2010. However, any tax due on land and buildings or business assets can be deferred and paid by ten annual instalments, though interest will still be charged. This is covered in Chapter 19. Interest on any outstanding inheritance tax unpaid by the due date will arise.

Delivering the return form to HMRC

There is a time limit for the personal representatives to file the completed inheritance tax return form, relating to the tax due on the estate held at the deceased's death, to the Capital Taxes Office of HMRC. This is 12 months following the month the individual died. Note that penalties can arise on any late or incorrect tax return forms.

Example

Inheritance tax return filing date

If Rosie died on 15 January 2010 and left an estate on which there is an inheritance tax liability, her personal representatives must complete the inheritance tax return form IHT400, together with any additional schedules and pages, and submit this to HM Revenue and Customs by 31 January 2011.

Following the submission of an inheritance tax return, an officer at the Capital Taxes Office will issue an assessment showing the amount of inheritance tax payable with details of how to pay the inheritance tax. This should be checked against any calculations that the personal representatives have made and any queries raised as soon as possible. The personal representatives have thirty days to appeal against a calculation for inheritance tax.

Making amendments or corrections to form IHT400

When the administration of an estate is started and the inheritance tax forms are completed, sometimes true asset values cannot be ascertained. These are often based on estimated valuations or based on provisional information. In that case, the personal representatives must be prepared to justify such estimates because HMRC may levy a penalty if it considers that an estimate was careless. Very often, as the administration progresses, these values can change. In addition, information may come to light or more assets or liabilities discovered and this can have a bearing on the original inheritance tax account submitted. Any amendments should be reported promptly to avoid a risk of penalties being levied by HMRC for failure to disclose relevant information. In these cases, the personal representatives then make an amendment or correction to the original inheritance tax form and this is done on form C4. You can download a copy of form C4, which is shown in Figure 12.2 on page 127 from:
www.hmrc.gov.uk/cto/c4_2.pdf

If any inheritance tax has been underpaid or overpaid as a result of these changes, this can then be either paid to the Capital Taxes Office or a refund can be claimed.

Scotland and Northern Ireland

The inheritance tax return IHT400 and all the supporting schedules apply to England and Wales, Scotland and Northern Ireland alike, so this chapter applies to the whole of the UK. The only variation is for Scotland and this is in relation to completing form C4 to make amendments and corrections to the inheritance tax return form. However, there is clear guidance for personal representatives on the form.

Corrective Account /Inventory

Fill in this form when
- *too much or too little Inheritance or Capital Transfer tax or Estate duty has been paid on form IHT200, or*
- *you have included your own estimate of value for an asset in a 'reduced account' and that asset has been redirected to a chargeable beneficiary as a result of an Instrument of Variation, or*
- *Confirmation in Scotland is required to obtain title to additional assets.*

Name and address of firm or person dealing with the estate

	IR CT reference
	Your reference
	Your telephone number

About the person who has died *(the deceased)*

Surname

Title & first name(s)

Date of birth   Date of death

Last known address

Postcode

I/We *(give the name and address of each person signing this form)*

state that

1. The information given on pages 2,3 & 4 and any attached schedules is a full statement of all known additions and amendments to the details already given in the original Inland Revenue Account/Inventory.
2. The corrected liabilities are shown on page 2.

Scotland only

3. Confirmation was obtained as an excepted estate.   No Yes

4. The estate with amendments remains as an excepted estate.   No Yes

Unless you are seeking Confirmation under the Excepted Estates regulations, you should send this form to IR Capital Taxes before lodging it with the Sheriff Clerk.

C4   1   0147220102DTP

Figure 12.2 Form C4 to make amendments or corrections to the original inheritance tax form (IHT400)

Scotland only.

Where the deceased died domiciled in Scotland, list the additions and deductions in the order of estate in Scotland (heritable estate first), estate in England and Wales and Northern Ireland and estate elsewhere.

Gross amount of the estate to which Confirmation has been obtained   £0.00

ADD: assets previously omitted, increased in value, or *(in Scotland only)* wrongly described

Use the description contained in the Account/Inventory. Where the deceased died domiciled in England and Wales or Northern Ireland list assets where tax may not be paid by instalments first. If there is not enough space, use continuation pages numbering them 2a, 2b etc.

	Value as last shown £	Value as corrected £
	£0.00	£0.00
	£0.00	£0.00
	£0.00	£0.00
	£0.00	£0.00
	£0.00	£0.00
	£0.00	£0.00
	£0.00	£0.00
	£0.00	£0.00
	£0.00	£0.00
	£0.00	£0.00
	£0.00	£0.00
	£0.00	£0.00
	£0.00	£0.00
Bring forward totals from continuation page C4(C)	£0.00	£0.00
Totals	£0.00	£0.00

Net increase in assets carried to page 4 **A1**   £0.00

Liabilities: previously omitted or to be adjusted

	Value as last shown £	Value as corrected £
	£0.00	£0.00
	£0.00	£0.00
	£0.00	£0.00
	£0.00	£0.00
	£0.00	£0.00
	£0.00	£0.00
	£0.00	£0.00
Bring forward totals from continuation page C4(C)	£0.00	£0.00
Totals	£0.00	£0.00

Net adjustment in liabilities carried to page 4 *(show a negative figure in brackets)* **L1**   £0.00

DEDUCT: assets wrongly included, reduced in value, or *(in Scotland only)* wrongly described

Use the description contained in the Account/Inventory. List assets where tax may not be paid by instalments first. If there is not enough space, use continuation pages numbering them 3a, 3b etc.

	Value as last shown £	Value as corrected £
	£0.00	£0.00
	£0.00	£0.00
	£0.00	£0.00
	£0.00	£0.00
	£0.00	£0.00
	£0.00	£0.00
	£0.00	£0.00
	£0.00	£0.00
	£0.00	£0.00
	£0.00	£0.00
	£0.00	£0.00
	£0.00	£0.00
	£0.00	£0.00
	£0.00	£0.00
Bring forward totals from continuation page C4(C)	£0.00	£0.00
Totals	£0.00	£0.00

Net decrease in assets carried to page 4 *(show a negative figure in brackets)* **A2** £0.00

Declaration

To the best of my/our knowledge and belief the information I/we have given and the statements I/we have made in this Account/Inventory are correct and complete.

I/We understand that I/we may be liable to prosecution if I/we deliberately conceal any information that affects the liability to inheritance tax, capital transfer tax or estate duty arising on the deceased's death, OR if I/we deliberately include information in this Account which we know to be false.

I/We understand that I/we may have to pay financial penalties if this Account is incorrect by reason of my/our fraud or negligence, OR if I/we fail to remedy anything in this Account which is incorrect in any material respect within a reasonable time of it coming to my/our notice.

Each person delivering this Account/Inventory and listed on page 1 must sign below to indicate that they have read and agreed the statements above.

Signed by	Signed by
Date	Date

Signed by	Signed by
Date	Date

3

Aggregate chargeable estate returned in form IHT200
(box J1) or shown on last calculation from IR Capital Taxes
(dated) **that has been paid**
Or
Net qualifying value from form IHT205 or (in Scotland) form C5. | **S1** | £0.00

Summary of amendments to the estate | £

Increase in assets *(box A1)*	£0.00
Decrease in assets *(box A2)*	£0.00
Adjustment to liabilities *(box L1)*	£0.00
Total *(show a negative figure in brackets)* **S2**	£0.00

Amendments to exemptions and reliefs

Assets in respect of which exemption or relief is deducted	Nature of exemption or relief	Adjustment to exemption/relief
		£0.00
		£0.00
		£0.00
		£0.00
		£0.00
		£0.00
		£0.00
		£0.00
		£0.00
		£0.00
		£0.00
		£0.00
		£0.00
		£0.00
		£0.00
		£0.00
Total *(show a negative figure in brackets)* **S3**		£0.00

Revised chargeable estate *(sum of boxes S1, S2 & S3)*	£0.00
Tax now due	£0.00
Tax previously paid	£0.00
Tax payable/(repayable) as a result of amendments	£0.00

If a repayment of tax is due, you should provide evidence to support the reduction in value.

For IR Capital Taxes use

4

13

How to value property for inheritance tax

This chapter explains how to value property for the purposes of completing the inheritance tax return

- Personal possessions and chattels
- Land and property
- Leases
- Bank and building society accounts
- Quoted shares and securities
- Unit trusts
- Unquoted shares and securities
- Government securities
- National Savings certificates and premium bonds
- Individual savings accounts
- Foreign assets
- Trusts
- Pensions
- Life assurance
- Business interests
- Jointly-owned assets
- Related property owned jointly with a spouse or civil partner
- Jointly-owned assets: Scottish law

One of the duties of the personal representatives is to obtain details of the assets and liabilities of the deceased. They must then deal with the administration of the estate and then distribute the assets to the beneficiaries of the estate in accordance with the will, or intestacy, if no will was left. The collation of the values of the assets and liabilities is also important for ascertaining whether there will be an inheritance tax liability. An estate may have a liability if the total value is above the inheritance tax threshold:

£312,000 for 2008–09
£325,000 for 2009–10
£325,000 for 2010–11

There can be a higher threshold before inheritance tax if the deceased's spouse died before their own death and this is covered in Chapter 16. There are special rules for valuing property when calculating the IHT liability and these are covered below, for each type of asset.

Personal possessions and chattels

The valuation of personal possessions and chattels is based on the expected value of its resale. This would be similar to cost less wear and tear, which is likely to be the amount expected on sale of the second-hand goods. It can be difficult to determine whether something is valuable, just because it is old, whereas sometimes newer property can be unique or a collector's item. It is best not to make any assumptions but check whether an expert opinion is worthwhile. Some property such as jewellery might need a professional valuer to take a look at and it is worthwhile taking a trip to a local jeweller for an opinion.

The valuation of a car would be its second-hand value or trade price. There are some websites that can give an idea. Alternatively, the car can be taken to a garage or car sales business to obtain a valuation. Classic cars may need a professional valuation.

Art is a unique area that could warrant an expert opinion. It would be worth visiting a few auctioneers with any pieces to gain some thoughts on whether any items need a specific valuation.

Land and property

All land and property that was owned by the deceased is part of their estate. Land and property often forms the largest part of most estates and the value of this is necessary for the calculation of inheritance tax. Examples of land and property include houses; buy-to-let property; land; commercial buildings; and leasehold property or leases. It is usually necessary to obtain a professional valuation of the property. It is vital to obtain the most accurate valuation possible as this will determine the amount of inheritance tax due, and HM Revenue and Customs often make their own valuation of property to ensure the correct amount of tax is collected.

Sources of information for the value of land and property include local newspapers; the Land Registry, to see how any similar houses in the area have sold; websites, advertising the sale of local properties; and local estate agents for a free valuation.

If the property is jointly owned, then later in this chapter we'll look at how this will affect the valuation.

If there was an outstanding balance on a mortgage on the land or property, then this can be secured on the property itself and should be deducted from the value of the property. Endowment mortgages and capital repayment mortgages are discussed in Chapter 6.

If land and property was valued too high

If, when land and property is sold during the administration of the estate, it fetches less than valued at the date of death, it is possible to claim relief for this. The land and property needs to have been sold within four years of the date of death of the individual. A claim for the loss that arises on the land and property can be submitted to HMRC and the inheritance tax can be recalculated on the revised values, taking into account any fall in value. A claim would be made on form IHT38, which is discussed in Chapter 22.

Leases

If the deceased was a tenant of a property, the tenancy agreement would usually expire, unless there is a joint tenant to continue with the agreement and take on the responsibility. The personal representatives should check any agreements in place at the time of death because agreements vary and it is important to check the implications of the death of the tenant to see how this will affect the estate. For instance, there could be penalties to pay or damage to pay for out of the estate, or in contrast there could be the return of a deposit which will increase the value of the estate. Such a lease would not normally have any value. But if it is a long lease that does not expire on the death, then the lease may be sold or transferred to someone else. In such a case, expert advice on its true market value should be sought.

Bank and building society accounts

The value of the funds invested will be the amount that will be in the deceased's estate for inheritance tax purposes. Any interest that has accrued up to the date of death on the funds invested should also be added to the valuation. Any cheques made out by the deceased, but not yet cashed must be taken into account, and any payments made into the bank that have not yet cleared in the account must also be taken into account when ascertaining the balance.

Quoted shares and securities

Quoted shares and securities are those which are listed on the London Stock Exchange or on another recognised stock exchange. The value of the shares is usually obtained by using the closing price on the day the person died. Many of these values are published in the financial pages of newspapers. Backdated copies of newspapers are often kept by libraries.

Also, there are websites that publish share information, including the companies relating to the shareholdings themselves.

The Financial Times website (www.ft.com) has an interactive share price service. On the home page, you can search for a quote on a company's current share price and from this display a larger 'interactive chart' of the share's price history, day-by-day. A summary below the chart gives the ex-div date and when the dividend was paid. For example, to discover the share price for Pearson plc on 1 February 2010:

■ Go to www.ft.com.

■ In the search box near the top right of the page, type in Pearson and click the 'Quotes' button. A drop-down list gives all the exchanges on which Pearson shares are traded. The main listing is on the London Stock Exchange, abbreviated to PSON:LSE. Click on this.

■ You will be taken to a summary page for the latest Pearson data. Above the graph is the last price and above this a pink toolbar. One button on this is 'Interactive Chart'. Click on this. Another window will open showing a graph of the share price over the past year. Your mouse will control a vertical line that scrolls across the chart. Simply move this until the date shown near the top left is 01/02/2010 and read off the prices. Opening, high and low prices are also shown.

■ If you require the share price for an earlier date, click on 'Custom Range' and set the start and end dates to view using the calendar. Once you have selected the period, the graph will change accordingly.

The price of shares tends to vary over the course of a trading day, so the valuation for IHT purposes will be based on one of two methods. First is the 'quarter-up method'. A quarter of the difference between the highest and lowest prices quoted on the day is calculated and then added to the lowest price. The mid-bargain price – this is the average of the highest and lowest marked bargain prices of the day. The two methods are performed and the *lower* share price is used to value the shares.

Example

Valuing shares

Patsy died and left a holding of 5,000 ordinary £1 shares in ABC plc in her estate.

On the day that she died, the shares were quoted at 810p-818p a share and there were three marked bargains for the day quoted at 806p, 807p and 814p. The calculation of the shares for the IHT calculation will be as follows:

The *lower* of:

■ Quarter-up method

$$810 + (818 - 810) \times \tfrac{1}{4} = 812p$$

■ Mid-bargain price

$$(806 + 814) \times \tfrac{1}{2} = 810p$$

Taking the lower of these two figures, the value of 5,000 shares = 5,000 × 810p = £40,500

Unit trusts

For IHT purposes, the units in a unit trust are valued at the 'manager's bid price'. If there are two listed prices, then the value of each unit will be the lower of the two published prices of the day. These should be obtainable from the fund manager if they are not listed.

If the person died on a day when the stock exchange was closed, you can use the closing price on either:

▥ the last day when the stock exchange was open before the person died; or

▥ the first day when the stock exchange was open after the person died.

Compare the prices of the two days and take the lower value.

If the deceased owned many shares, or relatively unknown shareholdings, it might be beneficial for the personal representatives to obtain a professional valuation from a stockbroker.

Unquoted shares and securities

Unquoted shares are usually those in a personal company. They are not listed on the stock market, hence why they are referred to as unquoted shares and securities. Most family companies or private companies are unquoted.

Because they are not listed, they are not generally available to the general public and are usually owned by the people running the companies. Unquoted shares and securities are more difficult to value, because it is not possible to look at the values of the shares on the listed stock exchange as you can with the quoted shares and securities. Valuation will depend on the type and size of the company and how tradeable they are on the open market. The value of unquoted shares and securities will be based on the following factors:

▥ company accounts;

▥ company turnover and cashflow;

▥ the company's dividend policy;

▥ the value of the company's asscts;

▥ the goodwill of the company;

▥ the economic climate;

▥ the size of the shareholding in relation to the whole issue of shares;

▥ shareholder voting rights;

▥ the company's dividend policy.

Sometimes, and depending on the size of the company, the company secretary or directors will monitor the value of the company shares at frequent intervals and may be able to provide a reasonable estimate of the value of the shares. However, this is not always feasible and it may be necessary to seek professional advice to ascertain the correct valuation of the shares.

Government securities

These securities are issued by the Treasury that are quoted on the stock exchange. The valuation of these securities is the same as for securities in general.

National Savings certificates and premium bonds

If there are any National Savings & Investments (NS&I) investments, such as savings certificates, these will be valued by NS&I. The personal representatives should complete form DNS904, which can be obtained from a post office, and send it to NS&I.

Premium bonds retain their original value, but NS&I should be notified on the death, so that any prize winnings can be taken into account.

National Savings & Investments has a website, www.nsandi.com or it can be contacted on 0500 007 007.

Individual savings accounts

Individual savings accounts (ISAs) are an efficient investment vehicle to minimise income and capital gains tax liabilities. However, for inheritance tax purposes, the value of the ISA is included in the estate and could be liable to inheritance tax.

The valuation of the ISA is obtained from the fund manager. If there is an element of cash investment within the ISA, then this can be valued easily and would probably be shown on a statement. The ISA is also likely to be made up of several investments of stocks and shares and the fund manager is likely to be keeping a record of these valuations. Any management fees are deductible from the fund value. If this cannot be provided, it is possible to value each shareholding in the same way as other shares, using the methods described above, depending on the type of share or security that is invested within the ISA wrapper.

If the shares and securities were valued too high

If, when the shares and securities are sold in readiness for distribution during the administration of the estate, they are sold for less than the value they were originally valued at the date of death, it is possible to claim relief for this. The shares need to have been sold within one year of the date of death of the individual. A claim for the loss that arises on the sale of shares can be submitted to HMRC and the inheritance tax can be recalculated on the revised values, taking into account any fall in value.

A claim would be made on form IHT35 and this is discussed in Chapter 22.

Foreign assets

Similar methods are used to value foreign property as they are in the UK. The personal representatives should find local professionals to advise on the best valuation of the property. Again, newspapers, websites and the estate agents in the location of the property should be a good start to obtaining an accurate valuation.

If the property needs to be valued or sold, then expenses may need to be incurred and these will be deductible from the estate, as a liability. For the purposes of inheritance tax, this deduction is limited to 5 per cent of the value of the foreign asset only.

If any tax has been paid abroad, all or some of this can be given as a tax credit against the UK inheritance tax liability on the property.

Trusts

If the deceased was a beneficiary of a trust, it is possible that some or all of the value of the trust will be included as part of their estate for inheritance tax purposes. There are several ways that a personal representative may have to include property from a trust in the deceased's estate when calculating the inheritance tax liability, and this is usually when the beneficiary has some ownership or entitlement to the trust property.

A bare trust is one where the beneficiary is entitled to both the income and the assets in the trust. Therefore, when they die, both income and assets are considered part of their estate. A personal representative needs to account for the value of the beneficiary's estate, including their stake in the bare trust, on form IHT400. This form will determine whether there is inheritance tax to pay or not.

If the deceased was entitled to the income from a trust, as the life tenant, then it is likely that the value of the **interest in possession** of the trust will be included in the estate. The personal representatives will need to obtain information from the trustee but it is more likely to be taxable as the deceased's estate if the trust was set up before 22 March 2006 or it was set up after 22 March 2006 and was either an 'immediate post death interest', a 'disabled person's interest' or a 'transitional serial interest'. Advice should be sought because this can be a complex area and additional tax compliance may need to be carried out if a trust has come to an end on the death of the 'life tenant'.

Pensions

If the deceased was receiving a pension from a scheme or policy, the payments may have been guaranteed for a certain period of time. If the guarantee period ends after the death, the payments will continue to be made to the estate, and the right to receive those payments is an asset of the estate.

You should ignore any pension that continues to be paid *directly* to the deceased's surviving spouse or civil partner from the pension provider.

If the deceased died before taking their retirement benefits, a lump sum may be payable under the pension scheme or pension policy.

It will depend on the type of pension policy and the benefits derived from the plans as to whether there will be an IHT liability on the value. It is recommended with any pension policy that the personal representatives contact the trustees or pension organisation to obtain confirmation of the valuation and the tax treatment of the value.

Life assurance

The personal representatives should contact the organisation providing the assurance policy for the valuation of the amount that will be paid out. They will require a death certificate which confirms the date of death. The valuation will largely depend on the type of policy that was taken out.

Business interests

If the deceased owned a business, or part of a business, this would also need to be valued. Often, the value of the business is not just the assets or the equipment but may include some goodwill. Goodwill is the difference of the total value of the business, less all the assets and equipment at that time. But essentially it is the extra that someone would pay for the business being set up already, the client base perhaps, future earnings that are expected, or the brand name. There are many different aspects that need to have careful consideration, particularly if the business will continue after the death of an individual, or whether the business will be broken up. It will also depend on the size of the business. Sometimes professional valuation is needed.

Jointly-owned assets

Care needs to be taken when valuing property that is owned jointly with another person, or more.

There are several legal ways of owning a property and assets: sole ownership; jointly, as joint tenants; and jointly, as tenants in common.

With sole ownership, the individual owned all of the asset. When valuing the estate for inheritance tax purposes, the whole value will be placed in the estate.

With joint tenants, the property is jointly owned by two or more persons, each owning a share in the whole asset. They all own the property jointly and equally and the deceased's share passes automatically to the other joint owners. However, the property still needs to be valued for the purposes of inheritance tax, but because the asset passes automatically to the other joint owners, the asset passes outside of the will or intestacy rules. If the co-owners wish to dispose of all or part of the property in their lifetime, they both have to agree to do so.

In the case of tenants in common, assets or property are owned jointly with one or more people but each share doesn't have to be equal and each tenant can give away their share however they want to. Each co-owner has a defined share in the property and can give their share away however they wish during their lifetime or on their death. There is no need to obtain permission or agreement from the co-owners. On the death of one of the owners, the value of the deceased's share is added into the estate and if there is no valid will, it is distributed in accordance with the intestacy rules along with the rest of the estate.

If the deceased owned assets or property jointly with other people, you need to work out the value of their share. You usually work out the value based on the proportion they owned. But sometimes different rules apply. In Northern Ireland, the terms are the same as for England and Wales but a tenant in common can also be called a coparcener.

Valuing jointly-owned assets

When jointly owned land or property is valued for the estate, the whole value of the asset needs to be determined. The value of the deceased's share will then be a proportion of the total value, based on their share. If the property was owned jointly with someone other than the deceased person's spouse or civil partner, the share of the land or property can be reduced, typically by 10–15 per cent, but this can vary depending on the type of property and the relationship of the deceased with the other joint owners. This reduction takes into account the fact that the sale of a share in a property is difficult, and sometimes unmarketable because the rest of the asset is owned by someone else.

For tax purposes, the income from a jointly-owned bank or building society account is usually equal unless an election is provided to HMRC to advise that the ownership is in different shares. However, for inheritance tax purposes, the value of the funds within a joint bank or building society account is based on the actual amount that belonged to the deceased person based on the amounts he or she paid into the account.

The deceased person's share of the insurance policy is generally half if there are two owners. The insurance company will be able to provide a valuation of the policy and then half of the value is to be included in the estate.

If the deceased owned any other property jointly with others, then the personal representatives will need to ascertain the value of the asset and take the deceased person's share of this valuation.

Related property owned jointly with a spouse or civil partner

If property is owned jointly with a spouse or civil partner, there are special rules to value the share of the property in the estate of the deceased. The valuation is based on the formula:

$$\text{Combined value of the related parties' assets} \times \frac{\text{Value of the deceased's asset}}{\text{The total of the two related parties' valuations}}$$

Example

Related party valuation of land

Maggie owned a plot of land worth £300,000. Her husband, Charlie, owns the adjacent plot of land which is worth £400,000. The combined plots of land are worth £1,100,000.

When Maggie died, the personal representatives have the task of valuing her share of land to calculate the amount of IHT payable on her estate.

The value will be calculated as follows:

$$£1,100,000 \times \frac{£300,000}{£300,000 + £400,000} = £471,429$$

Example

Related party valuation of shares

George died recently and left 10,000 of his shares in a company CC Ltd to his daughter, Abigail. CC Ltd is an unquoted investment company with an issued share capital of £1 ordinary shares owned as follows:

	Number of shares
George	10,000
Lucy (George's wife)	4,000
Gino (George's son)	6,000
Other unconnected persons	5,000
	25,000

CC Ltd shares were valued on George's death as follows:

	Price per share
	£
0 – 25% shareholding	1.20
26 – 50% shareholding	1.80
51 – 75% shareholding	3.00
76 – 100% shareholding	4.20

George and Lucy had a 56 per cent joint interest in the company, which would make their shares worth:

$$£3 \times 14,000 \text{ shares} = £42,000$$

The personal representatives would therefore value George's shareholding, using the related property rules, as:

$$£42,000 \times \frac{10,000 \text{ shares}}{14,000 \text{ shares}} = £30,000$$

Jointly-owned assets: Scottish law

In Scotland, the legal ownership of assets is slightly different. Joint tenants are called joint owners. Tenants in common are called common owners. The asset is not automatically transferred to the joint owner because there are strict rules in Scotland about providing for family members, whether or not a will has been left. These rules are covered in Chapter 5.

14

Overseas property

This chapter will explain how overseas property, included in an estate, should be dealt with

- Chargeability to inheritance tax
- Domicile
- Location of assets
- Valuation of overseas property
- Double taxation relief

Chargeability to inheritance tax

First, it is necessary to consider the chargeability of an individual to UK inheritance tax and this depends on whether they are domiciled or deemed to be domiciled in the UK, as follows:

- If domiciled in the UK: individuals are liable to IHT on their worldwide assets.

- If *not* domiciled in the UK: individuals are liable to IHT on their UK assets only.

Therefore, if a person is not UK domiciled or not deemed domiciled in the UK, their overseas assets are **excluded property** and not chargeable to UK inheritance tax, and only UK assets are brought into their IHT computation, for gifts during lifetime or on their death in their estate calculation.

Domicile

As shown above, one of the factors that determines whether an individual is chargeable to UK inheritance tax is whether they are domiciled in the UK or not. Therefore it is necessary to ascertain the correct domicile of the individual. 'Domicile' is a legal term that represents the permanent 'home-land' of an individual.

The ways the domicile of an individual can be determined are:

■ domicile of origin;

■ domicile of dependency;

■ domicile of choice;

■ deemed domicile.

The **domicile of origin** relates to the fact that an individual will acquire domicile status at the time of their birth, when they inherit the domicile of their father. Therefore, the permanent 'homeland' of the father determines the domicile status. If the father is unknown, the individual will take the domicile status of their mother.

Domicile of dependency is when an individual's father changes his own domicile before the individual has reached the age of 16. The individual's domicile status will follow that of the father.

If UK domiciled, from the age of 16 it is legally possible for an individual to change his domicile of origin to a **domicile of choice**. In practice, this is often difficult to do and it takes a considerable time to lose the original domicile status. The individual must take steps to show that they intend to make another country their 'homeland' and to sever all ties with the UK, which would show the genuine purpose of changing the domicile. Steps that would support a change of domicile status would be for the individual to sell all UK assets and purchase assets of the country intended to become their permanent home. In other words, to sever ties with the UK and to integrate into the new country.

This concept of **deemed domicile** applies for IHT purposes only. An individual is deemed to be of UK domicile if:

■ The individual has been resident in the UK for at least seventeen out of the preceding twenty tax years (including the tax year in which the transfer is made); or

▪ The individual was UK domiciled within the preceding three years. This would apply if the individual had been successful in changing their domicile status.

Location of assets

As we have seen above, the UK tax liability of a *non*-UK domiciled person is based only on their UK assets, and all their overseas property is excluded from the charge. It is therefore important to ascertain the location of the person's assets so that if the individual is non-UK domiciled, it can be determined which of their assets is located in the UK or overseas. The rules that determine the location of the assets are shown in Table 14.1.

Table 14.1 Determining the location of assets

Asset	*Location rule*
Land, buildings and leases (including a share in the land and buildings)	Where the land is physically located
Registered shares and securities	Where the shares or securities are registered or traded
Bearer shares and securities	Where the title document is kept
An interest in an unincorporated business or an interest in a partnership	Where the business is carried out
Chattels and personal possessions	Where the item is situated at the time of transfer, or death
Debts owed to the deceased	Where the debtor lives at the time of transfer or death
Bank accounts	The location of the branch which holds the account

Valuation of overseas property

For those individuals that are chargeable to IHT on overseas property, the valuation of the overseas property will need to be carried out. When calculating UK inheritance tax liabilities, the value of the overseas property must be converted into sterling. This is done by using the rate of exchange on the date of the transfer (if a lifetime gift) or the date of death. If there is more than one conversion rate on this particular day, then the rate that gives the lowest valuation should be used. Relief for expenses incurred overseas, in transferring the property or dealing with the property on death, are allowed but these are limited to 5 per cent of the value of the overseas property.

Double taxation relief

Sometimes, tax is payable in relation to the property in the overseas country where the property is situated. Usually, credit for this overseas tax paid may be given against the UK tax and this is known as double taxation relief (DTR). The amount of the double taxation relief given is the lower of:

■ The overseas tax paid, in the country where the property is situated.

■ The UK inheritance tax liability attributable to the overseas asset.

This can be calculated by taking an apportionment of the total liability in relation to the value of the overseas asset. The UK IHT attributable is calculated as:

Average rate of IHT payable × Value of the foreign asset brought into the estate (after deducting expenses)

If the individual has several overseas assets, separate calculations will need to be performed for each one to ascertain the credit available, being the lower of the overseas tax and the amount of UK inheritance tax, for each of the assets.

Example

Valuation and DTR

Steven was a UK-domiciled individual. He died recently and one of the assets within his estate at the time of his death was an overseas property and chargeable to inheritance tax. The property was valued at €350,000 and the exchange rate on the date of his death was €1 = £0.9009.

When the overseas property was sold following his death, so that the estate could be distributed to the various beneficiaries, some overseas legal expenses were incurred totalling £16,000. Overseas tax was also paid amounting to £63,000.

Steven had no nil rate band available to allocate against his estate because he had previously made a transfer into a trust during his lifetime that used this entirely.

The way this would be dealt with for UK inheritance tax purposes is as follows.

Valuation of the overseas property

The value of the property would be converted into sterling using the lowest conversion rate on the date of death. In this example it would be:

$$€350,000 \times 0.9009 = £315,315.$$

Expenses of up to 5 per cent are deducted, making the property's value £315,315 less £15,766 = £299,549.

UK tax on this asset would be at 40 per cent, which is £299,549 at 40 per cent = £119,820.

The double taxation relief

The UK tax on this asset would be at 40 per cent as above £126,126 and so the availability of double tax relief for the overseas tax paid in addition to the UK tax paid is the lower of:

■ UK tax: £299,549 at 40% = £119,820

■ Overseas tax paid = £63,000

Tax relief of £63,000 would therefore be available to deduct from the UK tax liability on the overseas asset.

15

Considering gifts made before death

This chapter will explain how important it is to consider gifts made before death

- The occasions of charge
- Three-step method for calculating IHT
- Reliefs available on lifetime gifts
- Gifts with reservation of benefit
- Pre-owned asset transfer rules

One of the objectives for a personal representative is to calculate whether there is an inheritance tax liability on the estate of someone that has died, and if so, to ensure that this liability is calculated correctly. Usually, the inheritance tax form is completed and this is submitted to HM Revenue and Customs which is happy to calculate any tax liability, if necessary, and inform the personal representatives how to pay. However, it is not unusual for the personal representatives to want to understand how the tax is calculated so they can ensure that the estate is dealt with correctly and in the best interests of the beneficiaries that will benefit from the estate value.

The occasions of charge

Not only is there inheritance tax on the death estate of an individual, there is sometimes an inheritance tax liability when a person makes gifts during their lifetime. This can affect the inheritance tax liability if they die within a certain time frame. There are three occasions of charge to IHT, as shown in Table 15.1.

Table 15.1 Occasions of charge to IHT

Timing of the event	IHT could be charged on
Lifetime gifts	Chargeable lifetime transfers (CLTs) at the time the gift is made. This is covered in Chapter 23
On the death of the individual	Additional tax on chargeable lifetime transfers (CLTs) and potentially exempt transfers (PETs) as a result of the individual's death within *seven years* of the gifts
	The IHT liability on the value of the individual's estate at the date of death

Everyone's estate is exempt from inheritance tax up to a certain threshold. This threshold is known as the **nil rate band**. The amounts are:

2008–09	£312,000
2009–10	£325,000
2010–11	£325,000

The main point at issue is that the personal representatives need to see how much of the deceased's nil rate band is remaining after any gifts made during the lifetime, before they can calculate the inheritance tax due on the death estate. They need to look back *seven years* from the date of death and ascertain whether there were any potentially exempt transfers or chargeable lifetime transfers that need to be deducted from the nil band. The amount of the available nil rate band remaining is then deducted from the estate before charging the remainder to tax.

Three-step method for calculating IHT

So, to calculate the correct IHT on all the lifetime gifts before death and subsequently the correct IHT on the death estate, it is necessary to perform three calculations:

■ IHT on the lifetime gifts.

■ Additional IHT on those lifetime gifts, as a result of the death of an individual, within seven years of making the gifts.

■ IHT on the death estate.

Step 1: IHT on lifetime gifts

There are three categories of lifetime gifts:

◼ exempt gifts;

◼ potentially exempt transfers (PETs);

◼ chargeable lifetime transfers (CLTs).

Exempt gifts include:

◼ Annual exemption of £3,000 each year.

◼ Gifts to a spouse or civil partner.

◼ Gifts to charity.

◼ Gifts to a political party.

◼ Gifts that represent normal expenditure out of income.

◼ Small gifts under £250.

◼ Wedding gifts.

◼ Transfers for family maintenance.

These exemptions are fully covered, with some examples, in Chapter 23.

A potentially exempt transfer (PET) is a gift made by an individual (the **donor**) to another individual (the **donee**) that is potentially exempt from tax. A PET is exempt at the time of the gift, during the donor's lifetime, but could become chargeable to inheritance tax if the donor dies within seven years of making the gift. This type of transfer applies to *all* types of asset transferred from the donor to a donee and that are not treated as a chargeable lifetime transfer (see below) and would include cash, shares and securities, land and buildings, and chattels and personal possessions.

A chargeable lifetime transfer (CLT) is a gift that is not a potentially exempt transfer (PET) and is not exempt. These transfers usually consist of transfers into a trust. The gross chargeable value of a CLT is calculated in the same way as the gross value of a PET and the value of the gift is immediately liable to inheritance tax:

◼ If the donee agrees to pay the lifetime tax, then the transfer is chargeable at the rate of 20 per cent.

◼ If the donor agrees to pay the lifetime tax, then the transfer is chargeable on the amount of the tax payable as well, making an effective tax rate on the gift of 25 per cent.

When calculating the IHT payable on a chargeable lifetime transfer, it is necessary to look back seven years *before the gift* and to work out the total value of any other gross chargeable transfers in that period.

Example

Patsy: IHT on a chargeable lifetime transfer

Patsy died on 1 March 2010. During her lifetime she had made the following gifts:

■ £50,000 to a registered charity on 24 December 2004.

■ £10,000 cash to her daughter on 22 January 2005.

■ £6,000 to her grandson on the occasion of his marriage, on 3 January 2006.

■ A transfer of cash of £410,000 into a discretionary trust on 21 April 2006 (the trustees were to pay any of the lifetime tax due).

■ A transfer of cash of £250,000 into a discretionary trust on 19 March 2007 (Patsy was to pay any lifetime tax due).

Patsy has never married and she died intestate.

We have to establish the amount of any lifetime tax paid so that we can then ascertain whether any additional tax is due as a result of Patsy's death.

24/12/2004	£
Gift to registered charity	50,000
Less charity exemption	(50,000)
	0

This gift is covered by the charity exemption and is therefore not chargeable.

22/01/2005	£
Gift of cash to daughter	10,000
Less annual exemptions:	
2004/05	(3,000)
2003/04 (because it is unused)	(3,000)
PET	4,000

This gift is a potentially exempt transfer (PET) and therefore is not chargeable to IHT during lifetime, but it is important to include gifts such as these to ascertain how the annual exemptions, and other reliefs where applicable, have been used.

3/01/2006	£
Gift of cash to grandson on marriage	6,000
Less marriage exemption (grandparent)	(2,500)
	3,500
Less annual exemptions:	
2005/06	(3,000)
2004/05 (previously used)	(0)
PET	500

As with the gift to the daughter, this gift is a potentially exempt transfer (PET) and so is not chargeable to IHT during lifetime.

21/04/2006		£
Gift to a discretionary trust		410,000
Less annual exemptions:		
2006/07		(3,000)
2005/06 – (previously used)		(0)
		407,000
Less nil rate band for 2006/07	285,000	
Reduced by any chargeable gifts in the previous 7 years	(0)	(285,000)
Chargeable lifetime transfer (CLT)		122,000
Lifetime tax due on the CLT at 20% (trustees are paying the tax)		24,400

So when performing the calculation of gift to the discretionary trust, we can see the importance of starting at the very beginning with the previous gifts to recognise that annual exemptions have been used.

19/03/2007		£
Gift to discretionary trust		250,000
Less annual exemptions:		
2006/07 – (previously used)		(0)
2005/06 – (previously used)		(0)
		250,000
Less nil band for 2006/07	285,000	
Reduced by any chargeable gifts in the previous 7 years	(285,000)	(0)
Chargeable lifetime transfer (CLT)		250,000
Lifetime tax due on the CLT at 25% (Patsy agreed to pay the tax)		62,500

Again, we now recognise that the annual exemptions have been used on a previous gift and we can calculate the use of the nil rate band clearly and correctly.

Having clear calculations prepared is necessary in case HMRC should ask for them to support tax return forms that have been submitted.

Dates for payment of lifetime tax

The date of payment of IHT for the chargeable lifetime transfer (CLT) is as follows:

Date of CLT	Due date
6 April to 30 September	30 April in the following year
1 October to 5 April	Six months after the end of the month in which the CLT is made

Step 2: IHT on lifetime gifts due to death within 7 years

As discussed, there may be additional IHT on lifetime gifts made, as a result of the death of an individual, within seven years of making the gifts. The rate of tax payable on death is 40 per cent on the excess over the nil rate band. The nil rate band available is matched against *all* lifetime gifts first, before computing the IHT on the value of the individual's estate at the date of death. Therefore, the death tax on lifetime gifts must be calculated before the death tax due on the estate.

Taper relief is available on the additional tax due on a lifetime gift if it becomes chargeable on death more than three years before the date of death. The rate of taper relief is shown in Table 15.2.

Table 15.2 Rate of taper relief

Years between the date of the gift and the date of death		
More than	*Not more than*	*Taper relief (%)*
0	3	Nil
3	4	20
4	5	40
5	6	60
6	7	80
More than 7 years before death		100

Lifetime IHT can be deducted from the death tax calculated and only the excess is paid on death. However, it should be noted that there can be no repayment of lifetime IHT paid, at the time of making the lifetime gifts.

Now that the calculations have been done for the lifetime IHT for the example of Patsy, we need to work through the method to ascertain the change in liability when death has occurred within seven years of the lifetime gifts. There may be additional IHT due as a result of the death.

Example

Patsy: additional IHT on lifetime gifts

24/12/2004	£
Gift to registered charity	50,000
Less charity exemption	(50,000)
	0

This gift remains covered by the charity exemption and no additional tax is due as a result of Patsy's death within seven years of making the gift.

22/01/05		£	£
Gift to daughter			10,000
Less annual exemptions:			
2004–05			(3,000)
2003–04 (previously unused)			(3,000)
			4,000
Less nil band for 2009–10		325,000	
Reduced by any chargeable gifts in the previous 7 years	(	0)	(4,000)
Chargeable, on death			Nil

We can see that the nil rate band will also now need to be re-allocated to all charge-able gifts and not just those that were chargeable during lifetime. This can only be recalculated by going back to the beginning.

3/01/2006		£
Gift of cash to grandson on marriage		6,000
Less marriage exemption (grandparent)		(2,500)
		3,500
Less, annual exemptions:		
2005–06		(3,000)
2004–05 (previously used)		(0)
PET		500
Less nil band for 2009–10	325,000	
Reduced by any chargeable gifts in the previous 7 years	(4,000)	(500)
Chargeable, on death		Nil

We can see that the nil rate band will also now need to be re-allocated to this gift.

21/04/06		£
Gift to discretionary trust		410,000
Less annual exemptions:		
2005–06		(3,000)
2004–05 (previously used)		(0)
		407,000
Less nil band for 2009–10	325,000	
Reduced by any chargeable gifts in the previous 7 years	(4,000 + 500)	(320,500)
Chargeable at death		86,500
Death rate of tax due at 40%		34,600
Less taper relief, 3–4 years before death, therefore 80% of the tax is due after 20% taper relief		(6,920)
Tax due as a result of Patsy's death		27,680
Less lifetime tax paid		(24,400)
Additional IHT due on death		3,280

This gift is now chargeable at the full death rate of 40 per cent but there is more nil rate band available because of the increase since 2006–07.

Taper relief is available where the death is more than three years after the gift. In this case, because the gift was between three and four years of the death, 20 per cent relief is available (see Table 15.2).

19/03/07		£
Gift to discretionary trust		250,000
Add on the tax that Patsy paid		62,500
Total value of the gift		312,500
Less annual exemptions:		
2006–07 – used		(0)
2004–05 – used		(0)
		312,500
Less nil band for 2009/10	325,000	
Reduced by any chargeable gifts in the previous 7 years	(325,000)	(0)
Chargeable to tax on death		312,500
Death rate of tax due at 40%		125,000
Less lifetime tax paid		(62,500)
Additional IHT due on death		62,500

To recap, the requirement is to calculate any IHT arising as a result of the death and that will include 'additional inheritance tax' due on the lifetime gifts. Using this method we calculate the amount due, and then deduct any lifetime tax paid to arrive at this figure, so we can now appreciate why it has been necessary to simply take a step back a little further and perform the lifetime calculation.

There is another example of why there may be an additional amount of IHT on a donor's death. This is where a gift of property made by a donor during their lifetime qualified for Business Property Relief. If the donee disposes of this property within seven years of the gift and the donor dies during that period, the recalculation of any additional inheritance tax will be performed, but the original gift will no longer qualify for the valuable Business Property Relief because it is no longer held, which could result in much more tax becoming payable. If there is property that qualifies for reliefs such as BPR, it is always beneficial to seek professional advice, because a significant amount of tax could be at stake.

Note that any tax due as a result of the person's death has to be paid within six months after the end of the month of death.

Step 3: IHT due on the death estate

Now that all the lifetime calculations have been performed, only then can the death estate computation be done. We would see how much of the nil rate band is available to set off against the death estate.

Example

IHT on Patsy's estate

Following on from the example above, at Patsy's death, she owned the following assets:

- A home in Sussex valued at £380,000.
- 1,000 shares in JBL Ltd, a quoted company with a share price of £3.00 on the date of Patsy's death.
- A holiday flat in Dorset valued at £275,000.
- £54,900 in investments, bank accounts and cash.
- £6,000 in personal possessions and antiques.

In this example, Patsy has never married and she died intestate, without leaving a will.

To calculate the tax due on the death estate, it is simply a matter of adding the total value of the assets at the date of death and deducting any remaining nil band available. Then, applying the death rate of tax of 40 per cent to the chargeable amount.

Assets held at death: 1/3/2010		£
Home in Sussex		380,000
Shares in JBL Ltd		
1,000 × £3.00		3,000
Holiday flat in Dorset		275,000
Investments, bank accounts and cash		54,900
Personal possessions and antiques		6,000
Total taxable estate		718,900
Less, nil rate band for 2009–10	325,000	
Reduced by any chargeable gifts in the previous 7 years	(325,000)	(0)
Chargeable estate		718,900
Tax due at the death rate 40%		287,560

In the example above, Patsy was not married and therefore all her estate was chargeable. A spouse exemption would be applicable in many other situations. Also, in other situations, IHT reliefs may apply such as charitable exemptions, and other rules may need to be applied such as domicile, the valuation of the property or business property reliefs. If there have been numerous gifts made during a lifetime, particularly any business assets, that need to be taken into account, it may be wise to seek professional advice or consult HMRC.

Summary

So the amount of inheritance tax due on Patsy's death is as follows:

Additional tax on lifetime gifts	(£3,280 + £62,500)	£ 65,780
Death estate IHT		£ 287,560
Total		£ 353,340

Reliefs available on lifetime gifts

If the value of a gift made during lifetime has fallen by the time the donor dies, relief is available. This means that any recalculation of IHT, as a result of the donor's death within seven years of the gift, may be recalculated using the reduced value.

Example

> **Fall in value of Nick's shares**
>
> Nick made a lifetime gift of a portfolio of quoted shares into a discretionary trust for his grandchildren in November 2007. At the time of making the gift, the value of the share portfolio was £116,000. Unfortunately, Nick died in June 2010. At this date, the value of the portfolio had fallen to £75,000. In this case, the lifetime calculation of the IHT due on the transfer of an asset into a discretionary trust would have been based on the value at that time, £116,000. However, the calculations have to be performed for any additional IHT due, in view of Nick's death within seven years of making the lifetime gift, under Step 2 above.
>
> The fall in value relief means that the recalculation can be based on the reduced value of £75,000.

Business and agricultural property reliefs

Some assets have the luxury of additional reliefs available to them that means the value of these assets can be reduced. The reliefs available are Business Property Relief (BPR) and Agricultural Property Relief (APR). These two reliefs are covered in more depth in Chapter 16 when calculating the inheritance tax liability on the death estate.

Gifts with reservation of benefit

Sometimes a person makes a gift of their property during their lifetime, with the intention of reducing their wealth to try and reduce any exposure to inheritance tax due on their death. However, when gifts are made to reduce one's estate, they have to be outright gifts. The donor cannot give away property and then still benefit from this gift, otherwise it would be a gift with reservation of benefit.

The most common examples of gifts with reservation of benefit are where the donor gifts:

■ the freehold interest in a house but still lives in the property;

■ shares but retains the right to receive the dividend income;

■ assets into a trust fund but names himself as one of the beneficiaries of the trust.

Example

Gifts with reservation of benefit

Harry gives his home, worth £250,000, to his son, Peter. However, Harry continued to live in the home for the remainder of his life, until he died in April 2010. In this case, the gift of the home falls into the rules for gifts with reservation of benefit. The value of the asset is still potentially subject to inheritance tax on Harry's death.

In these cases, the gift has not actually been fully made as they are not outright gifts. The effect of this is that the value of these gifts will still remain in the estate and could be liable to IHT. To prevent a double charge to tax, HMRC will only collect the higher of the tax on:

■ the value of the original gift becoming chargeable; and

■ the value of the asset being included in the estate.

Pre-owned asset transfer rules

There are similar rules for assets that are pre-owned assets. Assets that fall under these rules could be where someone has avoided the gift with reservation of benefit (**GWROB**) rules by gifting an asset, but can still enjoy a benefit from the gift, when it has changed into another asset. This is more understandable by looking at an example.

Example

Pre-owned assets

Harry gives cash of £200,000 to his son, Peter. Peter then used the cash to buy a house which his father then lives in. In this case, the gift with reservation of benefit do not apply as the asset has changed from cash to a house. However, under the pre-owned assets rules, the benefit/asset is chargeable.

The value of the benefit depends on the nature of the asset and is calculated as follows:

■ For property = the market rent, less any rent paid by the donor

- Chattels and other assets = (official rate of interest × market value of the asset)

Alternatively, the donor (Harry in the above example) can opt out of the annual income tax charge and instead include the asset within his IHT estate computation on death, applying the rules the same way as the gift with reservation of benefit rules.

16

Calculating inheritance tax liability on the death estate

This chapter shows how to calculate the inheritance tax liability on the death estate

- The chargeability of the deceased person
- Charges to inheritance tax on death
- Valuation rules in an estate computation
- The death estate computation
- Calculation of inheritance tax on the death estate
- Nil rate band for spouses
- Exempt beneficiaries taking the residue of the estate
- Business property reliefs
- Tax credit reliefs
- Date for payment of inheritance tax

We have established that part of the role of personal representatives is to complete the inheritance tax return forms and calculate any inheritance tax due. Quite often, it is possible to complete the forms and submit them to HM Revenue and Customs with a request for a calculation to be done. But for peace of mind, most personal representatives would want to understand how the tax was calculated so they can be sure the funds of the estate are being dealt with correctly. So this chapter will give a little detail of each step in calculating the inheritance tax liability of the estate that someone has left when they die.

The chargeability of the deceased person

Remember, the scope to IHT depends on whether the individual was domiciled or deemed to be domiciled in the UK as follows:

Status of the individual	Liable to IHT on transfers of
Domiciled in the UK	Worldwide capital assets
Not domiciled in the UK	UK capital assets only

All aspects of domicile and how to determine someone's domicile are covered in Chapter 14. Therefore, if the individual was not UK domiciled, overseas assets are **excluded property**, and only UK assets are brought into the estate computation.

Charges to inheritance tax on death

When the personal representatives are calculating the inheritance tax liability, there are two stages to the charge. There may be additional IHT arising on the potential exempt transfers and chargeable lifetime transfers made by the deceased, during their lifetime. This must be calculated first, as described in Chapter 15. Only then can the inheritance tax on the death estate be computed.

Valuation rules in an estate computation

All valuations are calculated in the same way, as described in Chapter 13. However, there are special rules for quoted shares and securities.

Quoted shares and securities are usually quoted 'cum dividend' or 'cum-interest'. However, if they are quoted on the stock exchange as 'ex-dividend' or 'ex-interest', they are valued at the price they would fetch on the open market if sold *plus* the right to the next dividend payment or interest payment, depending on what type of security it is.

Example

Ex-dividend shares

Sam died on 31 November 2009. He owned 1,000 ordinary shares in Stone plc at the time he died, which will now be in his estate. On 31 November 2009, the shares were quoted at between 610p and 618p 'ex-div'. A dividend of 20p per share was announced on 28 November 2009 and was paid on 1 January 2010. In this instance, each share will be valued for the purposes of the estate as follows:

Quarter-up rule = 610 + ((618 − 610) × ¼) = 612p

The value of each share is equal to the share price plus the dividend. So the total value of the shares is:

	£
Ex-dividend valuation (1,000 × 612p)	6,120
Plus net dividend payment (1,000 × 20p)	200
Value to include in the estate	6,320

The death estate computation

Table 16.1 overleaf is a proforma for calculating the value of the death estate. It shows all of the property, and makes a deduction for all the allowable expenses of the estate.

Calculation of inheritance tax on the death estate

Now that we have looked at how to piece together the death estate computation, with all the details of assets and liabilities that the personal representatives have compiled, the next stage is calculating the inheritance tax on the estate.

The value of any exempt legacies needs to be deducted from the estate before charging the estate to tax, as these are exempt from IHT. Exempt legacies will include:

■ Any amounts left to the spouse or civil partner, if applicable.

■ Any amounts left to charities.

Everyone's estate is exempt from inheritance tax up to a certain threshold. This threshold is also known as the 'nil rate band'. The amounts are as follows:

2008–09   £312,000
2009–10   £325,000
2010–11   £325,000

The personal representatives need to see how much of the deceased's nil rate band is remaining after any gifts made during the lifetime. They need to look back seven years from the date of death and ascertain whether there were any potentially exempt transfers or chargeable lifetime transfers that

Table 16.1 Proforma for calculating an estate's value

Free estate	£	£
Freehold and leasehold property	X	
Less: outstanding mortgages	(X)	
		X
Unincorporated business (specialist valuation may be required)	X	
Less: outstanding loans and liabilities	(X)	
		X
Shares: add the next dividend if quoted 'ex-div'		X
Securities: add the next dividend or interest payment if quoted 'ex-div' or 'ex-interest'		X
Motor cars		X
Chattels		X
Debts due to the deceased		X
Interest and rental income accrued to the date of death		X
Insurance policy proceeds		X
ISAs		X
Cash at bank and on deposit		X
Foreign assets (if UK domiciled)	X	
Less: additional expenses		
(subject to a max of 5% of probate value)	(X)	
		X
TOTAL ASSETS IN THE ESTATE		**X**
Less: Allowable deductions:		
Funeral expenses	X	
Legally enforceable debts	X	
Outstanding taxes (e.g. income tax, CGT, VAT, NICs)	X	
		(X)
NET ESTATE		**X**
Exempt legacies		
(e.g. to spouse or civil partner, charity, political party)		(X)
Net free estate		X
Gift with reservation (GWR)		
Market value of capital assets gifted subject to a reservation at the date of death		X
Gross chargeable estate		X

need to be deducted from the nil rate band, as detailed in Chapter 15. The amount of the available nil rate band remaining is then deducted from the estate before charging the remainder to tax.

Example

Valuation of Margaret's estate

Margaret was domiciled in the UK and owned the following assets when she died on 24 October 2009:

■ A house in Lowestoft valued at £517,000. Margaret has an outstanding mortgage of £48,000 on the property.

■ An overseas flat which is valued at £130,000 (converted into sterling). This is to be sold and there is likely to be overseas professional fees of £7,000 from the sale.

■ Chattels in the UK house worth £11,700 and a car worth £8,000.

■ Six thousand ordinary shares in OPC plc, a company quoted on the UK stock exchange. On 24 October 2009, the shares were quoted at 512p–528p a share.

■ £15,000 in 5% Treasury loan stock (government gilts), quoted at 80–84p 'ex-interest'. The interest is paid half yearly on 31 July and 31 January each year.

■ A cash ISA worth £17,600 and a few bank accounts with a credit balance totalling £1,900.

Margaret owed £350 income tax to HMRC and £21,000 to a credit card company.

The executors received a £45,000 life assurance lump sum from Margaret's life insurance policy and the funeral cost £3,240. In addition, there are unpaid professional fees of £2,700.

Under the terms of her will, Margaret left £100,000 to charities and the residue (remainder of her estate) to her grand-daughter Minsky.

Free estate	£	£	£
House in Lowestoft		517,000	
Less: outstanding mortgage		(48,000)	
			469,000
Overseas flat		130,000	
Less: additional expenses (restricted to 5%)		(6,500)	
			123,500
Shares in OPC plc (see below for calculation)			30,960
Treasury loan stock – gilts (see below for calculation)	12,150		
Add: next interest on gilts received gross	375		
(£15,000 × 5% × ½)			
			12,525
Motor car			8,000
Chattels			11,700
Life assurance policy proceeds			45,000
ISA			17,600
Bank accounts			1,900
Total assets in the estate			**720,185**
Less: funeral expenses			(3,240)
Credit card outstanding			(21,000)
Professional fees			(2,700)
Income tax			(350)
Net estate			**511,500**

Workings

Shares in OPC valuation = 6,000 shares × [512 + ((528 − 512) × ¼)] = £30,960
Treasury stock valuation = £15,000 × (80 + ((84 − 80) × ¼)) = £12,150

The rate of tax charged on the chargeable estate after all the exemptions and reliefs have been deducted is 40 per cent.

Example

IHT on Margaret's estate (UK domiciled)

	£
NET ESTATE	511,500
Less: exempt legacies to charity	(100,000)
Gross chargeable estate	411,500
Less nil band for 2009–10	(325,000)
Chargeable estate	86,500

Tax due: £86,500 at 40% = **£34,600**

Nil rate band for spouses

As we have seen above, everyone's estate is exempt from inheritance tax up to a certain threshold. This threshold is also known as the 'nil rate band'. The amounts are as follows:

2008–09	£312,000
2009–10	£325,000
2010–11	£325,000

Married couples and registered civil partners are also allowed to pass assets from one spouse or civil partner to the other during their lifetime or when they die without having to pay inheritance tax – no matter how much they pass on – as long as the person receiving the assets has their permanent home in the UK. This is known as spouse or civil partner exemption.

If someone leaves everything they own to their surviving spouse or civil partner in this way, it's not only exempt from inheritance tax but it used to mean they didn't use any of their own nil rate band. However, from 9 October 2007, it is possible to increase the nil rate band of the second spouse or civil partner by any unused nil rate band, when they die, even if they have re-married. It doesn't matter when the first spouse or civil partner died. The amount available for transfer is the *percentage* unused.

Example

Transfer of unused nil rate band

Sanjay died in March 2008, leaving an estate worth £500,000 to his wife, Linda.

At his death, Sanjay's estate was transferred to his wife Linda and no inheritance tax was due, since the estate was covered by the spouse exemption. But what this also means is that Sanjay hadn't used his nil rate band, which was £300,000 for the tax year 2007–08, the tax year in which he died. Therefore, none of his nil rate band had been used.

Linda died in August 2009 and left an estate worth £750,000, which included the wealth she had inherited from her late husband Sanjay.

At Linda's death, she is entitled to her own nil rate band of £325,000, plus the 100% unused nil rate band of her late husband, a further £325,000.

Therefore the amount chargeable to IHT is:

Estate value	£750,000
Less nil bands £325,000 + £325,000	(650,000)
Chargeable	100,000
Tax due at 40%	£40,000

This example shows that it isn't the unused *amount* of the first spouse or civil partner's nil rate band that is available, but the unused *percentage*.

How to make the claim

The executors or personal representatives of the second spouse or civil partner to die need to make a claim for the unused nil rate band of the first spouse civil partner and this is done by submitting a form IHT402 to HMRC with supporting information:

■ a copy of the first will, if there was one;

■ a copy of the grant of probate (or confirmation in Scotland) or the death certificate if no grant was taken out;

■ a copy of any 'deed of variation' which was used to vary the estate, if there was one.

A copy of these documents can be obtained from the court service or a general register office. The court service should be able to provide copies of wills or grants and the general register offices may be able to provide copies of death certificates.

The claim must be made within two years from the end of the month in which the second spouse or civil partner dies.

You can download a copy of form IHT402 from: www.hmrc.gov.uk/inheritancetax/iht402.pdf

A copy of the form is in Appendix B.

Exempt beneficiaries taking the residue of the estate

In most circumstances, the IHT on the estate value is 40 per cent on the excess over the nil rate band, as shown above. However, sometimes, a person's will requires that an exempt beneficiary such as a charity or a spouse will acquire the 'residue' (remainder) of the estate, after any legacies to non-exempt beneficiaries. If this is the case, it is not such a simple matter of deducting the exemption, nil rate band and then taxing the excess at 40 per cent; a special calculation is required, as in the example below.

Example

Exempt beneficiary calculation

Suzie died on 15 August 2009 leaving an estate worth £700,000. She had made no lifetime gifts. The terms of her will were as follows:

■ A legacy free of tax of £200,000 would go to her daughter Polly.

■ A legacy free of tax of £200,000 would go to her son Keith.

■ The remainder of her estate would go to her husband.

Suzie's estate calculation would look like this:

	£
The chargeable estate is £200,000 + £200,000	400,000
Since the remainder is covered by the spouse exemption	
Less 2009–10 nil band	(325,000)
Chargeable to tax	75,000

Tax at (the special calculation) 2/3 = £50,000

This special calculation then ensures the correct amount of tax is charged, as can be seen.

In this way, tax is assessed on not only the non-exempt legacies but also on the tax payable on those legacies out of the estate. The amount therefore available to the spouse, after tax, is £700,000 less tax-free legacies of £400,000, less the tax due of £50,000 = £250,000. This will, of course, be covered by the spouse exemption.

Gross chargeable estate	700,000
Less spouse exemption, as calculated above	(250,000)
Less nil band for 2009–10	(325,000)
Chargeable estate	125,000

Tax due: £125,000 at 40% = £50,000

Business property reliefs

Some assets attract additional reliefs. The reliefs available are business property relief (BPR) and agricultural property relief (APR).

Business property relief (BPR)

The types of property that will qualify for business property relief at a rate of either 100 per cent or 50 per cent are:

- An unincorporated business or interest in a partnership (100%).

- Unquoted trading company shares, including AIM-listed shares (100%).

- Unquoted trading company *securities* (such as debentures and loan stock) *provided* the donor has a controlling interest based on share ownership immediately before the gift (100%).

- Quoted trading company shares and securities provided the donor has a controlling interest immediately before the gift (50%).

- Land, buildings and items of plant and machinery which are used for the purposes of a trade in a partnership in which the individual is a partner or a company in which the individual has a controlling interest (50%).

Example

Business property relief

Stephanie, a single woman, has owned the following assets for more than two years before her death in February 2010:

- A 45% interest, valued at £45,000, in the ordinary share capital of A Ltd, an unquoted trading company. This asset qualifies for BPR at 100%.

- A 15% interest in the ordinary share capital of B plc, a quoted trading company. The 20,000 shares were valued on the stock exchange at 40p a share at the date of Stephanie's death. This asset doesn't qualify for BPR.

- A 20% interest in the debentures of C Ltd, an unquoted trading company. Although this holding is in an unquoted trading company, the asset is 'securities' which means that a controlling interest of at least 50% would be required for BPR to be due. The securities were valued at £15,000 at the date of Stephanie's death.

- A share in a partnership in which she worked one day a week as a consultant. BPR is due on this asset, as she is a partner. It is irrelevant how much time she works for the partnership. Relief is available at 100%.

- An office block, valued at £1,000,000 which Stephanie rents out to the partnership for use in the business. BPR of 50% is available to set against the value of the offices.

Stephanie's estate calculation would look like this:

	£
Shares in A Ltd (covered by BPR)	0
Shares in B plc: 20,000 × 40p	8,000
Securites in C Ltd	15,000
Share in a partnership (covered by BPR)	0
Share in a property used by the partnership (£1,000,000 less 50% BPR)	500,000
Gross chargeable estate	523,000

To qualify for business property relief, the individual must have held the property in question for a minimum period of ownership of two years. It is possible for property to qualify for BPR, despite not being owned for two years, if:

■ The donor has owned some type of relevant business property for a combined period of at least two out of the previous five years.

■ The property was acquired by inheritance from another person's estate, and at that time it qualified for BPR.

Agricultural property relief (APR)

The types of property that will qualify for agricultural property relief, at a rate of 50 per cent and 100 per cent, is:

■ 100 per cent on farm and agricultural land/assets occupied by the owner for two years and tenanted farm and agricultural land/assets if owned by the donor and occupied by someone for the purposes of agriculture for seven years (providing the terms of the tenancy met some conditions).

■ 50 per cent on most other agricultural land and assets.

Reliefs due on lifetime gifts and on the death estate

As long as conditions are satisfied, business property relief and agricultural property relief are both available when calculating inheritance tax on life-time calculations (see Chapter 15) and when calculating the inheritance tax due on the estate. However, for the reliefs to qualify when calculating the death tax, two additional conditions must be satisfied at the date of death:

■ The donee must still own the asset gifted.

■ The property must be relevant business (or agricultural) property at the date of the donor's death.

Excepted assets

Sometimes, assets that are shown in the above list that potentially qualify for BPR may only qualify for relief on part of the value if some of the asset is:

■ partly investment value;

■ not currently used for the purposes of trading.

When there is some investment element in the value of this asset, the BPR is restricted accordingly.

If any assets in the estate look as if they potentially qualify for the agricultural or beneficial business property reliefs, professional advice should be sought. Usually, the tax advantages of taking such advice far outweigh the professional costs.

Tax credit reliefs

Once the inheritance tax liability has been calculated, there may be some tax credit relief that could be set against this liability using quick succession relief (QSR) and double-taxation relief (DTR).

Quick succession relief (QSR)

QSR is likely to be due if a person inherited assets from another's estate and then died, themselves, within five years. The amount of quick succession relief available depends on the length of time between the date the deceased received the gift, and the date of his death. The personal representatives would give an appropriate percentage based on the timescale in Table 16.2.

Table 16.2 Rates of quick succession relief

Years between the date of first gift and the date of death		QSR (%)
More than	Not more than	
0	1	100
1	2	80
2	3	60
3	4	40
4	5	20

The amount of tax credit to then allocate against the estate liability is based on the amount of IHT due on the original estate. The example below shows how it works.

Example

Quick succession relief

Everett died on 26 August 2009 leaving an estate of £600,000. He had previously made no lifetime transfers. He had inherited a house in the UK on the death of his aunt, Orla, on 14 April 2008. The house was valued at £220,000. Orla's total estate was worth £510,000 and £79,200 IHT was payable.

The amount of quick succession relief available to Everett's estate is based on a proportion of the tax paid on Orla's estate as follows:

$$220,000/510,000 \times £79,200 = £34,165$$

The length of time between the gift from Orla's estate and Everett's subsequent death was between one and two years, therefore the percentage to be applied using Table 16.1 is 80%.

The amount of quick succession relief is therefore £34,165 × 80% = £27,332.

This will be given as a tax credit to reduce the IHT due on Everett's estate.

Double-taxation relief (DTR)

Sometimes, tax is paid on overseas assets that a person owned at the time they died. The valuation of these overseas assets is covered in Chapter 14, together with details on how tax credit relief is given for any overseas tax paid. As a recap, however, the amount of DTR given is the lower of:

▨ the overseas tax suffered.

▨ the amount of UK inheritance tax attributable to the foreign asset.

Example

Double-taxation relief (DTR)

Meredith died on 20 September 2009 leaving an estate of £600,000. She had previously made chargeable lifetime transfers which meant that no nil band exemption was available to her estate, and all was taxable at 40 per cent.

Within the assets of the estate, there is an overseas property that has been valued at £200,000. Tax of £30,000 was payable overseas on this property in view of Meredith's death.

The estate is able to claim the double-tax relief credit because tax has been paid in two countries. The amount of DTR given is the lower of:

■ the overseas tax suffered: £30,000;

■ the amount of UK inheritance tax attributable to the foreign asset, which is £200,000 at 40% = £80,000.

Therefore £30,000 can be set against the UK tax liability.

It should be noted that if an individual had several overseas assets, separate DTR calculations for each asset are required.

Date for payment of inheritance tax

The due date for inheritance tax to be paid to HMRC is six months after the end of the month in which the death occurred, unless the instalment option is available, on some assets.

Any inheritance tax paid late is liable to interest, which would run from the due date to the date the tax is paid. Details of how to pay inheritance tax and the possibility of paying by instalments are covered in Chapter 19.

Tax planning after death and deeds of variation

This chapter will explain post-death variations and when they can be beneficial

- Disclaimers
- Deeds of variation
- Considerations for making a deed of variation

Usually, when someone dies leaving a will, or their property is subject to the rules of intestacy when a will hasn't been left, the way in which the property is distributed is clear cut and carried out accordingly. However, there are occasions when the distribution of the wealth can be changed. Typical situations where this might occur are:

- When at least one or more of the beneficiaries does not wish to benefit from the estate and would rather pass on their share of the estate to another individual.
- For tax reasons, when it is found that a lower amount of inheritance tax could be payable, if the distribution of assets was arranged in a more tax efficient manner.
- All beneficiaries wish for a fairer distribution of assets.

Disclaimers

There is no obligation for a beneficiary of a will, or a beneficiary who will inherit under the intestacy rules, to accept their legacy. They can choose to disclaim the gift. However, if they choose to do this the amount of the legacy will be added to the residue of the estate and will be distributed as if the original beneficiary has died. This may not be a good way of redistributing a gift to another chosen individual, which is the desire in most cases. In these cases, a deed of variation may be more appropriate.

Deeds of variation

One change is made by way of a deed of variation (sometimes still called a deed of family arrangement) and this is used to alter the distribution of an estate. Conditions must be met for the deed of variation to apply for tax purposes:

■ The deed must be made within two years of the death.

■ The deed must be signed by all the beneficiaries of the estate before the change who stand to lose under it.

■ All parties to the change in distribution are alive, of sound mind and of age to sign a legal document. This usually means it is not possible to carry out any changes where the beneficiary or beneficiaries who stand to lose are minors. In this case, the matter would be heard in a court of law and it is unusual for a court to overturn a minor's interest. There is no problem with increasing the benefit to a minor.

■ The deed of variation will take effect from the death of the deceased.

■ If the IHT situation is to be varied, the deed must contain a statement that the variation is to have effect for IHT as if the deceased had made it.

■ If the deed is to be effective for CGT as if the deceased had made the variation, a separate signed statement to that effect must be included in the deed.

■ The deed must be entered into voluntarily and for no consideration. So, for instance, an original beneficiary cannot be paid for agreeing to the change.

Considerations for making a deed of variation

As we can see above, there are strict conditions to be met before a deed of variation can be made. Having said that, let's consider other issues that need to be addressed before to ensure that a deed of variation is the best way forward.

The first thing to note is that a deed of variation can slow down the administration process and is likely to incur professional fees as a legal document is required. However, the benefits often far outweigh the disadvantages.

Another advantage to changing the position at death might be to minimise tax liabilities. For instance, deeds of variation are useful to distribute assets to fully utilise the nil band, as in the example below.

Example

Utilising a nil rate band

Edwin died in June 2010 and left an estate of £1,000,000. He left a will stating that he wanted his entire estate to go to his wife, Ella.

Ella is already wealthy in her own right and felt she would like for her children to also benefit from Edwin's estate. She makes a deed of variation to change the original will so that £325,000 of the estate is passed to the children, with the remainder of the estate to herself.

In doing this, she hasn't created an inheritance tax liability as she has re-directed enough of the estate to be covered by the nil rate band of £325,000.

However, this may not be seen as quite so important now that the nil rate band is transferable between spouses/civil partners, in cases where the second person of a couple died on or after 9 October 2007.

Another advantage is to minimise the tax liability by distributing the assets in a different way.

Example

Distributing assets using business property relief

Chrystia died in May 2010, leaving the following assets:

Shares in her own personal unquoted company that qualify for BPR of 100%:	£550,000
A share in the family home:	£400,000
Cash, bank accounts and chattels:	£50,000
Total	£1,000,000

She made a will stating that £500,000 of the company shares should go to her husband, Seamus, and the remainder of the estate assets amounting to £500,000 to go to her children.

Under the will, £500,000 of the company shares were left to the husband, with the remainder of the shares and the assets left to the children. The situation would be as follows:

Shares to the husband	£500,000
Less BPR or spouse exemption	£(500,000)
Chargeable to IHT	0

The remainder of the shares to the children	£50,000
Less BPR	£(50,000)
Chargeable to IHT	£0
Plus the remaining assets:	
£400,000 share of the house and £50,000	£450,000
Less nil band	(325,000)
Chargeable	125,000

Tax due at 40% = £40,000

Make a deed of variation

If £500,000 of the company shares were left to the children, with the remainder of the shares and the assets left to the husband Seamus, the situation would be as follows:

The shares to the children	£500,000
Less BPR	£(500,000)
Chargeable to IHT	£0

The remainder of the shares to the husband	£50,000
Less BPR or spouse exemption	£(50,000)
Chargeable to IHT	0
Plus the remaining assets:	
£400,000 share of the house and £50,000	£450,000
Less spouse exemption	(£450,000)
Chargeable	0

Tax due at 40% = £0

Conclusion

The difference between the two scenarios, with a bit of planning and using the business property relief exemptions and the spouse exemption shows that tax of £40,000 can be saved. This can be achieved by making a deed of variation, so long as the conditions can be met.

Skipping a generation

More often than not, parents will leave their wealth to their own children. This means that the wealth of the children increases so that on their death, their estates are higher, on which to pay a potential 40 per cent tax if the total wealth exceeded the nil rate band.

The alternative to this is to skip a generation for inheritance tax purposes and pass property to grandchildren. Ultimately, they are likely to survive longer and there is likely to be a longer period of time before an additional IHT liability arises on the property.

Example

Skipping a generation

John died in August 2010 and left an estate with a value of £800,000. In his will, he left the entire £800,000 to his nephew Peter.

On learning he was named as the beneficiary of John's will, Peter decided that he was wealthy enough in this own right not to benefit from the inheritance. He already has a potential inheritance tax liability on his own property, should he die.

He therefore made a deed of variation to re-direct the inheritance to his own two children, so that they had the value of £400,000 each in their own estates.

By doing this, Peter has skipped a generation of inheritance tax. Rather than pay additional inheritance tax at 40 per cent on his additional wealth, should he accept the wealth, he has in fact diverted the value to his children, thus skipping a generation.

It is recommended that professional advice is sought before making a deed of variation, just to check that the claim is beneficial from a practical and tax issue. The benefit in seeking further advice usually far outweighs the fees in doing so. A solicitor will also be able to help with raising the legal paperwork correctly.

18

Excepted estates

This chapter will detail which estates fall into the category of 'excepted estates'

- Low value estates

- Exempt excepted estates

- Foreign domiciliaries

- Procedure in England, Wales and Northern Ireland

- The Scottish variant

- Summary

Essentially, the personal representatives of the deceased must deliver an account of the assets and liabilities of the estate. This is actioned by completing an inheritance tax form IHT400 and submitting this to the Capital Taxes Office. Any inheritance tax must then be paid by the personal representatives by the required date. However, there are occasions when an IHT400 will not be required. In these cases, an estate is described as an excepted estate:

- low value estates;

- exempt excepted estates;

- foreign domiciliaries.

Instead of completing form IHT400, the personal representatives file a brief return of information about the estate as a whole. If any of the above conditions are not satisfied, a form IHT400 must be delivered to HMRC. Further details of how to do this are discussed in Chapter 12.

Low value estates

These are estates where there can be no liability to tax because the gross value of the estate does not exceed the IHT nil rate band. The nil bands are as follows:

2009–10   £325,000
2010–11   £325,000

Generally, the conditions for these estates applying to deaths occurring after 1 September 2006, are that the deceased was domiciled in the UK and the gross value of the estate, including their share of jointly owned assets, and any transfers previously made in their lifetime does not exceed the nil rate band.

There are additional conditions:

■ If the estate includes any assets held in trust, they must be held in a single trust and the gross value must not exceed £150,000.

■ If the estate includes foreign assets, their gross value must not exceed £100,000.

■ If there have been certain transfers made in the deceased's lifetime, their chargeable value does not exceed £150,000.

■ The deceased had not made a gift with reservation of benefit.

■ A charge does not arise on an alternatively secured pension fund.

These are the general conditions for an estate to qualify as being an excepted estate. If there is any doubt, advice should be sought by the Capital Taxes Office which would confirm whether all conditions are met.

Exempt excepted estates

These are estates where there can be no liability to IHT because the gross value of the estate does not exceed £1,000,000 and there is no tax to pay because either of the following two exemptions or reliefs can be deducted against the assets:

■ the spouse or civil partner exemption (where both individuals have always been domiciled in the UK), and/or

■ charity exemption *only* (where the gift is an absolute gift to the organisation concerned).

No other exemption or relief can be taken into account. Generally, the conditions for these estates, that apply to deaths occurring after 1 September 2006, are:

■ The deceased was domiciled in the United Kingdom; and

■ The gross value of the estate, including their share of jointly owned assets, and any transfers previously made in their lifetime does not exceed £1,000,000 and the net chargeable value of the estate after the deduction of liabilities and the above exemptions does not exceed the IHT nil rate band.

As with the low value estates, there are additional conditions:

■ If the estate includes any assets held in trust, they must be held in a single trust and the gross value must not exceed £150,000 (unless the settled property passes to the spouse or civil partner or charity, when the limit is waived).

■ If the estate includes foreign assets, their gross value must not exceed £100,000.

■ If there have been certain transfers made in the deceased's lifetime, their chargeable value does not exceed £150,000.

■ The deceased had not made a gift with reservation of benefit.

■ A charge does not arise on an alternatively secured pension fund.

These are the general conditions for an estate to qualify as being an excepted estate. Again, if there is any doubt, advice should be sought from the Capital Taxes Office.

Foreign domiciliaries

The death of an individual who was not of UK domicile status, occurring on or after 6 April 2002, could also qualify as an excepted estate. The estate will qualify as an excepted estate if the deceased was:

■ domiciled outside the UK at the date of their death;

■ had never been domiciled in the UK during their lifetime;

■ had never been 'deemed' domiciled in the UK;

■ the value of their estate situated in the UK consists only of cash or quoted shares or securities passing under their will or intestacy or by survivorship and the gross value does not exceed these cash limits:

Deaths (all dates inclusive)	*Gross value of estate*
6 April 2002 to 31 August 2006	£100,000
1 September onwards	£150,000

These are the general conditions for an estate to qualify as being an excepted estate in relation to foreign domiciliaries. If in doubt, seek advice from the Capital Taxes Office.

Procedure in England, Wales and Northern Ireland

For low value estates and exempt excepted estates

Rather than completing the full inheritance tax form IHT400, the personal representatives can complete form IHT205 Return of Estate Information, and send it with their probate application and other documentation required (usually the death certificate and a copy of any will) to the probate registry. A copy of the form IHT205 can be found on the HMRC website: www.hmrc.gov.uk/cto/forms/iht205-2006-2.pdf

The notes booklet to help complete the form can also be found at: www.hmrc.gov.uk/cto/forms/iht206-2006-1.pdf

If no problems arise, the probate registry calls the personal representative for the usual interview, at which the personal representative swears an oath that the information in the application for the grant is true and correct. The personal representative also pays the probate fees.

The main advantage with an excepted estate, other than the reduced administration, is that the grant of probate is usually issued within a few weeks of the interview. Figure 18.1 shows form IHT205.

For foreign domiciliaries excepted estates

Rather than completing the tax form IHT400, the personal representatives would complete the inheritance tax form IHT207 Return of Estate Information. A copy of the form IHT207 can be found on the HMRC website:
www.hmrc.gov.uk/cto/forms/iht207-2006-2.pdf

The notes booklet to help complete the form can be found at: www.hmrc.gov.uk/cto/forms/iht208-2006-1.pdf

Figure 18.2 shows form IHT207.

HM Revenue & Customs

Return of estate information

Fill in this version of this form only when the person died on or after 1 September 2006.
Fill in this form where the person who has died ('the deceased') had their permanent home in the United Kingdom (UK) at the date of death and the **gross value of the estate for Inheritance Tax:**
• is less than the excepted estate limit, **or**

• is less than £1,000,000 **and** there is no Inheritance Tax to pay because of spouse, civil partner or charity exemption **only**.

√ ☐ ☐

About the person who has died

| Title | 1.1 | Surname | 1.2 |
| | | Other name(s) | 1.3 |
| | | Date of death
DD MM YYYY | 1.4 |

Marital or civil partnership status   Write whichever is appropriate a, b, c or d in the box 1.5

a. married or in civil partnership   *b.* single   *c.* divorced or former civil partner   *d.* widowed or surviving civil partner

Occupation 1.6   National Insurance number 1.7

Surviving relatives

| Husband/Wife or Civil Partner | √ 1.8 | Brother(s)/Sister(s) | √ 1.9 | Parent(s) | √ 1.10 |
| Number of children | 1.11 | Number of grandchildren | 1.12 | | |

The notes in booklet IHT206 will help you to fill in this form. You must answer questions 2 to 10.

About the estate

                                                                                                                              No   Yes

2. Within seven years of death did the deceased:

   a. make any gifts or other transfers totalling more than £3,000 per year, other than normal birthday, festive, marriage or civil partnership gifts, **or**   ☐ ☐

   b. give up the right to benefit from any assets held in trust that were treated as part of their estate for Inheritance Tax purposes (see booklet IHT206)?   ☐ ☐

   If you answer 'Yes' to either part of question 2, include the chargeable value of the gifts in box 14.1. But if this value is more than £150,000 or the assets do not qualify as 'specified transfers' (see IHT206) stop filling in this form. You will need to fill in form IHT400 instead.

3. Did the deceased make:

   a. a gift, on or after 18 March 1986, where they continued to benefit from, or had some right to benefit from, or use all or part of the asset? **Or**   ☐ ☐

   b. a gift, on or after 18 March 1986, where the person receiving the gift did not take full possession of it? **Or**   ☐ ☐

   c. an election that the Income Tax charge should not apply to: ☐ ☐

      – assets they previously owned, in which they retained a benefit, **or**

      – the deceased's contribution to the purchase price of assets acquired by another person, but in which the deceased retained a benefit?

   If you answer 'Yes' to any part of question 3, stop filling in this form. You will need to fill in form IHT400 instead.

4. Did the deceased have the right to receive the benefit from any assets held in a trust that were treated as part of their estate for Inheritance Tax purposes (see booklet IHT206)?   ☐ ☐

   If you answer 'Yes' to question 4 and the deceased:

   • *was entitled to benefit from a single trust, and*

   • *the value of the assets in that trust, treated as part of their estate, was less than £150,000*

   include the value of the trust assets in box 14.2. But if the value was more than £150,000, or there was more than one trust, stop filling in this form. You will need to fill in form IHT400 instead.

5. Did the deceased own or benefit from any assets outside the UK?   ☐ ☐

   If you answer 'Yes' to question 5 include the value of the overseas assets in box 14.5. But if the value of the overseas assets is more than £100,000, stop filling in this form. You will need to fill in form IHT400 instead.

IHT205(2006)   www.hmrc.gov.uk/inheritancetax/   *Helpline 0845 30 20 900*   HMRC 06/09

Figure 18.1 Form IHT205 for low value and exempt excepted estates

		No	Yes

6. Did the deceased pay premiums on any life insurance policies that were not for the deceased's own benefit or did not pay out to the estate? ☐ ☐

   If you answer 'Yes' to question 6, you must also answer question 11.

7. Did the deceased benefit from an alternatively secured pension fund (see IHT206)? ☐ ☐

   *If you answer 'Yes' to question 7 **stop filling in this form. You will need to fill in form IHT400 instead.***

8. Did the deceased benefit under a registered pension scheme, where:

   • the benefit was unsecured, **and**

   • they acquired the benefit as a relevant dependant of a person who died aged 75 or over? ☐ ☐

   *If you answer 'Yes' to question 8 **stop filling in this form. You will need to fill in form IHT400 instead.***

9. Was the deceased a member of a pension scheme or did they have a personal pension policy from which, in either case, they had not taken their full retirement benefits before the date of death? ☐ ☐

   If you answer 'Yes' to question 9, you must also answer question 12.

10. a. Was the deceased entitled to receive payments from a pension which continued to be paid after they had died (other than arrears of pension)? ☐ ☐

    b. Was a lump sum payable under a pension scheme or pension policy as a result of the death? ☐ ☐

    If you answer 'Yes' to question 10, see IHT206 to find out where to include the asset.

Do not answer questions 11 or 12 unless you answered 'Yes' to questions 6 or 9.

11. Within seven years of the death, did the deceased:

    a. pay any premium on a life insurance policy under which the benefit is payable other than to the estate, or to the spouse or civil partner of the deceased, *and if so* ☐ ☐

    b. did they buy an annuity at any time? ☐ ☐

    *If you answer 'Yes' to question 11(a), see IHT206 to find out how to include the premiums paid on this form. If you answer 'Yes' to **both** question 11(a) and 11(b), **stop filling in this form. You will need to fill in form IHT400 instead.***

12. At a time when they were in poor health or terminally ill, did the deceased change their pension scheme or personal pension policy so as to:

    a. dispose of any of the benefits payable, or ☐ ☐

    b. make any change to the benefits to which they were entitled? ☐ ☐

    *If you answer 'Yes' to question 12(a) or 12(b), **stop filling in this form. You will need to fill in form IHT400 instead.***

13. **Deceased's own assets (including jointly owned assets NOT passing by survivorship – see IHT206)**

    • *You must include the gross value for each item below, before deduction of any exemption or relief.*

    • *You must include all the assets that were part of the deceased's estate as at the date of death, ignoring any changes that may take place through an Instrument of Variation made after the death.*

    • *You must make full enquiries so that you can show that the figures that you give in this form are right. If you cannot find out the value for an item, you may include your best estimate.*

    Tick box to show estimated amount √

13.1	Cash, including money in banks, building societies and National Savings	13.1 £	☐
13.2	Household and personal goods	13.2 £	☐
13.3	Stocks and shares quoted on the Stock Exchange	13.3 £	☐
13.4	Stocks and shares not quoted on the Stock Exchange	13.4 £	☐
13.5	Insurance policies, including bonuses and mortgage protection policies	13.5 £	☐
13.6	Money owed to the person who has died	13.6 £	☐
13.7	Partnership and business interests	13.7 £	☐
13.8	Freehold/leasehold residence of the person who has died	13.8 £	☐

Address (including postcode)

Tick box to show estimated amount ✓

13.9	Other freehold/leasehold residential property	**13.9** £
	Address (including postcode)	
13.10	Other land and buildings	**13.10** £
	Address/location	
13.11	Any other assets not included above	**13.11** £
	Total estate for which a grant is required (sum of boxes 13.1 to 13.11)	**A** £
14.	**Other assets forming part of the estate**	
14.1	Gifts and other lifetime transfers (after deduction of exemptions)	**14.1** £
	Details of gifts	
14.2	Assets held in trust for the benefit of the deceased	**14.2** £
	Details of assets held in trust	
14.3	Share of joint assets passing automatically to the surviving joint owner	**14.3** £
	Details of joint assets	
14.4	Nominated assets	**14.4** £
14.5	Assets outside the UK (value in £ sterling)	**14.5** £
	Total (sum of boxes 14.1 to 14.5)	**B** £
	Gross estate for Inheritance Tax (A *plus* B)	**C** £
15.	**Debts of the estate**	
15.1	Funeral expenses	**15.1** £
15.2	Mortgage or share of a mortgage on a property in Section 13	**15.2** £
15.3	Other debts owed by the deceased in the UK	**15.3** £
	Total debts owing in the UK (sum of boxes 15.1 to 15.3)	**D** £
15.4	Debts payable out of trust assets	**15.4** £
15.5	Share of mortgage on a property owned as a joint asset	**15.5** £
15.6	Share of other debts payable out of joint assets	**15.6** £
15.7	Debts owing to persons outside the UK	**15.7** £
	Total of other debts (sum of boxes 15.4 to 15.7)	**E** £
	Total debts (D *plus* E)	**F** £
	Net estate for Inheritance Tax (C *minus* F)	**G** £

16.   *Use this space to provide any other information we have asked for or you would like taken into account.*

17.   **Exemptions (you should read IHT206 before filling in this section)**

In the box below, deduct any exemption for assets passing on death to:
- *the spouse or civil partner of the deceased, or*
- *a UK charity or for national purposes.*

Describe the extent of the exemption deducted. If for charities, etc give the name of the charity(s) or other organisation(s) benefiting. Where exemptions are deducted for particular assets, list those assets and show the amount deducted.

17.1

	H £	
Net qualifying value for excepted estates (G *minus* H)	**J** £	

17.2   Tax office and/or Income Tax reference number | 17.2 |

If you find something has been left out, or if any of the figures you have given in this form change later on, you only need to tell us if, taking all the omissions and changes into account:
- the figure at box G is now higher than the Inheritance Tax threshold, **and**
- there are no exemptions to deduct which keep the value at box J below the Inheritance Tax threshold.

If, at any time, the value at box J is more than the Inheritance Tax threshold, you must list any new items and the items that have changed in a Corrective Account (form C4) and send it to us with a copy of this form along with a cheque for the tax that has become payable.

The issue of the grant does not mean that there is no Inheritance Tax due on this estate.

The information I/we have given on this form is correct and complete to the best of my/our knowledge and belief. I/We have read and understand the statements above.

I/We understand that I/we may have to pay financial penalties and face prosecution if the answers to the questions or figures that I/we give in this form are false, or if the estate fails to qualify as an excepted estate and I/we do not deliver a Corrective Account within 6 months of the failure coming to my/our notice.

Full name and address	Full name and address
Signature	Signature
Full name and address	Full name and address
Signature	Signature

Summary

Gross estate in the UK passing under Will or by intestacy	**A** £	
Debts in the UK owed by the deceased alone	**D** £	
Net estate in the UK (A *minus* D)	**K** £	

www.hmrc.gov.uk/inheritancetax/   Helpline 0845 30 20 900

HM Revenue & Customs

Return of estate information

*Fill in this version of this form only when the person died on or after 1 September 2006. Fill in this form where the person who has died ('the deceased') had their permanent home abroad and their assets in the United Kingdom (UK) consisted of cash, or quoted stocks and shares **only**, the gross value of which was less than £150,000.*

About the person who has died

Title [1.1]   Surname [1.2]

Other name(s) [1.3]

Date of death [1.4]
DD MM YYYY

Marital or civil partnership status   Write whichever is appropriate a, b, c or d in the box [1.5]

a. married or in civil partnership   b. single   c. divorced or former civil partner   d. widowed or surviving civil partner

Occupation [1.6]

Domicile [1.7]

Last known usual address [1.8]

Postcode

Surviving relatives

Spouse or civil partner [1.9]

Brother(s)/sister(s) [1.10]

Parent(s) [1.11]

Number of children [1.12]

Number of grandchildren [1.13]

You should read the notes about each question in booklet IHT208 as you fill in this form.

About residence in the United Kingdom (UK)

No Yes

2. Was the deceased born in the UK?

3. Did the deceased live in the UK during their lifetime?
*If you answer 'Yes' to either question 2 or 3, **do not fill in any more of this form**. You will need to fill in form IHT400 instead.*

About the estate

4. Was the deceased receiving any benefit from any assets held by trustees who were resident in the UK?

5. Did the deceased make any gifts of UK assets within the seven years before the date they died?
*If you answer 'Yes' to either question 4 or 5, **do not fill in any more of this form**. You will need to fill in form IHT400 instead.*

6. Did the deceased own any asset(s) in joint names with another person or people?
If you answer 'Yes' to question 6, describe the asset(s) and give their value(s) in box 7. Read IHT208 to find out how to include these assets in the rest of this form.

7. Use this space to provide any other information we have asked for or you would like taken into account

IHT207(2006)   www.hmrc.gov.uk/inheritancetax/   Helpline 0845 30 20 900   HMRC 06/09

Figure 18.2 Form IHT207 for excepted estates of foreign domiciliaries

8. Assets in the United Kingdom

- *You must include the gross value for each item below.*
- *You must make full enquiries so that you can show that the figures that you give in this form are right. If you cannot find out the value for an item, you may include your best estimate.*

Tick the box to show estimates √

8.1	Cash, including money in banks and building societies	**8.1** £	
8.2	Stocks and shares quoted on the Stock Exchange	**8.2** £	
8.3	Assets held as tenants-in-common	**8.3** £	
	Total estate in the UK for which a grant is required	**A** £	
8.4	Share of joint assets passing automatically to the surviving joint owner	**B** £	
	Gross estate for Inheritance Tax (A *plus* B)	**C** £	

9. Debts payable in the UK

9.1	Debts owed in the UK by the deceased	**D** £	
9.2	Share of debts in the UK payable out of joint UK assets	**E** £	
	Total debts (D *plus* E)	**F** £	
	Net estate in the UK for Inheritance Tax (C *minus* F)	**G** £	

If you find something has been left out, or if any of the figures you have given in this form change later on so that the value in box G is more than £150,000, you must list any new items and the items that have changed in a Corrective Account (form C4) and send it to us with a copy of this form.

The issue of the grant does not mean that there is no Inheritance Tax due on this estate.

The information I/we have given on this form is correct and complete to the best of my/our knowledge and belief. I/we have read and understand the statements above.

I/we understand that I/we may have to pay financial penalties if the answers to the questions or figures that I/we give in this form are false, or if the estate fails to qualify as an excepted estate and I/we do not deliver a Corrective Account within six months of the failure coming to my/our notice.

Full name and address	Full name and address
Signature　　　　　　　　Date	Signature　　　　　　　　Date
Full name and address	Full name and address
Signature　　　　　　　　Date	Signature　　　　　　　　Date

Summary

Gross estate in the UK passing under Will or by intestacy	**A** £	
Debts in the UK owed by the deceased alone	**D** £	
Net estate in the UK　　　　　　　　**(A *minus* D)**	**H** £	

The Scottish variant

As with estates in England, Wales and Northern Ireland, the personal representatives of a Scottish estate must deliver an account of the assets and liabilities of the estate by completing an inheritance tax form IHT400 and submitting this to HM Revenue and Customs. Any inheritance tax must then be paid by the personal representatives by the required date. However, there are occasions when an IHT400 will not be required to be completed and this is for an estate described as:

- An excepted estate – with the conditions applying exactly as described earlier in the chapter; or
- A small estate.

In these cases, instead of completing the usual form IHT400, the personal representatives file a brief return of information about the estate as a whole using form C5. If any of the conditions are not satisfied for the estate to be either excepted or small, a form IHT400 must be delivered to HMRC. Further details of how to do this are discussed in Chapter 12.

Excepted estates

The conditions for an estate to be an excepted estate in Scotland, are the same as those described for England, Wales and Northern Ireland. The form that requires completion by the personal representatives is the form C5 (Figure 18.3 overleaf). A copy of form C5 can be found on the HMRC website:
www.hmrc.gov.uk/cto/forms/c5-2006-2.pdf

Small estates

Where an estate in Scotland does not exceed £30,000, it will be regarded as a small estate under the Confirmation to Small Estates (Scotland) Act. In cases such as these, the application for confirmation is made by the personal representatives using form C5 (SE), as shown in Figure 18.4 (page 195). A copy can be found on the HMRC website:
www.hmrc.gov.uk/cto/forms/c5-2006-2.pdf

HM Revenue
& Customs

Return of estate information

*Fill in this version of this form only when the person died on or after 1 September 2006. Fill in this form where the person who has died ('the deceased') was domiciled in the United Kingdom (UK) at the date of death and the **gross value of the estate for Inheritance Tax:***
- *is less than the excepted estate limit,* **or**
- *is less than £1,000,000 **and** after deduction of liabilities and spouse or civil partner and/or charity exemption **only (taking account of no other relief)** the estate is below the IHT threshold.*

About the person who has died

Surname	**1.1**
Other name(s)	**1.2**
Date of death DD MM YYYY	**1.3**

You should read the notes about each question in booklet C3 as you fill in this form. Everyone must answer questions 2 to 10 until or unless directed to fill in form IHT400.

About the estate

                                               No Yes

2. Within seven years of death did the deceased:
   a. make any gifts or other transfers totalling more than £3,000 per year, other than normal
      birthday, festive, wedding or civil partnership gifts, **or**
   b. give up the right to benefit from any assets held in trust that were treated as part of their estate
      for Inheritance Tax purposes (see booklet C3).
   If you answer 'Yes' to either part of question 2, give brief details in box 14 and include the chargeable value of the gifts in box 15.4. But if this value is more than £150,000 or the assets do not qualify as 'specified transfers' (see booklet C3) stop filling in this form. You will need to fill in form IHT400 instead.

3. Did the deceased make:
   a. a gift, on or after 18 March 1986, where they continued to benefit from, or had some right to
      benefit from, or use all or part of the asset, **or**
   b. a gift, on or after 18 March 1986, where the person receiving the gift did not take full possession
      of it, **or**
   c. an election that an Income Tax charge should not apply to
      – assets the deceased previously owned, but in which they retained a benefit, **or**
      – the deceased's contribution to the purchase price of assets acquired by another person,
        but in which the deceased retained a benefit?
   *If you answer 'Yes' to any part of question 3, **stop filling in this form. You will need to fill in form IHT400 instead.***

4. Did the deceased have the right to receive the benefit from any assets held in a trust that were
   treated as part of their estate for Inheritance Tax purposes? (see booklet C3)
   If you answer 'Yes' to question 4 and the deceased:
   • *was entitled to benefit from a single trust, and*
   • *the gross value of the assets in that trust treated as part of their estate was less than £150,000 at the date of death, give brief details in box 14 and include the gross value of the trust assets in box 15.5. But if the value was more than £150,000, or there was more than one trust, stop filling in this form. You will need to fill in form IHT400 instead.*

5. Did the deceased own or benefit from any assets outside the UK?
   If you answer 'Yes' to question 5 include the value of the overseas assets in box 15.7. But if the gross value of the overseas assets is more than £100,000, stop filling in this form. You will need to fill in form IHT400 instead.

6. Did the deceased pay premiums on any life insurance policies that were not for the deceased's
   own benefit or did not pay out to the estate?
   If you answer 'Yes' to question 6, you must also answer question 11 unless you answer 'Yes' to question 7 or 8.

7. Did the deceased benefit from an alternatively secured pension fund (see booklet C3).
   *If you answer 'Yes' to question 7, **stop filling in this form. You will need to fill in form IHT400 instead.***

C5(2006)   *www.hmrc.gov.uk/inheritancetax/*   *Helpline 0845 30 20 900*   HMRC 06/09

Figure 18.3 Form C5 for Scottish excepted estates

8. Did the deceased benefit under a registered pension scheme, where: **No   Yes**
    - the benefit was unsecured, **and**
    - they acquired the benefit as a relevant dependant of a person who died aged 75 or over?   ☐ ☐
    *If you answer 'Yes' to question 8, **stop filling in this form. You will need to fill in form IHT400 instead.***

9. Was the deceased a member of a pension scheme or did they have a personal pension policy
    from which, in either case, they had not taken their full retirement benefits before the date of death?   ☐ ☐
    If you answer 'Yes' to question 9, you must also answer question 12.

10. a. Was the person who has died entitled to receive payments from a pension which continued
       to be paid after they had died (other than arrears of pension) which you have not included
       in the Inventory form C1?   ☐ ☐
    b. Was a lump sum payable under a pension scheme or pension policy as a result of the death
       which you have not included in the Inventory form C1?   ☐ ☐
    If you answer 'Yes' to question 10, include the value in box 15.2 or explain in box 14 why it is not included.

Do not answer question 11 or 12 unless you answered 'Yes' to question 6 or 9.

11. Within seven years of the death, did the deceased:
    a. pay any premium on a life insurance policy under which the benefit is payable other than
       to the estate, or to the spouse or civil partner of the deceased, *and if so*   ☐ ☐
    b. did they buy an annuity at any time?   ☐ ☐
    If you answer 'Yes' to question 11(a), see booklet C3 to find out how to include the premiums paid on this form.
    *If you answer 'Yes' to **both** questions 11(a) and 11(b), **stop filling in this form. You will need to fill in form IHT400 instead.***

12. At a time when they were in poor health or terminally ill, did the deceased change any pension
    scheme or personal pension policy so as to:
    a. dispose of any of the benefits payable, or   ☐ ☐
    b. make any change to the benefits to which they were entitled?   ☐ ☐
    *If you answer 'Yes' to questions 12(a) or 12(b), **stop filling in this form. You will need to fill in form IHT400 instead.***

Only answer question 13 if you are deducting spouse or civil partner or charity exemption against the estate.

                                                                                   N/A
13. Has the *legitim* fund been either claimed or discharged **in full** following the death?   ☐ ☐ ☐
    If the total value of the legitim fund not already claimed or discharged following the death, when added to the remaining
    *chargeable estate, exceeds the excepted estate limit, **stop filling in this form. You will need to fill in form IHT400 instead.***
    You should calculate the *legitim* on the basis that any not already discharged will be claimed in full.
    Show this figure and the amount claimed in box 13 and adopt it when calculating the exemption in
    box D on page 3 (see booklet C3).   Value of undischarged legal rights   **13** £ _____

14. *If you answer 'Yes' to either questions 2 or 4 use the space below to give details of the gifts or the trust, or for your*
    calculation of legal rights to answer question 13. You may also include here any other information you consider relevant.

    [blank box]

15. Summary of estate

You must make full enquiries so that you can show that the figures that you give in this form are right. If you cannot find out the value for an item, you may include your best estimate

Tick the box to show estimates √

15.1 Assets Confirmed to (box 1.1 on C1)	**15.1** £	
15.2 Payments under a pension (not included for Confirmation)	**15.2** £	
15.3 Share of jointly held UK assets passing automatically to the survivor(s)	**15.3** £	
15.4 Gifts and other lifetime transfers	**15.4** £	
15.5 Assets held in trust for the benefit of the deceased (see booklet C3)	**15.5** £	
15.6 Nominated assets not included for Confirmation (see booklet C3)	**15.6** £	
15.7 Assets outside the UK including the deceased's share of jointly owned assets	**15.7** £	

Gross estate for Inheritance Tax (sum of boxes 15.1 to 15.7)	**A** £	
Total liabilities	**B** £	
Net estate for Inheritance Tax (A *minus* B)	**C** £	

16. Exemptions (you should read booklet C3 before filling in this section)

In the box below, deduct any exemption for assets passing on death to:
- *the husband, wife or civil partner of the person who has died, and/or*
- *a UK charity and/or for national purposes.*

You must calculate the exemption on the basis that any undischarged legal rights will be claimed in full. *If you are deducting charity exemption etc., give the name of the charity(s) or other organisations benefiting. Where exemptions are deducted for particular assets, list those assets and show the amount deducted.*

Continue on page 4

D £	

Net qualifying value of the estate (C *minus* D)	**E** £

Carry the values from boxes A, C and E to boxes 3A, 3B and 3C respectively on page 4 of form C1.

If you find something has been left out, or if any of the figures you have given in this form change later on, you only need to tell us if, taking all the omissions and changes into account:
- the figure at box C is now higher than the Inheritance Tax threshold, **and**
- there are no exemptions to deduct which keep the value at box E below the Inheritance Tax threshold.

If at any time, the value at box E exceeds the Inheritance Tax threshold, you must complete a Corrective Account (form C4), *which must be signed by all the executors,* and send it to us with a cheque for the tax that has become payable.

The issue of Confirmation does not mean that there is no Inheritance Tax due on this estate.

The information I have given on this form is correct and complete to the best of my knowledge and belief. I have read and understand the statements above.

I understand that I may have to pay financial penalties and face prosecution if the answers to the questions or figures that I give in this form are false, or if the estate fails to qualify as an excepted estate and I do not deliver a Corrective Account within six months of the failure coming to my notice.

Signature		Date	

HM Revenue & Customs — *Information about Small Estates*

Use this form only if the person died on or after 1 September 2006. Fill in this form where the person who has died ('the deceased') was domiciled in the United Kingdom (UK) and their estate qualifies as a Small Estate under the Small Estates Acts.

About the person who has died

Surname   1.1

Other name(s)   1.2

Date of death   1.3
DD MM YYYY

You should read the notes overleaf as you fill in this form.

About the estate

	No	Yes
2. Did the deceased benefit from an alternatively secured pension fund from a registered pension scheme at the time of their death?	☐	☐
3. Did the deceased benefit from an unsecured pension under a registered pension scheme as a relevant dependant of a scheme member who died aged 75 or over?	☐	☐
4. Did the deceased make any gifts over £3,000 in any one or more of the seven years before they died?	☐	☐
5. Did the deceased give away any asset but keep back an interest in it?	☐	☐
6. Was the deceased entitled to benefit from any assets held in trust?	☐	☐
7. Did the deceased own any asset(s) in joint names with anyone, which passed by survivorship? (If the assets were held with, and passed to, the deceased's surviving husband, wife or civil partner you may answer 'No' – see overleaf.)	☐	☐
8. Had the deceased nominated any assets in favour of someone else during their lifetime? (If the assets were nominated in favour of the deceased's surviving husband, wife or civil partner you may answer 'No' – see overleaf.)	☐	☐

We look at the forms that are submitted to us from the Sheriff Clerk's Office or the Commissary Office and may write to you. If you do not hear from us with any questions within 60 days from the date of Confirmation, you may assume that we have no questions about the answers you have given.

If you become aware of any changes to the estate you only need to tell us if the total estate confirmed to plus any assets and/or gifts as above is more than the taxable threshold. (You can find out the current threshold by phoning the Helpline on **0845 30 20 900**.) In that case you must fill in a formal Inheritance Tax Return on form IHT400.

The information I have given on this form is correct and complete to the best of my knowledge and belief. I have read and understand the statements above.

I understand that I may have to pay financial penalties and face prosecution if the answers to the questions or figures that I give in this form are false, or if the estate fails to qualify as an excepted estate and I do not deliver a Corrective Account within six months of the failure coming to my notice.

Signature   Date

C5(SE)(2006)   *www.hmrc.gov.uk/inheritancetax/*   *Helpline 0845 30 20 900*   HMRC 06/09

Figure 18.4 Form C5 (SE) for small Scottish estates

Notes

2 and 3.

A person must be aged 75 or over to benefit from an Alternatively Secured Pension (ASP). An ASP is an unsecured pension for the benefit of a person who is aged 75 or over.

An unsecured pension is a fund in a registered pension scheme that has been earmarked to provide benefits for a person but has not been used to purchase pension benefits or an annuity.

A registered pension scheme is a pension scheme or arrangement registered under Section 153 Finance Act 2004.

Answer 'Yes' to question 3 if the deceased was a relevant dependant of a member of a registered pension scheme and became entitled to the unsecured pension benefit on the death of the scheme member aged 75 or over. A relevant dependant is the scheme member's spouse or civil partner or a person who is financially dependent on them.

4. Gifts

It is not just outright gifts, such as giving a cheque for £10,000 to someone, which are relevant for Inheritance Tax. The law says that there is a gift whenever there is a 'loss to the donor' (the donor is always the person making the gift). This can happen in different ways. For example, an individual may sell a house to a relative for less than they could sell it on the open market. This will be a loss to the donor. A person may hold some shares that give them control of a company. They may give only a small holding to a relative, but losing control of the company reduces the value of their other shares by an amount which is greater than the saleable value of the holding in its own right. The amount of the loss to the donor is the value of the gift for Inheritance Tax purposes. There are other ways of making gifts too, such as giving away rights to a pension which is not yet payable.

You do not need to take into account gifts between husband and wife, civil partners, or that do not exceed £3,000 in any one year, or those that are no more than £250 in any year to any one individual. You need only consider gifts with no reservation of benefit within seven years of the deceased's death.

5. Gifts with reservation of benefit

Sometimes the person making the gift may keep an interest in the asset being given away, or the person receiving the gift may not take full ownership or possession of the assets. Such a gift is called a 'gift with reservation of benefit'. The most common occurrence of this is where a parent gives the family home to the children but goes on living in it, or where the parent buys a house but puts the title in the name of their children.

Where the person who has died has made a gift with reservation, the Inheritance Tax law says that the asset should be included and valued as part of the deceased's estate at death, although the asset itself may not be in the estate when they died. The rule applies to gifts with reservation of benefit made on or after **18 March 1986.**

6. Assets held in trust

A trust is an obligation on one or more people (the trustees) to deal with the assets for the benefit of another person. A trust may be in the form of a deed or a Will. Examples of when a person will benefit from assets held in trust are when they do not own the assets but they have the right to:

- receive income from assets, for example dividends from shares or interest from a bank or building society account but not the assets themselves
- receive payments of a fixed amount each year, often in regular instalments
- live in a house without paying rent.

In deciding how to answer this question it does not matter whether the trustees are resident in the UK or abroad. You must take all trusts into account.

7. Assets owned in joint names

The deceased may have owned an asset, such as a house, which is in their name and that of someone else 'and the survivor'. You may not always need Confirmation to the asset, but we will need to know what the deceased's share was and (if it is a bank or building society account) how much they contributed to it. You need to take the value of this into account when working out the gross estate for Inheritance Tax to put in at box 3A on page 4 of the Inventory form C1, **but**, because there is no Inheritance Tax to pay between spouses or civil partners, you may still answer 'No' if the deceased was survived by a husband, wife or civil partner and the asset passes to him or her.

8. Nominated assets

The deceased may have nominated an asset in favour of someone else during their lifetime. An example would be friendly society funds or payment of a death benefit. The deceased may have done this so that the person who benefits can get access to the funds immediately on the death and the funds may not be listed in the Inventory. The asset must still be taken into account for Inheritance Tax at box 3A on page 4 of the C1, but if it passes to the surviving husband, wife or civil partner, you can still answer 'No', because there is no Inheritance Tax to pay between spouses or civil partners.

Our booklet C3 has more help and detail about what you need to do.

www.hmrc.gov.uk/inheritancetax/   Helpline 0845 30 20 900

Obtaining confirmation for an excepted estate in Scotland

If the conditions are met for an excepted estate or a small estate, there is no requirement to complete the inheritance tax form IHT400 and form C5 is completed, as discussed. Confirmation is then applied for using the inventory form C1. Whoever completes the inventory form C1, confirmation application form, should indicate on page 4 that the estate falls within the excepted or small estate confirmation regimes. If it is a small estate which conforms to both descriptions both boxes on page 4 should be ticked 'yes'.

The application for confirmation is dealt with in further detail in Chapter 8.

A copy of form C1 can be found on the HMRC website: www.hmrc.gov.uk/cto/forms/c1_2_lined.pdf

The notes booklet to help complete forms C1 and C5 can be found at: www.hmrc.gov.uk/cto/forms/c3-2006-2.pdf

Once form C1 is completed and the sheriff clerk or commissary clerk has all the other documentation required (such as, the death certificate and a copy of any will), confirmation will usually be issued. On granting confirmation, form C1 is sent to the Capital Taxes Office of HMRC in Edinburgh for retention. This is slightly different from the corresponding procedure for excepted estates in the rest of the UK.

Summary

There are various forms to be completed and the correct one depends on where the deceased lived and the reason for the estate to be an excepted estate. Table 18.1 details the correct forms.

Table 18.1 Forms for excepted estates

Country where the deceased lived	IHT forms if the estate is likely to be an excepted estate	IHT forms if the estate is unlikely to be an excepted estate
England and Wales	Probate application PA1 (Figure 8.1)	Probate application PA1 (Figure 8.1)
	IHT205 (Figure 18.1)	IHT400 (Figure 12.1)
		IHT421 (Figure 8.2)
Northern Ireland	IHT205 (Figure 18.1)	IHT400 (Figure 12.1)
		IHT421 (Figure 8.2)
Scotland	C1 (Figure 8.3)	C1 (Figure 8.3)
	C5 (Figure 18.3)	IHT400 (Figure 12.1)

19

Paying inheritance tax

This chapter will detail when inheritance tax due can be paid in instalments

- Obtaining an inheritance tax reference number

- Payment due date

- Methods of payment

- Payments from the deceased's bank account (direct payment scheme)

- Payments by instalment

- Interest on overdue IHT

- How inheritance tax is attributable to beneficiaries

Once the inheritance tax liability has been calculated and form IHT400 has been completed, the personal representatives are responsible for paying the tax to HM Revenue and Customs. If there is a tax liability, the personal representatives must first obtain an inheritance tax reference number and payslip. The reference number will be unique to the estate and should be used on all payments of IHT and correspondence with HMRC. They will also send a pre-referenced payslip, which you should use to pay the tax.

Of course, if there is no IHT to pay on the estate, it is not necessary to obtain a reference number. In these cases, HMRC will allocate you a reference number when it receives your forms and paperwork as part of the probate process (or confirmation in Scotland).

Obtaining an inheritance tax reference number

As explained, the first thing the personal representatives must do before they can pay any inheritance tax and submit the form IHT400, is obtain an inheritance tax reference number. The reference is made up of 10, 11 or 12 characters and starts with a letter 'F' for England and Wales, 'N' for Northern Ireland or 'ST' for Scotland, for example F123456/09X, N12345/09X or ST010446/08X.

Application for the reference number should be made at least three weeks before the date you expect to make your payment. You can obtain the number by post or online.

Applying by post

The personal representatives will complete form IHT422 (Figure 19.1).

If you are based in England, Wales or Northern Ireland, send IHT422 to:

HM Revenue & Customs
Ferrers House
PO Box 38
Castle Meadow Road
Nottingham
NG2 1BB

If you are based in Scotland, send it to:

HM Revenue & Customs
Meldrum House
15 Drumsheugh Gardens
Edinburgh
EH3 7UG

Once the form has been processed and a reference number allocated to the estate, the personal representatives will be notified. They should use the unique reference number on all payments of inheritance tax and correspondence with HMRC. HMRC will also send a pre-referenced payslip, which should be used to pay the tax.

Applying online

The reference number can also be obtained by applying online. The following link will take you to the relevant page on the HMRC website: www.hmrc.gov.uk/inheritancetax/online.htm

Application for an Inheritance Tax reference

Schedule IHT422

When to use this form

Fill in this form if there is any Inheritance Tax (IHT) to pay on the estate. You will need an IHT reference number before you can make a payment. If you intend to pay by cheque, you will also need an IHT payslip.

You can apply for an IHT reference and payslip online. Go to our website at **www.hmrc.gov.uk/inheritancetax/**

If you do not have access to the Internet you can get an IHT reference and a payslip by filling in this form and posting it to the address to which you intend to send the form IHT400. We will send the reference and payslip (if required) to you by post.

You must fill in all the details we request or we may not be able to allocate a reference.

Where to send this form

Use the following address if you intend to apply for a grant of representation in England & Wales or Northern Ireland:

HM Revenue & Customs Inheritance Tax
PO Box 38
Castle Meadow Road
Nottingham   DX: 701201
NG2 1BB   Nottingham 4

Use the following address if you intend to apply for Confirmation in Scotland:

HM Revenue & Customs Inheritance Tax
15 Drumsheugh Gardens
Edinburgh   DX: ED 542001
EH3 7UG   Edinburgh 14

Deceased's details

Surname *in capital letters*

First name(s)

Any other names the deceased was known by

Date of birth *DD MM YYYY*

National Insurance number (if known)

Date of death *DD MM YYYY*

Country in which you will be applying for probate/Confirmation

England or Wales   Scotland

Northern Ireland

Your details

I wish to pay Inheritance Tax by transferring money from the deceased's bank or building society account(s) and am applying for a reference number only

I wish to pay Inheritance Tax and am applying for both a reference and a payslip

I am an agent acting for the executors/administrators of this estate

I am the executor/administrator of this estate

Enter your name and address

Your reference, if any

◄ *The reference and any payslip will be sent to this address*

IHT422   Page 1   HMRC 09/08

Figure 19.1 Form IHT422 to apply for an IHT reference number by post

It is helpful to gather information that you will need before completing the form, as none of the information can be saved to return to the form later, the application must be done in one go. Information that you will enter on screen will include:

■ full name of the person who has died;

■ date of death;

■ date of birth;

■ national insurance number.

HMRC will process the online application and send the reference number by post to the personal representatives, together with the pre-referenced payslips to enable the form IHT400 to be submitted and the tax to be paid.

Payment due date

The due date for inheritance tax to be paid to HMRC is six months after the end of the month in which the death occurred, unless the instalment option is available, on some assets. So, for example, if someone died in January 2010, any inheritance tax liability would need to be paid to HMRC by 31 July 2010.

Any inheritance tax paid late is liable to interest, which would run from the due date to the date the tax is paid.

Methods of payment

There are many ways of paying the inheritance tax due, and these include:

■ online or telephone banking;

■ cheque, by post;

■ CHAPS transfer;

■ Bank Giro.

You can use the following link to obtain details from the HMRC website, depending on the method that you wish to use:
www.hmrc.gov.uk/payinghmrc/inheritance.htm#2

Payments from the deceased's bank account (direct payment scheme)

If you're paying inheritance tax on an estate, you can pay some or all of the tax due by arranging to have money transferred from the deceased's bank or building society accounts directly to HMRC using the inheritance tax direct payment scheme. This can be particularly helpful and essential if much of the capital is unable to be accessed, due to the banks and building societies not being able to release the funds until the grant of probate has been received.

You will need to:

1 Contact the banks or building societies that you would like to transfer the money from. Ask them what they need to see to grant you power as a personal representative, to arrange for the transfer, and how long the transfer will take once they have everything they need. To avoid delays, it is best to do this before you apply for the grant of probate.

2 Apply to HMRC for an inheritance tax reference number, as discussed earlier. You will need to put the reference number on the direct payment scheme application form, so you will need to do this in good time too.

3 Fill in form IHT423 Direct Payment Scheme (Figure 19.2 on page 205). You will need a separate form for each bank or building society that will be transferring funds. You can obtain the form from the HMRC website:
www.hmrc.gov.uk/inheritancetax/iht423.pdf

4 Send form IHT423 to the banks and building societies. At the same time, send form IHT400 Inheritance Tax Account, form IHT421 Probate Summary (form C1 Confirmation in Scotland) and any supplementary pages or supporting documents to HMRC. If you are based in England, Wales or Northern Ireland:

HM Revenue & Customs
Ferrers House
PO Box 38
Castle Meadow Road
Nottingham NG2 1BB

If you are based in Scotland:

HM Revenue & Customs
Meldrum House
15 Drumsheugh Gardens
Edinburgh EH3 7UG

5 The bank or building society will transfer the money to HMRC.

6 Once HMRC receives notification of payment, the payment and your form IHT400 inheritance tax account will be linked. If all is in order, HMRC will stamp and return form IHT421 Probate Summary (or form C1 Confirmation in Scotland) to you.

Payments by instalment

It may be possible to pay the inheritance tax over ten equal annual instalments, but it depends on the type of asset. The instalments would start on the normal due date (six months after the month of death). Assets qualifying for the instalment option include:

■ Land and buildings anywhere in the world.

■ Quoted shares or securities where the donor has a controlling interest (at least a half shareholding) in the company.

■ Unquoted shares or securities where the donor has a controlling interest (at least a half shareholding) in the company and some minority holdings in unquoted shares.

■ An unincorporated business (sole tradership) or a share in a partnership.

The personal representatives indicate on the form IHT400 Inheritance Tax Account that they wish to pay in instalments.

Good reasons for paying any tax by instalments are often down to cash-flow. Sometimes, the beneficiaries are able to keep the assets themselves when they benefit from an estate but there could be inheritance tax due on these assets that has to be paid, which might force the sale of these assets. Therefore, if there is the option of paying the IHT by instalments, then this often gives the chance for the beneficiary to keep the asset but still pay the IHT within the allowed timescale.

Another good reason for the IHT on some assets to be paid by instalments is so that the personal representatives can pay the immediate IHT due with the funds available so that the grant of probate may be obtained. Once this has been obtained, then more of the assets can be released for sale as necessary and if chosen, the full amount of IHT can be paid.

Opting to pay by instalments initially gives the personal representatives a little more scope and time to sort out the administration.

Direct Payment Scheme
Bank or building society account
Schedule IHT423

When to use this form

Fill in this form if you want to pay the Inheritance Tax that is due, by transferring money from the deceased's bank or building society account(s).

Please fill in a separate form for each account.

Help

Please read the guidance notes on the Direct Payment Scheme in the IHT400 Notes before filling in this form.
For more information or help or another copy of this form:
• go to **www.hmrc.gov.uk/inheritancetax/**
• phone our Helpline on **0845 30 20 900**
  – if calling from outside the UK, phone **+44 115 974 3009**.

Where to send this form

The form should be sent to the bank or building society concerned and not to HM Revenue & Customs Inheritance Tax.

Name of deceased

Date of death *DD MM YYYY*

IHT reference number

Transfer details

I/We have applied for a grant of representation or Confirmation for the estate of the deceased and request that the amount shown below is transferred from the deceased's account to HM Revenue & Customs to pay the Inheritance Tax due.

Deceased's account details

Name of bank or building society

Sort code

Account number

Building society account roll or reference number

Amount to be transferred

In words

In figures

£

Transfer to HM Revenue & Customs

Name of bank

Citi

Sort code

0 8 – 3 2 – 1 0

Account number

1 2 0 0 1 1 3 6

Please turn to page 2 to sign the Declaration. It is important that everyone who is applying for the grant of representation or Confirmation to the estate of the deceased signs this form.

Figure 19.2 Form IHT423 for the direct payment scheme

Declaration

The amount shown on page 1 is required to pay all or part of the Inheritance Tax due. If HM Revenue & Customs needs to repay the tax paid before the grant or Confirmation is issued they are authorised to return the money to the account shown on page 1.

First representative

Surname

First name(s)

Postcode

Rest of address, including house number/flat number

Signature

Date *DD MM YYYY*

Second representative

Surname

First name(s)

Postcode

Rest of address, including house number/flat number

Signature

Date *DD MM YYYY*

Third representative

Surname

First name(s)

Postcode

Rest of address, including house number/flat number

Signature

Date *DD MM YYYY*

Fourth representative

Surname

First name(s)

Postcode

Rest of address, including house number/flat number

Signature

Date *DD MM YYYY*

IHT423   Page 2

Interest on overdue IHT

Interest on inheritance tax paid late will run from the due date of payment to the date the tax is paid:

■ When paying IHT by instalments, interest could run from the due date to the date the tax is paid.

■ Where IHT is paid by instalments on land and buildings, interest will accrue on the IHT outstanding from the date of the first instalment.

■ Where IHT is paid by instalments on other assets, interest will only accrue if the instalments are paid late.

Example

Payment of tax on instalment and non-instalment property

Sunil died on 1 December 2009 and on his death, his estate was valued at £600,000. The estate was made up of a house worth £400,000, investments in bank accounts and a portfolio of shares, none of which he had a controlling interest in. This means his tax liability is likely to be as follows:

Property	£400,000
Investments	£200,000
Total	£600,000
Less nil band	
For 2009–10	(£325,000)
Taxable estate	£275,000
Tax due at 40%	£110,000

Of this tax liability, a proportion of the £110,000 will relate to the £400,000 property and can be paid in instalments. In addition, there will be a proportion of the £110,000 tax liability that relates to the investments. So, for the property:

£400,000 / £600,000 × £110,000 = £73,333 can be paid by 10 equal instalments.

And for the investments:

£200,000 / £600,000 × £110,000 = £36,667 will be due by the usual due date.

If any inheritance tax is overpaid, interest will be paid by HMRC together with the overpayment. The interest will run from the date the tax is overpaid.

How inheritance tax is attributable to beneficiaries

It is important for the personal representatives to calculate the IHT obviously, but the next stage is then to consider, once it has been paid out of the estate, how the remaining funds are to be distributed. To start allocating the legacies and the residue to the appropriate beneficiaries, the personal representatives need to consider who has had to suffer the appropriate inheritance tax.

Example

The will pays the IHT

Sometimes a beneficiary will be allocated a legacy (gift) and in the will this may be stated as free of tax. In this case therefore, you can see that the full amount of the legacy would be payable to the beneficiary and any IHT due on that part of the estate has to come out of the residue of the estate before it is then paid out to the other beneficiaries.

Once the amount of inheritance tax has been calculated, it needs to be decided among the beneficiaries who will actually suffer the tax. The general rules are set out in Table 19.1.

Table 19.1 Deciding who pays the IHT

	Paid by	*Suffered by*
UK assets specifically gifted free of tax	The executors pay out of the estate funds	The residuary legatee (i.e. the person who is left 'the rest of the assets' in the will) *unless* the will states otherwise
Overseas assets specifically gifted	The specific legatee (i.e. the person who is left the overseas asset) subject to any contraindication in the will	The specific legatee (all of the benefit of any double taxation relief available goes to this person)
The rest of the free estate (residue)	The executors pay out of the estate funds	The residuary legatee
Gift with reservation (GWR)	The donee who received the gift	The donee who received the gift

The amount actually allocated to the beneficiaries is based on the portion of the tax attributable to the gift they will receive, using the following apportionment:

$$\frac{\text{IHT payable on the estate (after QSR)}}{\text{Gross chargeable estate}} \times \text{their portion of the estate}$$

Example

Allocating the IHT

Chinwe died on 12 January 2009 leaving the following estate:

Free estate	£
House in UK	650,000
Flat in Cyprus (assume no overseas death duties payable)	180,000
Shares in ABC plc (a 3% interest in the company)	56,000
Chattels, car and bank accounts	57,500
	943,500
Less: allowable deductions	(24,300)
Gross chargeable estate	919,200

In her will, Chinwe leaves the flat in Cyprus to her nephew, the shares in ABC plc to her god-daughter and the rest of her estate to her daughter. So the personal representatives will need to:

■ Calculate the IHT due on the estate.

■ Determine who is responsible for paying the tax.

■ Determine who will ultimately suffer the tax and have this deducted from their share of the estate.

IHT on the death estate	£
Gross chargeable estate	919,200
Nil rate band	(325,000)
Taxable amount	594,200
IHT payable on estate at 40%	237,680
Due date of payment	31 July 2009

Average rate of IHT on estate: (237,680 ÷ 919,200) × 100 = 25.8572%

Allocation of the IHT payable

		£	Paid by	Suffered by
Flat in Cyprus	£180,000 × 25.8572%	46,544	Nephew	Nephew
Shares in ABC plc	£56,000 × 25.8572%	14,480	Executors	Daughter*
Rest of free estate	£683,200 × 25.8572%	176,656	Executors	Daughter
		237,680		

*The shares are left in the will to the god-daughter but she does not bear the tax on the gift, the tax is borne by the daughter (i.e. the residuary legatee).

The HMRC website has an IHT400 calculation that takes you through the steps of working out the liability, the tax that may be paid by instalments and the interest that may be due:

www.hmrc.gov.uk/inheritancetax/iht400-calc.pdf

Form IHT400 is shown in Appendix B.

When probate has been granted

20

Distributing the estate

This chapter will detail when and how the estate should be distributed

- Dealing with the assets once the grant has been obtained
- Protecting the personal representatives
- Estate accounts
- Distributing the legacies and the residue
- Form IHT30: clearance certificate
- Insolvent estates

Dealing with the assets once the grant has been obtained

Once the grant is received, the personal representatives will then be able to deal with the assets. They will begin to close the bank accounts and receive the funds. This process may also involve selling assets or transferring assets directly to some of the named beneficiaries. If there is a house or other property to sell, then this can take place in the usual way. The transfer of assets can be done by providing the appropriate forms and official copies of the grant to the asset holders.

The personal representatives will also carry out the following duties:

- Pay any outstanding liabilities of the estate.
- Pay any cash legacies.

■ Finalise the inheritance tax, income tax and capital gains tax relating to the deceased, to the date of death.

■ Finalise the inheritance tax, income tax and capital gains tax relating to the estate, following death.

The inheritance tax position in particular can take some time to deal with. HM Revenue and Customs is entitled to raise any queries to ensure that the assets and liabilities have been correctly valued and that any reliefs that are claimed are properly due.

Protecting the personal representatives

The personal representatives are obliged to deal with the estate correctly and responsibly and if they fail to do this, they are personally liable to replace funds that they have otherwise failed to protect. It is vital, therefore, that the personal representatives take steps to protect themselves, and to ensure that there is evidence that they have dealt with the estate to the best of their ability. These steps would include the following:

■ Ensure they act precisely in accordance with the will, or intestacy rules if there is no will.

■ Advertise (by placing notices or statutory advertisements) in local newspapers where land is owned for any unknown creditors and claimants (possible beneficiaries to the estate).

■ Advertise (by placing notices or statutory advertisements) in the London Gazette for any unknown creditors and claimants (possible beneficiaries to the estate).

■ Check identities and relationships of any of the creditors and beneficiaries.

■ Check that no beneficiaries are undischarged bankrupts.

■ Obtain an inheritance tax clearance certificate form IHT30 (detailed below).

■ Check the possibility of claimants under the Inheritance (Provision for Family and Dependants) Act 1975.

■ Keep sufficient funds back for any uncertain or potential claims.

■ Obtain a receipt from all the recipients of the estate funds, including beneficiaries.

The estate should not be distributed for at least two months after the advertisements. If there is thought to be any possibility of a claim being made by someone under the provisions of the Inheritance (Provision for Family and Dependants) Act 1975, the distribution should be deferred until six months from the date of the grant of probate (in England & Wales). If any claim is made then distribution should be further deferred until this has been dealt with.

> The executors' year is the expression used to describe the length of time that it usually takes, that is **reasonable**, to ensure that the administration is dealt with correctly and that care has been taken to ensure no further creditors or beneficiaries will be entitled to any of the estate. There is no legal requirement that an estate be fully dealt with within a year.

Estate accounts

Once the personal representatives are happy that they have dealt with all of the administration of the estate, estate accounts are usually prepared to summarise the financial position and show what is left over to be distributed to the beneficiaries who are entitled to the residue of the estate. Although these accounts strictly only need to be approved by the personal representatives, it is often wise to have them approved by the residuary beneficiaries too. They will want to know that the estate has been dealt with correctly and fully and will want to know how the balance to them has been calculated. Obtaining their approval at this stage can avoid any queries or disputes later.

Distributing the legacies and the residue

When any estate accounts have been approved, the final task of the personal representatives will be to distribute the balance of the estate to the beneficiaries. The beneficiaries should be asked to sign a receipt.

Pecuniary legacies are the gifts of money that are stated in the testator's will. For example, the will might state: 'I give Mr Jenkins a gift of £1,000 for the hard work that he has put into maintaining my garden.' These gifts can be paid out of the cash funds of the estate once the bank accounts are collected in and assets are sold.

Specific legacies are the gifts of property, other than cash, that have been gifted out in a testator's will. For example, the will might state: 'I give to my daughter my jewellery box and jewellery.' These gifts can be transferred to the beneficiary accordingly, once the personal representatives are sure that all liabilities of the estate are covered. It is important to obtain a receipt once the gift has been transferred.

The **residue** of the estate is what is left after the pecuniary and specific gifts have been paid out. The residue is paid out to the residuary beneficiaries in accordance with the testator's will, or intestacy. Once the assets, or the funds from the sale of the assets have been distributed to the beneficiaries of the estate, the ownership is now that of the beneficiary or beneficiaries. From this point on, any income and gains arising from these assets or capital funds will be assessable on the beneficiary and the responsibility for reporting the income and gains is thus with the beneficiary.

Form IHT30: clearance certificate

When HMRC is satisfied that all the necessary forms have been received and that the inheritance tax and interest due have been paid, it will send you a letter confirming this. However, if the personal representatives want to be extra sure that the estate record is fully up to date and closed with HMRC, they can apply for a **clearance certificate** IHT30 (Figure 20.1 on page 218). Once this is received, the estate can come to an end and the assets distributed to the beneficiaries. This certificate is the reassurance that the personal representatives need to confirm that all inheritance tax is paid to date. It must be noted however, that this certificate purely confirms that all tax is paid up to date, based on the information submitted and is not an insurance policy should it be found that further tax should have, in fact, been paid. You can find a copy of this form at: www.hmrc.gov.uk/CTO/forms/iht30.pdf

Insolvent estates

An estate is insolvent if the assets are insufficient to pay off its expenses, debts and liabilities. This means that the creditors, the people or organisations owed, cannot be paid in full and there is nothing to pay to any beneficiaries. Statute law under the Insolvency Act 1986 and the Administration of Insolvent Estates of Deceased Persons Order 1986 decides the order in which the debts and liabilities are paid, and these are as follows:

- Reasonable funeral expenses and administration expenses.
- Specially preferred debts, such as money belonging to a friendly society.
- Preferential debts, such as tax liabilities, NIC liabilities and repayments of state pension.
- Ordinary debts.
- Deferred debts, such as family loans.

In cases where there is sufficient funds to pay all liabilities and there is some value in the estate to pay some legacies, but not all, there is again special treatment. The personal representatives should pay out the specific legacies first, then the pecuniary legacies and, if any value remains, this will then be the residue to distribute accordingly. However, if there is insufficient value to make all legacies, they will have to abate (reduce) the legacies. It is advisable to seek professional guidance in these cases to ensure the distribution is carried out correctly to avoid the decisions of the personal representatives being questioned or disputed.

Application for a clearance certificate

Inheritance Tax Act 1984 s239(2) or Finance Act 1975 sch.4 para.25(2) or Finance Act 1894 s11(2)

Name and address of the person to whom IR
Capital Taxes should send the certificate.

IR CT reference *(if known)*

Your reference

Telephone number

- Send this form to us only when you believe
  that all the inheritance tax due has been paid.
- Fill in **one section only** of sections A, B or C.
- Section B is for a liability arising on death in
  respect of a lifetime transfer. Section A is for any
  other liability arising on death, most commonly
  in respect of the deceased's own estate or the
  coming to an end on death of an interest in
  possession in settled property.
- Fill in section D by entering the relevant date(s)
  and tick either the 'Yes' or 'No' box as appropriate.

IR Capital Taxes, P.O. Box 38, Ferrers House,
Castle Meadow Road, Nottingham, NG2 1BB,
(DX 701201 Nottingham 4).   **Tel: 0115 974 2400.**

IR Capital Taxes, Meldrum House, 15 Drumsheugh
Gardens, Edinburgh EH3 7UG (DX ED 542001
Edinburgh 14).   **Tel: 0131 777 4050/4060.**

IR Capital Taxes, Level 3, Dorchester House,
52-58 Great Victoria Street, Belfast, BT2 7QL.
(DX 2001 NR Belfast 2).   **Tel: 028 9050 5353.**

**Please send the completed form in duplicate to
the IR Capital Taxes office dealing with the estate.**

Section A   Liability arising on a death

Full name of the person who has died.

Date of death.

Title under which the property is taxable
(e.g. 'Will of the deceased' or 'Settlement dated...').

Section B   Liability in respect of a lifetime transfer

Full name of the person who **made** the transfer.

Date of death.

Please give details of the transfer, including the date
on which it was made.

Section C   Liability in respect of a settlement without an interest in possession

Full title and date of the settlement.

Please give brief details, including the date of the
chargeable event.

Section D   Application in respect of property or transfers of value included in:

Original account(s) or inventory(ies) dated

Corrective account(s) or inventory(ies) dated

Calculation(s) of tax from IR Capital Taxes dated

Have there been changes to the value since the above?
If you have answered 'Yes', please give details on a separate sheet.   Yes   No

IHT30 (PDF) Version 2.0.0.2

Figure 20.1 IHT30, the clearance certificate application form

Section E   Repayment

A repayment cheque can only be paid into the account of the person(s) to whom the cheque is made payable. If you believe that a repayment of tax may be due, please state the name(s) of the person(s) to whom any repayment cheque should be made payable. This information is only required if a repayment of tax is claimed.

Section F   Declaration by the appropriate person(s)

To the best of my/our knowledge and belief, the information given above is correct. I am/We are not aware of any other information which I/we should disclose. I/We apply for a statutory certificate of discharge.

Name

Signature

Capacity*

Date

Name

Signature

Capacity*

Date

*Capacity i.e. Executor, Administrator, Transferee, Trustee. Professional agents must not sign this form on behalf of the appropriate person(s).

Section G   Certificate (for official use only)

The Commissioners of Inland Revenue discharge the above named applicant(s) from any (further) claim for tax or duty on the value attributable to the property at section D, on the occasion specified at section A, B, or C **except for any tax which is being paid by instalments.**

The certificate is not valid unless IR CT stamp this box.

Signed by

(name stamp or block capitals)

Signature

for and on behalf of the Commissioners.

Date

This certificate does not itself constitute a determination of values of individual items for any other Revenue purpose. In particular, the issue of the certificate does not necessarily mean that values have been "ascertained" or that values may be taken as market values for capital gains tax within the provisions of section 274 and paragraph 9, schedule 11, Taxation of Chargeable Gains Act 1992. This certificate is not valid in certain circumstances, such as in the case of fraud or failure to disclose material facts or if further tax becomes payable as a result of an instrument of variation - see section 239 (4) Inheritance Tax Act 1984.

113507062000DTP

21

Estate accounts

This chapter will detail when it can be necessary and advantageous for estate accounts to be prepared

- When estate accounts are beneficial
- When estate accounts are necessary
- An estate where gifts have been made to charity
- Format for the accounts

Once the personal representatives are content that all aspects of the estate have been administered, the role is then to distribute the estate to the beneficiaries. Estate accounts will sometimes be prepared to summarise the financial position and show what is to be distributed.

When estate accounts are beneficial

Professional administrators would usually prepare a set of estate accounts as a matter of course in dealing with the estate, but for those individuals who are dealing with the estate personally, this can still be beneficial. Estate accounts can provide:

- Clarity: the accounts show the summary of the wealth and how it has been distributed in a more simplified manner than a box of paperwork.
- Legality: sometimes estate accounts are necessary.
- Reassurance for all beneficiaries that the estate has been dealt with completely and correctly.

■ Protection for the executors or personal representatives: even where the estate accounts are not necessary, they can still provide protection for the administrators, should a query arise.

HMRC would not normally need to receive a copy of the estate accounts. However, if it makes an enquiry into any of the returns submitted by the personal representatives in relation to the position at death and the administration period, it might require information that is usually detailed by the accounts. Estate accounts could therefore be useful in such cases.

When estate accounts are necessary

Beneficiaries of an estate are those who will receive assets or wealth by inheritance, from the deceased person's estate. They have a right to know how the estate administration has been dealt with and how the assets of the estate have been distributed. In this respect, the personal representatives are legally obliged to provide the beneficiaries with this information. Residuary beneficiaries receive the estate accounts and can be asked to approve these before the final distribution of the estate.

An estate where gifts have been made to charity

When a charity benefits from a person's estate, the Charity Commission requires the charity to ask for estate accounts. This is not so that the administration may be questioned, but more for reassurance that all matters have been completed so that the charitable trustees dealing with the charity may be sure that they have received all that is due to the charity. The charity is required to give a final approval and receipt to the administrators of the person's estate and to do this, it will need the following information:

■ A copy of the will and any codicils.

■ A schedule of assets and liabilities of the estate.

■ A copy of an independent valuation of any significant assets, particularly land and property.

■ Estate accounts (preferably before any distributions of property to any beneficiaries).

■ Tax deduction certificates, relating to any income that has arisen during the administration period.

Format for the accounts

There is no set format, or legal requirement for the estate accounts to be presented in any particular way, as long as they can be understood, and are readable. The simplest way of providing this information is normally by a set of estate accounts, which would show:

- The capital assets and liabilities at the date of death. This would account for the total value of the estate at death.

- An income account. This would give details of all income such as interest, dividends, rents and so on, that has been received on assets since the date of death.

- An expenditure account. This would include any inheritance tax, administration expenses and pecuniary legacies that have been deducted from the value of the estate before any distributions can be made.

- A distribution account. This would show how the net estate has passed to the beneficiaries.

There is an example of a set of estate accounts that can be adopted in Appendix C.

Revisions and amendments to the estate

This chapter will detail when and how the personal representatives can make a claim for the reduction in value of assets sold after death

- Relief for a loss on sale
- Land and property
- Notes for completing form IHT38
- Shares
- Notes for completing form IHT35
- The effect on inheritance tax
- Tax planning

Relief for a loss on sale

When property has been sold after death and the value has fallen since the date of death, it is often possible to claim for the relief of this loss on sale. If the claim can be made, this can reduce the amount of inheritance tax that was originally paid on the value of the estate. The claim for the loss on sale applies to the following:

- Land and property where the asset has been sold within four years of the death.
- Shares, where these have been sold within one year of the death.

A claim would be submitted by the personal representatives to HM Revenue and Customs, for the original inheritance tax computation to be reduced by the loss on sale. The value of the land or property in the IHT computation is substituted for the original value, and it is just the value of the land and property, no expenses can be deducted.

Land and property

If the personal representatives sell any land or property in the estate within four years of the death for less than the value on which inheritance tax was paid, the claim for the relief for this loss can be made to HMRC on form IHT38 (Figure 22.1). The form can be obtained from:
www.hmrc.gov.uk/cto/forms/iht38.pdf

But once the relief is claimed, the sale price of *all* interests in land sold within the four-year period must be substituted for their date of death value. This includes those interests sold for more than the date of death value. The exception is property sold for a higher price in the fourth year.

Notes for completing form IHT38

There are notes on the form which help the personal representatives to complete the claim, and some additional points to make. On page 1:

■ The claim must be made on a sale that has occurred within four years of the death.

■ The claim must be made by the personal representatives.

■ The date of sale is usually taken as the date of the exchange of contracts.

■ The claim is based on the sale value, and no expenses can be deducted from this.

■ No claim can be made if the reduction in the value between death and the sale of the land or property is less than £1,000 or 5 per cent of the value used at the date of death.

■ The claim is not valid if the sale of the land and property, after death, is to a beneficiary or a relative of a beneficiary.

Claim for relief
Loss on sale of LAND

Name of deceased	Date of death	IR CT reference

Name and full postal address of the person IR Capital Taxes should contact.

Your reference (if any)

Your telephone number

When you have completed this form, please send it to the IR Capital Taxes office with which you have been corresponding. If you have not yet been in correspondence about this estate, please send it to: IR Capital Taxes, Ferrers House, PO Box 38, Castle Meadow Road, Nottingham NG2 1BB. If using the DX postal system, send it to DX 701201 Nottingham 4.

Notes

1. This form is for claiming relief when you sell land or buildings which were part of the deceased's estate. The sale must occur within **4 years** of the date of death (3 years if the date of death was on or before 15 March 1990). *This period may be extended if the sale is to an authority with compulsory purchase powers.*

2. You may only make the claim if you are the **'appropriate person(s)'**. The 'appropriate person(s)' are those liable for the inheritance tax on the value of the land or buildings (for example, the executors, the administrators, trustees or donees). If there is more than one group of people liable for the tax, the 'appropriate persons' are those who are actually paying the tax. You must say on page 4 of this form in what capacity you claim the relief (eg executor, administrator, trustee or donee). If you are a beneficiary you are unlikely to be an 'appropriate person'. *All appropriate persons must sign this form. We cannot accept a claim signed by agents.*

3. You must include on page 2 every interest in land or buildings you sold in that capacity during the four (or three) year period *(see note 1, above)*. The trustees of a settlement are treated as a single, continuing body of persons. So are the personal representatives of the deceased. We advise you not to make a claim until **all** items to be sold have been sold. **You cannot withdraw a claim for relief** if it proves to be disadvantageous following any subsequent sale.

4. You may claim provisional relief within four months of the last qualifying sale unless you intend to purchase an interest in land during those four months. *If we give provisional relief, we may review it later.*

5. The date of sale or purchase is usually the date contracts are exchanged or, in Scotland, when missives are concluded.

6. The relief is based on the gross sale price but restricted by the net price of any purchase. So you must exclude any expenses relating to a sale or purchase (eg commission, stamp duty, legal fees).

7. Relief is not available if the sale price differs from the value on death by less than £1,000 or 5% of the value on death, whichever is lower.

8. The relief is not given if the sale is to a beneficiary or the relative of a beneficiary. Any profit from such a sale or exchange may reduce the relief on a qualifying sale.

9. If land is purchased between the date of death and four months after the last qualifying sale within the four (or three) year period *(see note 1)*, relief may be restricted.

10. Special rules apply to a lease or interest in a lease with less than 50 years to run at the date of death. Please show the unexpired term at the date of death in the 'Tenure' column overleaf.

If you need help completing this form, please telephone IHT helpline 0845 3020 900

IHT38 (PDF) Version 2.0.0.   1

Figure 22.1 Claim form IHT38 for losses on land sales

Claim for relief

Please give details of the interests in land to which your claim for relief relates. Attach a separate sheet if you need more space.

Address or description of the property	Tenure *(see note 10)*	Value at the date of death £	Date of sale *(see note 5)*	Gross sale proceeds *(see note 6)* £	Name of each purchaser
		0		0	
		0		0	
		0		0	
		0		0	
		0		0	
	Total	£0	Total	£0	

Please answer the following questions by ticking the boxes marked 'Yes' or 'No'.
If 'Yes', please give additional information in the space provided in each box below.
Attach a separate sheet if you need more space and show clearly which question number(s) it refers to.

1. Did either the purchaser or any relative of the purchaser have any beneficial interest in the sold property between the deceased's death and the sale?   **Yes** **No**

2. Do any sale prices represent less than the best consideration you could reasonably have obtained at the date of sale? *If 'Yes', please explain why you accepted a lower price and state the best price that you could reasonably have obtained.*   **Yes** **No**

2

3. Did you sell any other 'interests in land' in this estate within the four (or three) years *(see note 1 on page 1)* immediately following the death?
If 'Yes', please include details on page 2.
If you intend to make further sales of interests in land, please give full details below or attach a separate sheet. *(See note 4 on page 1)*   **Yes** ☐ **No** ☐

4. Did you purchase any 'interests in land', in the same capacity, between the death and four months after the last of the sales referred to opposite or at 3 above?
Please note that you cannot make any claim for relief if less than 4 months has passed since the last date of sale and you intend to purchase any interest in land in the same capacity within those 4 months (see note 4 on page 1).   **Yes** ☐ **No** ☐

5. Were the interests in land different in any respect when sold than they were at the date of death?   **Yes** ☐ **No** ☐

6. Was the land in which any sold interests subsisted in a different state and with different incidents (eg burdens, easements) than it was at the date of death?   **Yes** ☐ **No** ☐

7. Has any statutory compensation become payable to any person since the death in respect of any interest in land involved in this claim?   **Yes** ☐ **No** ☐

8. Have the vendors or their relatives acquired a right to repurchase the sold property?   **Yes** ☐ **No** ☐

9. Has anything been received since the death under any insurance claim relating to the interests in land?   **Yes** ☐ **No** ☐

If you have answered 'Yes' to any of the above questions then relief may not be due, or if it is due, it may be restricted.

3

Repayment

Since the Cheques Act 1992, all cheques are 'not negotiable'. This means that they can only be paid into an account in the name(s) of the person(s) in whose favour a cheque is drawn. Please state here the name of the person(s) to whom any repayment cheque should be made payable.

This claim will not be dealt with unless one of the boxes below has been ticked.

Declaration by the appropriate person(s) (see note 2 on page 1)

To the best of my knowledge and belief, the details given on this form and attached schedule(s) are true and complete.

1. ☐ I undertake not to sell or exchange further land in the four years after the date of death in my capacity as the appropriate person and/or I undertake not to make purchases of land ending four months after the last sale included in this claim in my capacity as the appropriate person.

    or

2. ☐ If further sales or exchanges are intended, I understand that the relief granted will be **provisional** and I undertake to provide details of any further sales or exchanges and any purchases made to the IR: Capital Taxes. I understand that a clearance certificate cannot be issued until the relief is final.

	Name	
	Signature	
	Capacity (see note 2)	
	Date	

	Name	
	Signature	
	Capacity (see note 2)	
	Date	

4

On page 2, the personal representatives will show the original value used for the land and property and the revised value on the sale. The questions on page 3 are checking the validity of the claim and whether any of the instances mentioned on page 1 will apply. On page 4:

■ The declaration can only be signed by the personal representatives because they are the only individuals able to make the claim.

■ It is important that they realise that once a claim has been made for this, it cannot later be withdrawn.

Important note

If more than one property or a number of interests in land are in the estate and are purchased or sold, or likely to be purchased or sold within four years of the death, it is important that the personal representatives take professional advice as a claim could affect the overall IHT liability. Once a claim for a loss on sale has been made, it cannot be withdrawn.

Shares

If the personal representatives sell any qualifying shares in the estate within one year of the death for less than the value on which inheritance tax was paid, then a claim can be made to reduce the value of the shares for inheritance tax. For the shares to qualify, they must be:

■ quoted shares and securities on the London Stock Exchange;

■ holdings in an authorised unit trust;

■ shares in a common investment fund.

All investments sold within one year of the death must be taken into account when calculating the value by which the estate has fallen in value, and therefore a claim is not possible for just the shareholdings that have made a loss. If the personal representatives buy replacement qualifying investments during the one-year claim period, the original loss claim will be reduced in accordance with the investments purchased. The claim can be made to HMRC on form IHT35 (Figure 22.2 overleaf). The form can be obtained from:
www.hmrc.gov.uk/cto/forms/iht35.pdf

Claim for relief
Loss on sale of SHARES

Inland **Revenue**
Capital Taxes

Name of deceased	Date of death	IR CT reference

Name and full postal address of the person
IR CT should contact.

Your reference (if any)

Your telephone number

When you have completed this form, please send it to IR Capital Taxes office with which you have been corresponding. If you have not yet been in correspondence about this estate, please send it to: IR Capital Taxes, Ferrers House, PO Box 38, Castle Meadow Road, Nottingham NG2 1BB. If using the DX postal system, send it to DX 701201 Nottingham 4.

Notes

1. This form is for claiming relief when you sell **'qualifying investments'** which were part of the deceased's estate **within 12 months of the date of death.** Include all qualifying investments sold, not just those sold at a loss. Generally, **'qualifying investments'** are:
    *   shares or securities quoted or listed on a recognised stock exchange at the date of death
    *   holdings in authorised unit trusts.
    *They **do not** include any holdings in **unquoted** private companies.*
    Shareholdings in AIM companies are regarded as "unquoted" for (and only for) the purposes of business relief, loss on sale relief and instalments.

2. A **sale** includes an appropriation made by the personal representatives in satisfaction of a pecuniary legacy, with the consent of the legatee, and where there is no power of appropriation without that consent.

3. You may only make the claim if you are the **'appropriate person(s)'.** The 'appropriate person(s)' are those liable for the inheritance tax on the value of the investments (for example, the executors, the administrators, the trustees or donees). If there is more than one group of people liable for the tax, the 'appropriate persons' are those who are actually paying the tax. You must state on page 4 of this form in what capacity you claim the relief (eg executor, administrator, trustee or donee). If you are a beneficiary you are unlikely to be an 'appropriate person'. *All appropriate persons must sign this form. We cannot accept a claim signed by agents.*

4. You may claim provisional relief within 12 months of the date of death. *If we give provisional relief, we may review it later.*

5. The date of sale or purchase is the contract date unless either was made as a result of an option. If so, state the date the option was granted.

6. The relief is based on the gross sale price but restricted by the net cost of any purchase. So you must exclude the expenses of the sales and any purchase you make (eg commission, fees).

7. The value of qualifying investments at the date of death, sale or purchase must:
    *   take into account interest on Government Stocks (gilts), loan and debenture stocks;
    *   exclude dividends due but unpaid.

8. A 'capital payment' includes:
    *   money or money's worth which is not income for income tax purposes;
    *   the proceeds of any sale of 'rights'.

9. A change in a holding (eg as a result of a bonus or rights issue) is one which gives rise to a 'new holding' as defined by s126 Taxation of Chargeable Gains Act 1992.

10. The market value of any investment for capital gains tax purposes is the value at the date of death **after** adjustment for this relief.

If you need help completing this form, please telephone IHT helpline on 0845 3020 900

IHT35 **(PDF)** Version 2.0.0.   1   144711122002DTP

Figure 22.2   Form IHT35 to claim for losses on shares

Claim for relief

1. Please give details of the qualifying investments *(see note 1)* to which your claim for relief relates. *Attach a separate sheet if you need more space.*

Full description of holding (including the number of shares or amount of stock held)	Date of death		Sales		
	Price	Value £	Date (see note 4)	Price	Gross proceeds (see note 5) £
		0.00			0.00
		0.00			0.00
		0.00			0.00
		0.00			0.00
		0.00			0.00
		0.00			0.00
		0.00			0.00
		0.00			0.00
		0.00			0.00
		0.00			0.00
		0.00			0.00
		0.00			0.00
		0.00			0.00
		0.00			0.00
		0.00			0.00
		0.00			0.00
		0.00			0.00
		0.00			0.00
		0.00			0.00
		0.00			0.00
	Total A	£0.00		**Total B**	£0.00

Net Loss (Total A minus total B) = **C** £0.00

2. Have there been any purchases of 'qualifying investments' *(see note 1 on page 1)* by the claimant(s) in the same capacity between the date of death and two months after the latest sale shown in part 1 above?

Yes ☐   No ☐

If 'Yes', complete the table below. If 'No' go straight to part 3 overleaf. *If you need more space, please attach a separate sheet clearly marked as referring to part 2.*

Description of holding	Purchases		Restriction of relief
	Date	Sum paid (excluding expenses)	
		0.00	
		0.00	If there have been any purchases , the relief is restricted
			To calculate the restriction (**E**), show
		0.00	$\dfrac{D \text{ (purchases)}}{B \text{ (proceeds)}} \times C \text{ (net loss)} = E$
		0.00	Total **E** £0.00
			Net loss (**C**) - restriction (**E**) = **Allowable loss**
		0.00	
Total **D**		£0.00	Allowable loss £0.00

3. Please answer the following questions about the 12 month period following the date of death:

   a) Have any qualifying investments *(see note 1 on page 1)* been exchanged (with or without payment)?   Yes ☐ No ☐

   b) Have any capital payments *(see note 8 on page 1)* been received for any **sold** qualifying investments?   Yes ☐ No ☐

   c) Have any 'calls' been paid on any of the **sold** qualifying investments?   Yes ☐ No ☐

   d) Have there been any changes in the holding *(see note 9 on page 1)* of any of the **sold** qualifying investments?   Yes ☐ No ☐

   e) Has any option to buy or sell qualifying investments been acquired or exercised (whenever the option was acquired)?   Yes ☐ No ☐

*If you answer 'Yes' to any question, **you must** give details. If you need more space, attach a separate sheet.*

Repayment

Since the Cheques Act 1992, all cheques are 'not negotiable'. This means that they can only be paid into an account in the name(s) of the person(s) in whose favour a cheque is drawn. Please state here the name of the person(s) to whom any repayment cheque should be made payable.

This claim will not be dealt with unless one of the boxes below has been ticked.

Declaration by the appropriate person(s) (see note 3 on page 1)

To the best of my knowledge and belief, the details given on this form and attached schedule(s) are true and complete.

1. ☐ I undertake not to sell or exchange further qualifying investments in the 12 months after the date of death in my capacity as the appropriate person and/or I undertake not to make purchases of any qualifying investments in the two months after the date of the last sale included in this claim in my capacity as the appropriate person.

   or

2. ☐ If further sales, exchanges or purchases are intended, I understand that the relief granted will be **provisional** and I undertake to provide details of any further sales or exchanges and any purchases made to the IR: Capital Taxes. I understand that a clearance certificate cannot be issued until the relief is final.

	Name	
	Signature	
	Capacity *(see note 3)*	
	Date	
	Name	
	Signature	
	Capacity *(see note 3)*	
	Date	

4

Notes for completing form IHT35

There are notes on the form which help the personal representatives to complete the claim, and some additional points to make. On page 1:

■ The claim must be made on a sale of shares that has occurred within one year of the death.

■ The claim is for qualifying investments only, as defined earlier in the chapter.

■ The claim must be made by the personal representatives.

■ The date of sale is usually taken as the contract date.

■ The claim is based on the gross sale price, but needs to be restricted by the cost of any purchase (so excluding the expenses of sale and repurchase).

On page 2, the personal representatives will show the original value of the shares, used for the original inheritance tax calculation, together with the revised values on the sale of the shares. The questions on page 3 are checking the validity of the claim and whether any qualifying investments were also purchased during the one year period following death. If so, there will be a restriction of the relief. The declaration on page 4 can only be signed by the personal representatives as they are the only individuals able to make the claim. It is important to realise that a claim within the one-year period is only provisional, so that if any further purchases have been made, the claim for the loss may be restricted.

Important note

When making a claim for the loss on the sale of shares within one year of death, *all* sales of shares must be taken into account and not just the ones that have made the loss. It would be wise therefore, for the personal representatives to sell just the shares that have made a loss, within the first one year of death, make the claim, and then sell the remaining shares thereafter. Professional advice would be recommended if there are large, valuable or numerous shareholdings to consider as a claim such as this will have an effect on the inheritance tax liability.

The effect on inheritance tax

A claim made for the loss on land and property or on shares will affect the level of IHT, as these two examples show.

Example

Claim for the loss of value on a house

Gareth died in March 2010 and the personal representatives obtained a valuation of his home, which was £500,000 at the date of his death. The personal representatives completed the IHT return form IHT400 with the valuation of £500,000 and paid the correct amount of IHT to HMRC. However, during the administration of the estate, the housing market took a downturn and when the property was sold, two years later, the proceeds of the sale were £450,000. This is £50,000 less than the amount declared for inheritance tax purposes.

The personal representatives can complete a claim form IHT38, detailing the sale of the property and the proceeds received. The claim form is then submitted to the Capital Taxes Office that dealt with the inheritance tax return, and the value can be amended. On doing this, the probate valuation is amended to £450,000 and a repayment of inheritance tax of £50,000 at 40% = £20,000 can be obtained.

Example

A claim made for the loss on shares

Scott also died in March 2010 and the personal representatives obtained a valuation of his two shareholdings, as follows:

ABC plc   £40,000
XYZ plc   £60,000

The personal representatives completed the IHT return form IHT400 with the valuations of £100,000 and paid the correct amount of IHT to HMRC. However, during the administration of the estate, the valuation of the two shareholdings had fluctuated and when the shares were sold, a few months later, the proceeds of the sale were as follows:

ABC plc   £45,000
XYZ plc   £30,000

The personal representatives can complete a claim form IHT35, in view of the fact that the shares in XYZ plc have decreased. However, in doing this, they have to detail all of the sales. To see if this is still beneficial, it is necessary to take both shareholdings into account, as follows:

ABC plc: a gain of £45000, less £40,000   £5,000
XYZ plc: a loss of £60,000, less £30,000   (£30,000)

Therefore, an overall loss of £25,000. The tax repayable at 40 per cent is £10,000. A repayment of inheritance tax could also be due on the submission of the claim form to the Capital Taxes Office that dealt with the IHT return.

Tax planning

The two examples above give food for thought on how to structure the sales of land and property or qualifying shares. If there is a drop in the value of the land or property, ensure this is sold within four years of death to enable the claim to be made. If there are several properties, give careful consideration to whether the claim is beneficial, as all of the revised values will be amended, not just the one that has reduced in value.

If there is more than one shareholding and only some of them have fallen in value, consider whether the claim is beneficial, as shown by the example above. One way to plan around this is to sell the shareholdings that have fallen in value within the first year of death, to make the claim. Any shareholdings that have grown in value can be sold outside the twelve-month period, and be excluded from the calculation. The investment prospects and other practical matters of the administration also have to be taken into account.

part 5

Lifetime planning

23

Lifetime planning to reduce an inheritance tax liability

This chapter will suggest ways in which inheritance tax can be reduced, using tax planning during lifetime

- Making lifetime gifts
- Lifetime gifts: be sure you consider all taxes
- Using the inheritance tax nil rate band
- Making a tax-efficient will
- Taking out insurance to cover any IHT liability

The saying is true 'There is nothing more certain than death and taxes'. And to top this, on death there is often a tax liability to inheritance tax. So what can a person do to minimise the potential inheritance tax that could be due on their estate, when they die? Among other things, an individual can minimise exposure to IHT by:

- Making lifetime gifts.
- Making a tax efficient will.
- Taking out some insurance to cover any potential IHT liability.

Making lifetime gifts

When someone is very wealthy, they may feel happy about the thought of making lifetime gifts without this affecting their own standard of living. Making lifetime gifts is an excellent way of reducing one's wealth which, in effect, will then reduce their wealth in their estate when they die, and therefore reduce any inheritance tax due on that estate. There are three categories of lifetime gifts:

■ exempt gifts;

■ potentially-exempt transfers (PETs);

■ chargeable lifetime transfers (CLTs).

Exempt gifts

Exempt gifts are those that can be made during a person's lifetime that have no IHT consequence. There is no IHT due at the time of making the gift, and there is no IHT due when the donor dies.

The first example of exempt gifts is that each individual has an exemption of £3,000 a year. Any unused part of this annual exemption can be carried forward, but to the next tax year only.

Example

Use of the annual exemption

Gregory has made gifts of £5,000 to each of his two god-children in 2009–10 and 2010–11. In the first year, 2009–2010, the position is as follows:

Gifts £5,000 × 2 =	£10,000
Less annual exemption for 2009–10	(3,000)
Less annual exemption for 2008–09 (unused)	(3,000)
Remaining gifts	4,000

This amount of £4,000 is now a potentially exempt transfer (PET), which is explained later, and subject to other reliefs and exemptions.

In 2010–11, the position is as follows:

Gifts £5,000 × 2 =	£10,000
Less annual exemption for 2010–11	(3,000)
Less annual exemption for 2009–10 (used)	(0)
Remaining gifts	6,000

This amount of £6,000 is also now a potentially exempt transfer (PET), which is explained later, and subject to other reliefs and exemptions.

Furthermore, any gift to a spouse or civil partner is exempt from IHT during the donor's lifetime and transfers made on death in a will or via intestacy. It should be noted though that if a UK-domiciled individual makes a transfer of value to their non-UK spouse or civil partner, the exemption is limited to £55,000. Anything over this amount is then subject to other reliefs and exemptions being available.

All gifts to registered charities in the UK are exempt from IHT during the donor's lifetime and transfers made on death in a will.

All gifts to a qualifying political party are exempt from IHT during the donor's lifetime and transfers made on death in a will. A qualifying political party is a party that following the last general election has at least two elected MPs, or one elected MP and at least 150,000 votes cast for that political party.

Gifts that represent normal expenditure out of income offer the potential to reduce one's estate significantly provided certain criteria are met. Gifts out of income are exempt from IHT during lifetime and no IHT will be due on the subsequent death. The exemption applies where the gifts are unconditional (with no ties attached), and the donor can show that the gifts:

■ form part of their usual expenditure, and so are regular outgoings;

■ are made out of income the donor receives, and not their capital funds;

■ leave the donor with sufficient income to maintain their normal standard of living.

This is a useful exemption for grandparents who would like to reduce the value of their estates and contribute to the upbringing of their grandchildren and pay for school fees.

Example

Gift of school fees each year

Silke pays £10,000 towards the school fees for her grandchild each year, and has done for the last few years. She has income from a portfolio of shares of around £30,000 a year. In this case, it can be seen that the criteria are likely to be met:

■ The payments form part of Silke's usual expenditure and are regular outgoings.

■ The payments can be made out of income, and not capital, as there is sufficient income to cover the payments.

■ It is likely that the remaining income that Silke receives is sufficient to maintain her normal standard of living.

In this case, the gifts of school fees payments are covered by the exemption and the gifts will be free of inheritance tax during Silke's lifetime and no IHT will be due, should she die.

Example

Gift of school fees

Paris paid £4,000 towards the fees for a school trip for her grandchild. She has income from a portfolio of shares of around £25,000 a year. In this case, it can be seen that one of the criteria is unlikely to be met because the payment does not form part of Paris's usual expenditure and is not a regular outgoing. In this case, the gift of the school trip is not covered by the exemption and the gifts will be subject to other exemptions and reliefs being available.

Small gifts to individuals of £250 or less, per individual for each tax year, are exempt from IHT.

Example

Gift of £200

Tia made a gift of £200 to her friend Chardonnay. In this case, the gift is under the £250 small gifts exemption and the gift will be free of inheritance tax during Tia's lifetime and no IHT will be due, should Tia die.

Example

Gift of £400

Maria made a gift of £400 to her friend Zinnie. In this case, the gift is over £250 and therefore the gift will not be covered by the small gifts exemption. The gift could still be free of inheritance tax during Maria's lifetime and on her death, but this will be subject to other exemptions and reliefs being available. The point here is that, for the gift to be covered by the small gifts exemption, it must be under £250.

Gifts to individuals on the occasion of their marriage are also completely or partially exempt from IHT by the wedding exemptions, as follows:

Relationship of the donor to one of the couple:	Limit (£)
Parent	5,000
Grandparent	2,500
One of the couple to the other	2,500
Anyone else	1,000

If the gift exceeds the limit, only the excess is chargeable.

Example

Gift of £4,000

Sapphire made a gift of £4,000 to her son Daniel on the occasion of his marriage. In this case, the gift is under the £5,000 marriage exemption and the gift will be free of inheritance tax during Sapphire's lifetime and no IHT will be due, should Sapphire die.

Example

Gift of £4,000

Ruby made a gift of £3,000 to her grandson Daniel on the occasion of his marriage. In this case, the gift is over the £2,500 wedding exemption for a grandparent. The gift will still receive the wedding exemption of £2,500 and the remaining part of the gift (£3,000 less £2,500 = £500) could still be free of inheritance tax during Ruby's lifetime and on her death, but this will be subject to other exemptions and reliefs being available.

The point here is that the wedding exemption can still be used, even if the gift made exceeds the amount of the exemption.

Transfers for family maintenance, such as when capital is provided for a family on divorce or dissolution of a civil partnership, are also exempt from inheritance tax.

Potentially exempt transfers (PETs)

A potentially exempt transfer (PET) is a gift that is made by an individual (the donor) to another individual (the donee) that is potentially exempt from tax. A PET is exempt at the *time* of the gift, during the donor's lifetime, but could become chargeable to inheritance tax if the donor dies within seven years of making the gift.

Example

> **Potentially exempt transfer**
>
> Emerald made a gift of £50,000 cash to her daughter Gem. This is a potentially exempt transfer and at the time of making the gift of cash, no inheritance tax is payable.
>
> So long as Emerald survives the gift for at least seven years, there will still be no inheritance tax payable on the gift. However, should Emerald die within seven years of making this gift, the value of the gift must be taken into account when calculating the inheritance tax liability of Emerald's estate and her gifts within seven years. Often, the use of taper relief on the death estate inheritance tax calculation reduces the tax sufficiently for the gift(s) to be worthwhile.

This type of transfer applies to *all* types of asset transferred from one individual (the donor) to another individual (the donee) provided it does not fall into the category of a 'chargeable lifetime transfer' (see below for details) and would include things such as cash, shares and securities, land and buildings, and chattels and personal possessions.

So you can see that making a gift of property can often be useful in reducing the donor's estate, and can reduce the inheritance tax accordingly, providing the donor survives seven years. In addition, even if the donor does not survive the full seven years, the inheritance tax can still be greatly reduced by the use of taper relief on the death calculation. This is explained further in Chapter 16.

Despite the fact that a PET does not become chargeable unless the donor subsequently dies, the value of a PET needs to be fixed at the time of the gift, in case it is required to be taken into account when calculating IHT on other lifetime gifts. The value of a potentially exempt transfer is calculated as follows:

	£
Value of the estate before the gift	X
Less value of the estate after the gift	(X)
Transfer of value (or **diminution in value**)	X
Less: **Reliefs** if applicable (explained later)	(X)
Less: **Exemptions**	
Marriage exemption	(X)
Annual exemption – current tax year	(X)
– preceding tax year (if unused)	(X)
Value of the PET	X

In other words, the measure of the value of a PET is not its value to the recipient but the extent to which the gift reduces the value of the donor's estate. These two values can sometimes be different, for example, if the gift is of one item from a set, where the value of the set is greater than the sum of the separate values of each item in the set; or where some of the shares that gave the donor a controlling interest in a company were given away so that he no longer had a controlling interest.

Chargeable lifetime transfers (CLTs)

A chargeable lifetime transfer (CLT) is a gift which is not a potentially exempt transfer (PET) and is not exempt. These transfers usually consist of transfers into a discretionary trust or a relevant property trust. The gross chargeable value of a CLT is calculated in a same way as the gross value of a PET and the value of the gift is then immediately liable to inheritance tax:

■ If the donee agrees to pay the lifetime tax, then the transfer is chargeable at the rate of 20 per cent.

■ If the donor agrees to pay the lifetime tax, then the transfer is chargeable at the rate of 25 per cent.

Example

A chargeable lifetime transfer where the donee pays any IHT liability

Crystal made a gift of £500,000 cash into a discretionary trust for her grandchildren during the tax year 2010–11. The trustees of the trust have agreed to pay any IHT out of the gift. The value of the gift is as follows:

	£
Transfer of value (or **diminution in value**)	500,000
Reliefs if applicable (explained later)	(0)
Exemptions	
Marriage exemption, in this not applicable	(0)
Annual exemption – current tax year	(3,000)
– preceding tax year (if unused)	(3,000)
Value of the CLT	494,000

Everyone's estate is exempt from inheritance tax up to a certain threshold. This threshold is also known as the 'nil rate band'. The amount for 2010–11 is £325,000. Assuming that Crystal's nil rate band of £325,000 is available to set against this transfer, there would be a charge to IHT during her lifetime, at the time of this transfer as follows:

Transfer value	£494,000
Less nil rate band	(325,000)
Chargeable	169,000

Tax due on the gift at 20%
(as the trustees have agreed to pay the tax)

= £33,800

Example

CLT where the donor pays any IHT liability

Assuming that Crystal made the gift (see page 247), but also agreed to pay any IHT arising on the gift during her lifetime:

Transfer value	£494,000
Less nil rate band	(325,000)
Chargeable	169,000

Tax due on the gift at 25% = £42,250

Lifetime gifts: be sure you consider all taxes

This chapter discusses the advantage of saving inheritance tax by making lifetime gifts. It is clear in most cases how beneficial this can be because it can reduce the donor's potential liability to inheritance tax. However, it is important to consider other taxes when making lifetime gifts of whole assets, or partial assets. Depending on the type of asset, such as land and buildings, there may be other tax liabilities to consider, such as capital gains tax, VAT and stamp duty. Therefore, it is vital to take additional advice that covers the influence of all taxes and looks at the whole tax picture, before any lifetime planning is carried out.

Using the inheritance tax nil rate band

All individuals have a threshold/nil rate band before they have exposure to inheritance tax on their death, as follows:

2009–10	£325,000
2010–11	£325,000

It is possible for an individual to give away these amounts during their lifetime, which will reduce their own wealth for inheritance tax purposes. Should the individual survive seven years, and subject to the inheritance legislation staying the same, they will then be entitled to a further nil rate band that could be utilised against their remaining wealth or continue to make lifetime gifts with the further nil rate band.

Example

Using the inheritance tax nil rate band during lifetime

Benji is wealthy with an estate valued at about £1,000,000. He has not made any gifts of property or wealth to date and has therefore not currently used his nil rate band of £325,000 during 2010–11.

Option 1

If he were to die in say, 10 years' time, having made no gifts during his lifetime, he would be chargeable to IHT on his wealth as follows (using today's rates for the illustration):

His estate	£1,000,000
Less the nil band	(£325,000)
Chargeable to IHT	£675,000

Tax due at 40% = £270,000

Option 2

If Benji was to make lifetime gifts up to the value of his nil rate band, £325,000 in 2010–11, then this would use the nil rate band for the next seven years and wouldn't be then available to set against his wealth at death. However, if he were to die in 10 years' time, as above, he would be chargeable to IHT on his wealth as follows (using today's rates for the illustration):

His estate (£1,000,000 less £325,000 that was covered by the original nil rate band)	£675,000
Less a new nil rate band as Benji survives seven years from lifetime gift Chargeable	(325,000)
	350,000

Tax due at 40% = £140,000

Conclusion:

A saving of inheritance tax of £325,000 at 40% = £130,000

Making a tax-efficient will

There are ways in which an individual can draw up their will to minimise inheritance tax. Although not exhaustive, the following are examples of this. Everyone's estate is exempt from inheritance tax up to the nil rate band. The amounts are as follows:

2008–09	£312,000
2009–10	£325,000
2010–11	£325,000

When drawing up a will, it is essential to use as much of the nil rate band as possible.

If an individual is married or in a civil partnership

Married couples and registered civil partners are allowed to pass assets from one spouse or civil partner to the other during their lifetime or when they die without having to pay inheritance tax – no matter how much they pass on – as long as the person receiving the assets has their permanent home in the UK. This is known as spouse or civil partner exemption.

It used to be that when transferring wealth from spouse to spouse on death, there would be a waste of the nil rate band of the person that had died. However, since 9 October 2007, it has been possible for a spouse or civil partner to use any unused nil rate band from their own spouse or civil partner. If someone leaves everything they own to their surviving spouse or civil partner in this way, it's not only exempt from inheritance tax but it also means they haven't used any of their own inheritance tax threshold, or nil rate band. It is therefore available to increase the inheritance tax nil rate band of the second spouse or civil partner when they die – even if the second spouse has re-married. It doesn't matter when the first spouse or civil partner died (although there are some special rules if it was before 1975).

> To transfer the unused threshold, the executors or personal representatives of the second spouse or civil partner to die need to complete a form IHT402 and send this together with supporting documents to HMRC. See Chapter 16.

Another suggestion is to give assets in the will to friends and relatives to the value of the nil rate band and gift the rest of the estate to a spouse or civil partner, which means that the nil rate band will cover the legacies that would normally be chargeable, and the remaining estate is covered by the spouse exemption. Additional savings would be achieved by gifting any chargeable estate to charities.

If an individual is not married or in a civil partnership

Individuals who are not married do not have the luxury of transferring their estate to a spouse and therefore the use of the nil band is more important. In these cases, some inheritance tax can be saved just by ensuring that the assets of the couple are jointly owned, or that the wealth of the couple is equalised so that they can each use their nil rate bands, should they die.

Example

Individuals who are not married or civil partners

Lucie and Aiden are an unmarried couple and have lived together in a relationship for many years. They have acquired assets together over the years that are valued at £800,000, but these have always been in Aiden's sole name, and they are unaware of the effect this can have on their inheritance tax position should they die. They have always intended for each other to inherit the assets, should one of them die.

Situation 1

If they were to die, with the situation as it stands, then using today's tax rates for an illustration, the inheritance tax position would be as follows:

Lucie

	£
Her estate (nothing in her name)	0
Less the nil rate band	(325,000)
Chargeable to IHT	0

Tax due at 40% = £0

However, it can be seen that Lucie's nil rate band of £325,000 is not being used.

Aiden

	£
His estate (all in his name)	800,000
Less the nil rate band	(325,000)
Chargeable	475,000

Tax due at 40% = £190,000

Situation 2: equalise the estates

If the assets were put into joint names, the inheritance tax position would be as follows:

	£
Lucie's estate	400,000
Less the nil band	(325,000)
Chargeable	75,000

Tax due at 40% = £30,000

Aiden's estate would be exactly the same as the above, and therefore a further £30,000 would be due, making a total liability for both estates of £60,000.

Conclusion

The difference between the two scenarios, with a little bit of planning and using Lucie's nil rate band, shows that tax of £190,000 less £60,000 = £130,000 can be saved. This example shows the inheritance tax advantage of holding assets in joint names for couples that are not married or in a civil partnership. This is an important consideration when assets are acquired by the partners. In addition, if assets are already held by one of the partners, then there are likely to be taxation implications when those assets are transferred into joint names and it is important that the effect of other taxes, such as capital gains tax and stamp duty, are considered before a transfer is made. It is vital to take additional advice that covers the effect of all taxes and looks at the whole tax picture before any lifetime tax planning is carried out.

Business property reliefs

Another way to minimise tax liability is by the use of any business property relief (BPR) on assets that qualify. Then, use the nil rate band as much as possible and so only suffer inheritance tax at 40 per cent on the remainder of the estate where exemptions can't be used.

The details of whether an asset qualifies for the favourable business property relief is covered in Chapter 16.

Example

Using business property reliefs

Danielle has the following assets:

Shares in her own personal unquoted company that qualify for BPR of 100%:	£550,000
A share in the family home:	£400,000
Cash, bank accounts and chattels:	£ 50,000
Total	**£1,000,000**

She is drawing up a will with her solicitor and would like £500,000 to go to her husband, Amir and £500,000 to go to her children, but has no preference how this is achieved.

Option 1

If £500,000 of the company shares were left to the husband, Amir, with the remainder of the shares and the assets left to the children, the situation would be as follows:

The shares to the husband	£500,000
(Less BPR or spouse exemption)	£(500,000)
Chargeable to IHT	£0
The remainder of the shares to the children	£50,000
(Less BPR)	£(50,000)
Chargeable to IHT	£0

Plus the remaining assets:

£400,000 share of the house and £50,000	£450,000
Less nil band	(325,000)
Chargeable	125,000

Tax due at 40% = £50,000

Option 2: gift the assets qualifying for BPR to non-exempt beneficiaries

If £500,000 of the company shares were left to the children, with the remainder of the shares and the assets left to the husband Amir, the situation would be as follows:

The shares to the children	£500,000
(Less BPR)	£(500,000)
Chargeable to IHT	£0
The remainder of the shares to the husband	£50,000
(Less BPR or spouse exemption)	£(50,000)
Chargeable to IHT	£0

Plus the remaining assets:

£400,000 share of the house and £50,000	£450,000
Less spouse exemption	(450,000)
Chargeable	0

Tax due at 40% = £0

Conclusion

The difference between the two scenarios, with some planning and using the business property relief exemptions and the spouse exemption, shows that tax of £50,000 can be saved. There is also still scope to use the £325,000 nil rate band in this example, which serves to emphasise how a little planning can make a big difference.

As with all tax planning and when drawing up legal documents, it is advisable to seek specialist tax advice to ensure you are minimising your estate in the most beneficial way, subject to your wishes. In addition, it is advisable to seek professional advice when drawing up your will. It would be a catastrophe if a will left at the time of death caused more uncertainty or complications than leaving none at all, so it is always advisable to take extra care.

Taking out insurance to cover any IHT liability

One of the problems with having a large estate, and one where there is an inheritance tax liability on death, is that the estate can be depleted considerably by the tax payable. Once the nil band (£325,000 in 2010–11) is exceeded, the tax is potentially 40 per cent, which is a sizeable chunk. However, it is possible for the individual to take out insurance cover that will pay out on death, to cover all or part of this tax liability. The insurance policy should be set up and written into trust, so it does not form part of the death estate for inheritance tax purposes, and the proceeds can be paid direct to the beneficiaries of the trust. Moreover, the policy premiums, if paid regularly out of surplus income, will be exempt gifts for IHT purposes. This can be done by drawing up a written deed, or in many cases, completing a form provided by the insurance provider. This is common practice and most insurance advisers should be able to assist with the type of policy suited to the circumstances and assist with writing the policy into trust.

Writing insurance policies into trust is covered in more detail in Chapter 25.

Protecting lifetime gifts

As we have seen, some gifts can be made during lifetime to reduce the value of an estate, that would be potentially exempt transfers, which means that the gift will be exempt providing the donor survives seven years. Of course, there is always the risk that the donor may die within the seven-year period and these lifetime gifts would then be brought into the inheritance tax calculation. In these cases, it is often beneficial for the donor to take out life insurance to cover the potential IHT due on the lifetime gifts, should they not survive the seven-year period.

The type of insurance is known as a gifts inter vivos policy and runs for seven years. The policy is set up in trust to ensure that the funds fall outside the donor's estate for tax purposes. The beneficiaries nominated in the trust document are normally the heirs to the estate.

Help with the administration process

The order of play is that the assets of a person who has died cannot be released, sold or transferred to the beneficiaries until the inheritance tax has been paid. But, of course, the IHT liability might be difficult to pay if there are no liquid funds. Rather than expecting the personal representatives to take out a loan to cover the temporary cash-flow issue, some people like to take out enough insurance cover to ensure their IHT liability can be paid to ease the burden for the personal representatives and beneficiaries.

24

The benefits of making a will

This chapter suggests reasons why making a will is preferable to dying intestate

- Choosing how the estate is distributed
- Choosing personal representatives
- Executors can act immediately
- Guardians can be appointed for minors
- Tax planning advantages
- Special wishes and the funeral
- How to draw up a will
- Where to keep a will
- Living wills
- Law in Northern Ireland and Scotland

We would all agree that there are happier and far more interesting activities to do during our lifetime than think about what might happen should we die. However, those of us who have had to deal with the death of a member of the family or friend will appreciate that leaving individuals to do such work, with no knowledge of the deceased's wishes, can make the situation more stressful.

Choosing how the estate is distributed

If a person dies without making a will, and therefore dies 'intestate', the law states how their property will be dealt with and this may not be how the individual would have wished. Unfortunately, in all but a few cases where all beneficiaries agree to change the situation, there is nothing that can be done. The rules covering intestacy under the Administration of Estates Act 1925 are in covered in detail in Chapter 5 for England and Wales as well as Scotland and Northern Ireland. As is demonstrated there, there is a fixed sequence of inheritance, which may not match the deceased's wishes, so it is apparent as to why it is preferable to make a will during one's lifetime, rather than leave it to the law to decide how one's property is to be distributed:

■ Without a will, the estate will be distributed according to statute law and no-one has control over how the property can be distributed.

■ If a will is made, the individual has a say in how their estate is dealt with. The testator can choose who will benefit from their estate, and ensure that any friends and charities can be included in the beneficiaries if wished, that wouldn't otherwise benefit under the intestacy rules.

■ Consideration may need to be given around situations involving separated spouses and between half brothers and sisters in connected families.

Cohabitees

Cohabitees where no marriage or civil partnership has taken place would not benefit automatically from a partner's estate should their partner die without having made a will. To establish a claim, the surviving partner would have to rely on the provisions for dependants, which may not be applicable or be expensive to enforce, so these are beneficiaries who can be included by making a will.

Same-sex registered civil partnerships are treated in the same way as married couples under the rules of intestacy if no will is made.

Joint ownership

If property is held in joint names with another person, it may pass automatically to that person upon death, depending on whether it is held jointly as tenants in common or joint tenants. This ownership is discussed in Chapter 13. If the distribution of the jointly-owned property is intended to be to someone other than the joint owner, the title deeds need to be checked, and changed if necessary to ensure the asset is held as tenants in common. If there is any doubt about the way joint property is held, legal advice should be sought.

Choosing personal representatives

If a person dies without making a will, the personal representatives who have to deal with the property in the estate are determined by statute law. So, one advantage of making a will is that chosen executors can be named in the will. Anyone can be nominated as an executor provided they are at least eighteen years of age and of sound mind.

Executors might be professionals that the testator has chosen to act, especially if the estate is large or complex. Otherwise, a named executor may be a close friend or member of the family. Usually, the testator would consult the named executor, just to gain their agreement.

When choosing an executor to deal with the estate, it is wise to consider their suitability. Consider whether they will be able to take on the task of collecting in the assets, paying all liabilities, completing all the forms necessary, and distributing the balance of the estate. There is the option for professional assistance but there would be fees that would need to be paid out of the estate. It would also be wise to consider the availability of an executor. Dealing with an estate can take a considerable time and, for instance, it would not be a good idea to nominate an executor who lives overseas for an estate of property in the UK.

The choice of executor can also depend on whether there will be fees incurred. If the executor is a professional, such as a solicitor, then it is likely that considerable fees will need to be paid from the value of the estate. However, if the executor is a member of the family, then fees are not likely to be so much of an issue. Again, this would largely depend on the size and complexity of the estate and the testator's wishes.

Usually, two executors are chosen, but there can be up to four.

Executors can act immediately

As a will would state who the executors of the estate are, there is no need for anyone to make an application to deal with the estate as an administrator. Therefore considerable time can be saved in the process of dealing with the estate, as the named executor(s) can start acting immediately, arrange the funeral and start collecting in all the information necessary to deal with the estate.

Guardians can be appointed for minors

If the testator has young children, a will can state named guardians who would care for them after the death of the testator. Of course, it is advisable to consult the prospective guardians to ensure that they are willing to take on this role, should they be needed.

Tax planning advantages

Once an individual's estate exceeds the nil rate band for inheritance tax, the property within the estate is liable to tax at a rate of 40 per cent. The nil rate bands currently legislated for are:

2008–09	£312,000
2009–10	£325,000
2010–11	£325,000

Careful planning with the help of a solicitor or tax professional can reduce the level of inheritance tax which will be paid. It provides an opportunity to assess the assets within the estate and consider what steps can be taken to minimise the inheritance tax liability.

Skipping a generation

More often than not, parents will leave their wealth to their own children. This means that the wealth of the children increases so that on their death, their estates are higher, on which to pay a potential 40 per cent tax if the total wealth exceeded the nil band.

One alternative to this is to skip a generation for inheritance tax purposes and pass property to grandchildren. Ultimately they are likely to survive longer and there is likely to be a longer period of time before an additional IHT liability arises on the property.

Examples are detailed in Chapter 23.

Special wishes and the funeral

Special wishes that can be included in a will include organ donation and notifying particular people. In the former case, there should be an organ donation card. However, in the will, it can be stated whether any donation can be made for medical purposes.

The will can include provisions for how the testator would like their funeral to be arranged. In addition, whether they would like to be buried or cremated.

How to draw up a will

First, it is important to know that when a will is to be drawn up, there are certain conditions that have to be met for it to be valid. These conditions are detailed in Chapter 4. Once the testator (person making their will) is happy that the will can be prepared and meet these conditions for the will to be valid, it is then up to them how they go about getting the will drawn up.

There are several ways to draw up a will. A will can be prepared using a pre-printed will form available from stationers – there are many examples on the market. Alternatively, it is possible to prepare one from scratch in the form of a written document. Some websites also offer will-writing services. There are certain conditions that must be met for a will to be valid, as discussed in Chapter 4, and so it is essential to check that the home-made will is valid to avoid any complications later.

Drawing up a will with the help of a solicitor or other qualified or experienced professional can ensure that the will document is valid and the conditions are met for the will to be valid. It is likely that solicitors or other professional will writers will also be able to help with any tax planning and minimising your inheritance tax liabilities. This very often justifies the cost of seeking this professional advice. A reputable professional can be found from the Law Society website.

The Citizens Advice Bureau and Age Concern can assist with the drawing up of a will, or if outside their scope of assistance, they will be able to recommend a good professional to approach.

Where to keep a will

A will may not be required for many years after it is made, so it is essential that it is stored safely and that it can be found after death. The main storage providers are:

- solicitors (a charge may be made);
- banks (a charge may be made). Note that a will should not be stored in a safety deposit box because the box cannot be opened until

probate has been granted and probate can't be granted without the original will.

▪ The Principal Registry of the Family Division (PRFD). You can deposit your will with the PRFD through any probate registry in England and Wales for a one-off fee of £15.

▪ Keep it safe yourself.

Wherever the will is kept, it is essential that family or friends are aware that it exists and can access the document straight away.

Living wills

Living wills are different to the usual will that one draws up for the event of their death. A living will is a document that stipulates an individual's wishes in relation to medical treatment. A living will is the chance to let your relatives and doctors know your wishes, in the event of an illness that renders you incapable of communicating. You can state how you would like to be treated and whether you would like medical treatment to be withdrawn at any stage in illness. It is important to note that a living will is not legally binding, but it can be persuasive. It is always best to take legal advice if drawing up a living will, since this will involve decisions that other people will be involved with at a time that you are living. Sometimes these requests may conflict with the aims of the people involved.

Every adult with mental capacity has the right to agree to or refuse medical treatment. Living wills can include general statements about the wishes, which aren't legally binding, and specific refusals of treatment called 'advanced decisions' or 'advance directives'.

General written statements

A general written statement (sometimes called an 'advance statement') can set out which treatments you feel you would or wouldn't like to receive should you lose mental capacity in the future. Advance statements aren't legally binding, but health professionals do have to take them into account when deciding on a course of action. Family and friends can also use them as evidence of your wishes. A statement could include:

▪ treatment you would be happy to have, and in what circumstances;

▪ treatment you would want, no matter how ill you are;

▪ treatment you would prefer not to have, and in what circumstances;

■ someone you would like to be consulted about your treatment at the time a decision needs to be made;

■ a specific refusal of treatment, which has a different legal status;

■ why you've made your decision about how you do or don't want to be treated;

■ what you understand about the treatment you're agreeing to or refusing;

■ why you're making these decisions now.

You could also make your views known verbally, for example, when discussing treatment with a doctor, but having it written down may make things clearer for everyone.

It is important that your living will is entered into your medical notes so that in an emergency it is found and acted upon. Consider sending a copy to your doctor, to any hospital treating you and to your nearest relatives. If your living will is verbal, make sure close relatives or friends are aware of your wishes. You should consider reviewing your living will regularly to make sure you're happy with it, particularly if your situation changes.

Law in Northern Ireland and Scotland

The law on intestacy in Northern Ireland and Scotland is different from that in England and Wales, and this is covered in Chapter 5.

For deaths in Northern Ireland, the rules of intestacy and how an estate should be distributed according to statute law, are governed by the Administration of Estates Act (Northern Ireland) 1955.

The Scottish Executive's 'Rights of succession' guide explains what happens if someone dies in Scotland without making a will. Details of this guide can be found at:
www.scottishlaw.org.uk/lawscotland/succ.html

Some points to note are that in Scotland:

■ Marriage doesn't revoke a will, but the Scottish law states that the spouse can take up to half of the estate.

■ Having children after a will has been made will make it invalid.

■ Divorce doesn't invalidate a gift to the ex-spouse.

If an individual lives in Scotland and they want to make a will, they can contact a solicitor or voluntary organisations such as Age Concern Scotland or the Citizens Advice Bureau for advice.

25

Trusts

This chapter will briefly explain the types of trust and how
they can be useful

What is a trust?

A trust is a separate entity (ownership) entirely, that can be set up by an
individual, in accordance with the instructions and wishes they stipulate in
a written document, called the trust deed. The person that creates a trust is
called a settlor and in creating the trust they will have transferred some of
their wealth or assets into the trust. This is the trust property or the capital
of the trust fund. It is important to understand that the ownership of the
assets is then changed from the original owner, the settlor, to become
owned by the trustees for the trust. The trust property is managed by trustees, and these people are usually chosen, or nominated, by the settlor of

the trust, in the trust deed, at the time of creating the trust. The trustees will manage the trust property on behalf of the beneficiaries, who are the named individuals that the settlor has stated on the trust deed that they would like to benefit from the trust (Figure 25.1).

Generally, all types of property can be transferred into a trust. Trusts can be used for a number of reasons which will be apparent throughout the chapter. One of the reasons for setting up a trust is for tax planning, however, there are other practical reasons. The concept of trusts is well used in the UK and is governed by UK law, but trusts are not always used or recognised in other parts of the world.

The tax treatment of trusts is the same throughout the UK. The detail given in this chapter applies equally to England and Wales, Scotland and Northern Ireland. However, there are differences in terminology in relation to Scottish trusts and these are covered at the end of the chapter.

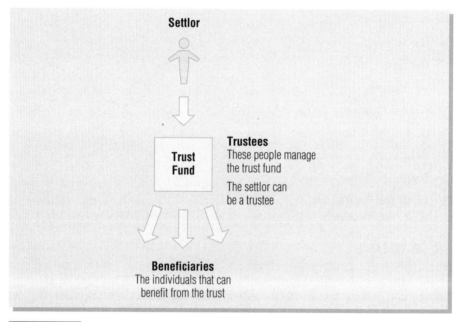

Figure 25.1 The structure of a trust

The settlor

The settlor is the person who creates the trust and passes some of their property, regardless of what type of asset this is, into the trust. The ownership of the property is thus legally transferred into the hands of the trustees, who manage the trust fund, and so the property no longer belongs to the settlor. This transfer means that the settlor has given away their property into the trust. The settlor can still influence how the assets are managed though, by being one of the trustees. It is possible for the settlor to still benefit from the property within the trust but this removes any of the tax advantages of setting up the trust, so needs to be considered carefully, if the aim of the trust is to reduce any potential inheritance tax liability.

It is possible for two persons to be settlors of the same trust and one example of this is where a married couple might put a jointly owned property into trust.

The beneficiaries

The beneficiaries of a trust are those that can benefit from the trust in some way. When the settlor transfers property into the ownership of a trust, they must define who the beneficiaries are. There can be just one, or there can be more than one beneficiary. The beneficiaries can be specifically named individuals, such as 'Miss Lucinda Green' or they can be a class of beneficiaries, such as 'my grandchildren'.

It is possible for a trustee to be a beneficiary but unless there are a number of trustees, there could be a conflict of interest between this beneficiary and other beneficiaries and therefore this is rare. Not all beneficiaries have the same entitlements under a trust and it depends on the type of trust as to how they can benefit.

The trustees

As we have seen, the trustees are there to manage a fund that has been put into a trust by the settlor, in accordance with the instructions, rights and powers set out in a deed. The trustees are the legal owners of the property. However, they cannot benefit from the income or the capital of the trust unless they are named as beneficiaries of the trust. The property is held in their names, as the legal owners, so that they can manage the property as if they were the owners, but in accordance with the wishes of the settlor.

The trust deed states the powers and rights of the trustees and governs how the appointment of new or replacement trustees should take place. Usually, the appointment of new or replacement trustees would be with the agreement of the settlor during their lifetime, and then this responsibility passed to the existing trustees after the settlor's death.

Most trusts have between two and four trustees, although there is no limit to the number of trustees there can be, unless the trust assets happen to include land, when the maximum number of trustees permitted is four. Anyone who is aged at least 18 and of sound mind can be a trustee. Sometimes, a trust can be managed by a company that acts as a trustee. Many offshore trusts are managed in this way.

Powers of trustees

The trust deed stipulates what the trustees can and cannot do with the fund. Examples of this might be:

■ What assets they are allowed to invest in, or those they are not permitted to invest in.

■ Whether they are able to make distributions of income or capital of the trust fund to the beneficiaries. This can also be governed by the type of trust in place.

■ Whether they can charge for their services. This is usually the case if the trustees are professional firms or if they are corporate trustees. If a trustee is not permitted to charge for their services, they are usually able to recover their expenses incurred while carrying out the role of trustee.

Trustees' responsibilities

A trustee must take the role of managing the trust fund responsibly, and they have key duties, such as:

■ To act unanimously if there is more than one trustee.

■ Not to make a personal profit from the trust (except to the extent that a professional trustee is authorised to charge for his or her services).

■ Provide accounts showing how the trust fund is managed, if asked by a beneficiary of the trust.

■ To act with a duty of care. The Trustee Act 2000 governs how trustees must handle investments if there are no stipulations in the trust deed.

■ Trustees must carefully consider the type of investment used for trust property, including how risky this might be.

■ As we have seen, trustees are deemed to own the trust property as if they were the beneficial owners, but they must consider the interests of the beneficiaries, since it is ultimately their wealth and not that of the trustees.

■ Trustees must regularly review the trust's investments to ensure they are the most appropriate to meet the wishes and intentions of the settlor, and to seek investment advice where necessary or appropriate.

■ Northern Ireland has similar legislation (Trustee Act (Northern Ireland) 2001) in force and, since 2006, so has Scotland.

The trustees must ensure that they take account of the beneficiaries of the trust, and this will vary from trust to trust, depending on the reasons for it being created. For instance, we will soon look at the types of trust but if there is a mixture of beneficiaries, or where some beneficiaries would benefit from income and others would benefit from the capital of the trust, all of these interests must be taken into account when deciding how to invest the trust fund.

Anyone can create a trust, either during their lifetime or in a will. For a trust to be valid the following conditions must be met:
■ The intentions of the person creating the trust must be clear.
■ The assets to be held in trust must be clearly defined.
■ It must be clear who the beneficiaries of the trust are.

The main types of trust

There are many types of trust, and the main ones are:

■ bare trusts;
■ discretionary trusts;
■ life interest trusts (also named interest in possession trusts);
■ immediate post-death interest trusts;
■ trusts for children.

Bare trusts

A bare trust is one where the trustees are not actually the legal owners of the trust property but merely hold the asset as a 'nominee' for a person. The legal ownership of the property still lies with the beneficiary and so the trustees hold the legal title of the asset or assets on behalf of the beneficiaries only.

Discretionary trusts

A discretionary trust is one whereby the trustees are able to distribute the income or the capital of the trust fund to the trust beneficiaries, at their absolute discretion (Figure 25.2). The beneficiaries would be named individuals, or a class of beneficiaries as detailed above, but no one of them has the right to receive any income or capital at all. If they do receive anything from the trust fund, it would be at the discretion and decision of the trustees. Trustees in England and Wales have a right to accumulate all income of the trust fund for the lifetime of the trust, which can be up to 125 years.

Discretionary trusts are very often used in tax planning. All individuals have a threshold/nil rate band before they have exposure to inheritance tax on their death, as follows:

2009–10   £325,000
2010–11   £325,000

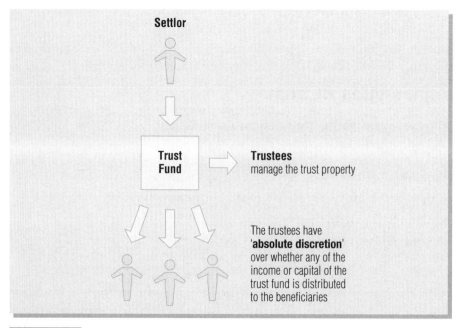

Figure 25.2   The structure of a discretionary trust

It is possible for an individual to put these amounts into a trust and in doing so, will reduce their own wealth for inheritance tax purposes. Should the individual survive seven years, they will then be entitled to a further nil rate band that could be used against their remaining wealth. The discretionary trust is a useful vehicle to enable the settlor to gift property into trust and away from their own estates, but still have a certain amount of control over the assets as a trustee.

Life interest (interest in possession) trusts

A life interest trust usually has two stages in its trust life. First, the trust will be created and a beneficiary is named as the life tenant. There can be more than one life tenant.

■ The beneficiary of a life interest trust, the life tenant, has a right to the income from the trust property, or the right to use the trust property personally during his/her lifetime.

■ The beneficiary (life tenant) is not normally able to benefit from the actual capital of the trust fund itself in this case, only the income generated from the capital. In some cases, however, the trustees have a discretionary power to pay capital to the life tenant as well.

Second, on the death of the life tenant, the capital fund of the trust property is then transferred to the beneficiaries that have been nominated, by the settlor, on the trust deed as the individuals to ultimately receive the capital (Figure 25.3 overleaf):

■ The beneficiaries that ultimately receive the trust fund after the life tenant has died are called the **remaindermen.**

■ During the lifetime of the life tenant, who has the right to the income or use of the trust property, the remainderman (or remaindermen if there is more than one) is said to have a reversionary interest.

■ During the lifetime of the life tenant, remainderman or remaindermen have no right to any income from the trust and usually receive nothing until the death of the life tenant.

Life interest trusts are often used to enable a settlor to give an individual the use of a property or income, but without making a gift of the whole asset. The asset or the asset value itself can then be preserved so that the settlor can pass this on to other individuals. An example of how a life interest trust is commonly used is when a settlor wishes for their spouse or civil partner to benefit from an asset during their lifetime, but wants the asset itself to ultimately pass to children, particularly if they are from a previous relationship. These trusts can often appear in wills for this reason. Many trusts created on the death of a settlor are created with the surviving spouse or civil partner being given the right to continue to live in the settlor's share of the family home. Then, on the death of the spouse or civil partner, that asset then passes to children.

With this type of trust, and because there are different beneficiaries to owe the duty of care to – the life tenant at the present time, and the preservation of the trust capital for the future beneficiaries – care must be taken in choosing appropriate investments for the trust.

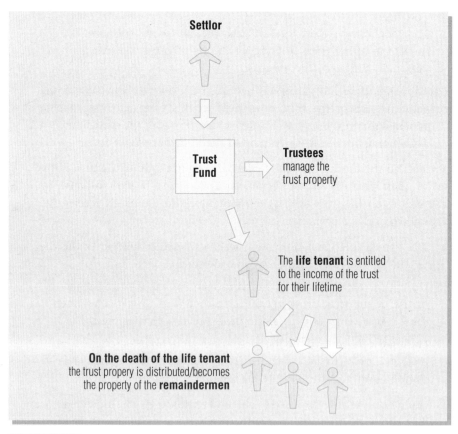

Figure 25.3   The structure of a life interest trust

Example

Life interest trust for a widow

Where a life interest trust has been set up with a widow as life tenant and her children as the remaindermen, it would not generally be appropriate for the trustees to invest with the sole objective of maximising immediate income, e.g. by purchasing relatively high-yielding stocks such as government gilts priced above par. Similarly, a pure growth portfolio, with minimal income, would be unsuitable for the life tenant. In recessionary times with consequent low interest rates, trustees will find it difficult to balance the interests of various types of beneficiaries.

Other types of trust

Settlor interested trusts

Many trusts are set up with the aim of saving tax. Using a trust is one way to use tax legislation, in a legal manner, to minimise potential tax liabilities, such as inheritance tax. However, when a settlor creates a trust and is able to benefit directly from the trust as a beneficiary or is able to benefit from the trust indirectly if their spouse or civil partner is a beneficiary, then there is anti-avoidance tax legislation in place that renders any tax planning void. Therefore, most trusts that are now set up specifically exclude the settlor and their spouse or civil partner as being able to benefit in any way.

To gain the full tax advantages, the property must be completely given away by the settlor, albeit in a trust, and they should not be able to benefit. The only way they can still have a say in what happens to the original value is by being a trustee and having control over how the trust fund is managed for others.

Accumulation and maintenance trusts

Accumulation and maintenance (A&M) trusts were often used which had IHT advantages under s71 of the Inheritance Tax Act 1984. However, due to changes in the tax legislation in 2006, these trusts can no longer be created. The IHT advantages can now only continue for A&M trusts:

■ created before 22 March 2006, with gifts made before 22 March 2006;

■ that were amended before 5 April 2008 to comply with the requirements contained in the Finance Act 2006.

The legislation that came into play by the Finance Act 2006 required that for these trusts, by 5 April 2008, the trust beneficiaries must become absolutely entitled to the trust property by the time they are aged eighteen. If this condition was not stipulated by the trust deed, or changes were not put into place by amending the trust terms, the tax advantages would not be able to continue under the new legislation.

Immediate post-death interest trusts

An immediate post-death interest trust (IPDI) is one where a life interest trust is set up via a will on the death of the testator. The concept behind the IPDI trust is broadly the same as described for the life interest trusts.

Trusts for children

The Finance Act 2006 has effectively replaced old accumulation and maintenance (A&M) trusts created in wills with 'bereaved minors trusts' and '18 to 25' trusts. These can only be created by a deceased parent (not a grandparent) via a will or intestacy. These are also subject to an IHT exit charge if absolute entitlement is given any later than age eighteen (but by twenty-five at the latest).

Protective trusts

This type of trust would be useful where a settlor would like to gift property to an individual but is mindful of that individual being, or becoming bankrupt, or perhaps in an unsettled relationship with the possibility of someone else in some way taking over the beneficiary's benefits from the trust. With the assets in a protective trust wrapper, they cannot be enjoyed by anyone without the authority of the trustee(s).

It should be noted however that a settlor cannot establish a protective trust for their own benefit, with the objective of being protected from their own creditors or bankruptcy, as the law renders the trust ineffective.

Overseas trusts

If an individual is not UK domiciled and is not deemed to be UK domiciled by their residence in the UK of seventeen out of twenty tax years, then we have seen that only their UK assets would be potentially chargeable to UK inheritance tax. What this also means is that their overseas assets could escape liability to inheritance tax. Therefore the use of overseas trusts can be a good tax planning tool for non UK-domiciled individuals to keep their assets overseas and outside their UK estates for UK inheritance tax.

Overseas trusts do not currently have any tax advantages for a UK-domiciled individual since all of their worldwide assets would be potentially liable to inheritance tax. Unless, of course, the trust property has been completely given away to other named beneficiaries and the settlor cannot benefit at all, which would be no different to the setting up of a UK trust.

Specialist advice is recommended for the creation of overseas trusts, as this area of trusts is complex and would inevitably involve tax issues abroad.

Charitable trusts

To be a charitable trust, the trust must be purely for charitable purposes and for the public benefit, from creation. Broadly speaking, a charitable trust is a trust established for the public benefit. Its purposes must be *solely* charitable. For example, a trust that gives a life interest to an individual beneficiary with the reversionary interest passing to the National Trust would not be a charitable trust. In the nineteenth century, the courts classified charitable purposes into four qualifying categories:

- the relief of poverty;
- the advancement of education;
- the advancement of religion;
- other purposes beneficial to the community.

The Charity Commission now states that a trust is charitable if it:

- is for a purpose that was previously accepted as charitable (as above);
- also now meets the requirement that the purpose benefits the public such as for the following reasons:
  - prevention and relief of poverty;
  - citizenship and community advancement;
  - other purposes beneficial to the community;
  - the promotion of human rights;
  - conflict resolution and reconciliation;
  - the advancement of education;
  - religion;
  - health;
  - amateur sport;
  - environmental protection and improvement;

■ science, culture;

■ arts and heritage;

■ the promotion of the efficiency of the Armed Forces of the Crown;

■ the promotion of animal welfare.

Charitable trusts also benefit from special rules. First, they have no time limit and can exist with no restriction on when the trust should end. Second, the investment income and capital gains of charitable trusts are normally free of UK taxes. Finally, gifts to UK charities are free of IHT and are therefore used by individuals to reduce their exposure to inheritance tax liability.

Statutory trusts

These are trusts that are established by law. An example would be a trust set up under the rules of intestacy which was in place to manage the property that was left to minors who cannot manage trust property themselves.

Using trusts for tax and practical reasons

Now that we have seen what a trust is and how a trust can be established and managed, we can explore some of the ways in which a trust can be used for tax planning as well as for practical reasons. Tax planning is the term used to describe how we can organise our finances, wealth, assets in such a way that minimises exposure to inheritance tax. It is the legal way of using the tax legislation in a favourable manner.

Discretionary will trusts: using the nil rate band

Most individuals have wills that simply pass all their property to their spouses or civil partners on death. In this case, there is no IHT payable on the first death since this transfer is exempt from IHT. Furthermore, since 9 October 2007, the surviving spouse or civil partner (who may have bene-fited from the initial transfer) is now entitled to any unused portion of the IHT nil rate band of the deceased spouse or civil partner, which ensures that both of the couples' nil bands are available to use. This treatment applies even where the first spouse/civil partner died before 9 October 2007.

The result of this means that for married couples or civil partners, there will be no liability to IHT if their joint estate is under £325,000 × 2 = £650,000 for 2009–10 and 2010–11.

This is fine if the intention is that the spouse or civil partner only is to benefit. In cases where the first spouse wishes for other individuals to benefit, it is possible to set up a discretionary trust for other beneficiaries. If this amount is within the nil rate band, then there is still no IHT payable on the death, despite not using the spouse exemption opportunity.

Example

Discretionary trust for children

Ed made a will during his lifetime. In the will, he stipulated that a discretionary trust be set up for his adult children, to the value of the nil rate band. The remainder of his estate is to go to his wife of five years, Eleanor. Unfortunately, Ed died on 16 February 2010. He left an estate valued at £450,000.

In this case, Ed died during 2009–10 which means that on his death, £325,000 will go into trust for his adult children. This amount is normally a chargeable amount as it is not covered by any exemptions such as spouse exemption. However, as the amount is £325,000 this is covered by the nil rate band and no IHT is payable.

The remainder of Ed's estate (£450,000 − £325,000 = £125,000) is then transferred to Eleanor. This is covered by the spouse exemption and therefore no IHT is payable.

Discretionary will trusts: when assets are likely to increase

It can be beneficial to leave assets in a discretionary trust if the assets are likely to increase in value at a higher rate than the IHT nil rate band. This would result in a tax saving because if they were in the hands of the surviving spouse, it is possible that these assets would exceed the two nil rate bands available on the second death. By putting these assets into trust on the first death, they are outside the estate of the surviving spouse or civil partner and therefore any rise in value will not be charged on the second death. The surviving spouse or civil partner could still be a beneficiary during their lifetime at the discretion of the trustees, but the trustees would carry out the management of the trust in accordance with the settlor's wishes.

Example

If Eleanor dies ...

Using the example of Ed and Eleanor, Ed had two options:

1   Pass all of the assets to Eleanor, his wife. If this was the case, she would have the total assets in her estate on her own death but be able to use any unused nil rate band that Ed was entitled to.

2 Create a discretionary trust on his death, by way of his will, as discussed in the previous example. In this case, £325,000 went into trust and the remaining value of £125,000 was passed to Eleanor.

If Eleanor subsequently died on 20 April 2010 leaving her own estate valued at £350,000, and the value of the assets that were originally in Ed's estate had increased to £600,000, the effect would have been as follows:

Under option 1, the IHT due on Eleanor's death would be:

Eleanor's personal wealth	£350,000
Add inherited from Ed (originally £450,000 but now valued at £600,000)	£600,000
Total	**£950,000**
Less Eleanor's nil band: 2010–11	(325,000)
Less Ed's unused nil band: 100%	(325,000)
Chargeable to IHT at 40%	300,000 = £120,000

Under option 2, the IHT position on Eleanor's death would be:

Eleanor's personal wealth	£350,000
Add inherited from Ed	
125,000/450,000 × 600,000	£166,667
(the remainder went into trust separate to Eleanor's estate)	
Total	**£516,667**
Less Eleanor's nil band: 2010–11	(325,000)
Less Ed's unused nil band: 0%	(0)
Chargeable to IHT at 40%	191,667 = £76,667

Using this example, we can see that not only does the nil rate band discretionary trust offer many practical reasons for putting in place, but that it can potentially save IHT too. This does, of course, depend on the values of assets and the amounts put into the trust, and specialist advice is recommended to ensure that the concept is worthwhile from a tax point of view, but to also ensure that any documentation is drafted correctly.

Discretionary will trusts: where a remarriage might occur

Any assets left to a surviving spouse or civil partner would become their property, so that if they should remarry, or enter another civil partnership, this may exclude the children of the first spouse or civil partner from ever benefiting. However, where assets are left to a discretionary will trust, particularly using the nil-rate band at the time, not only will the testator be using their own nil rate band, but also they will have provided for their other nominated beneficiaries.

Example

Stuart died on 4 March 2010 and he left a will stating that all of his estate should be transferred to his wife, Naomi. He didn't leave any assets to their two adult children, or their grandchildren. Naomi remarried a few years later but unfortunately died soon after, without leaving a will.

In this case, Stuart's estate was transferred absolutely to his wife Naomi so it was owned entirely by her. When Naomi died, she didn't leave a will which meant that she died intestate, and therefore potentially all of her estate could go to her new husband, thus excluding the children of Stuart and Naomi, subject to the value of the estate and the intestacy rules.

This may be the intention or wishes of an individual, however Stuart could have considered creating a trust which provided for Naomi during her lifetime, but preserved the value to eventually be passed on to their children, so they could also benefit.

Immediate post-death interest (IPDI)

The protection of assets for other beneficiaries can also be achieved by using an IPDI rather than a discretionary trust described above, and therefore providing for a surviving spouse too. However, the difference with this type of trust in contrast to the use of the discretionary trust is that the value of the IPDI would be included in the estate of the surviving spouse. This still might not be liable to IHT if the combined values of the trust along with the survivor's own estate at the second death were within the combined total of the unused nil rate band of the first spouse or civil partner to die plus that of the survivor. However, if these values are likely to be higher, using a discretionary trust could ensure the value of the trust is out of the estate of the surviving spouse or civil partner.

Two-year discretionary will trust

A testator might not always be certain about who they would like to benefit from their estate when they die. However, this shouldn't restrict someone from making a will. Therefore, the inclusion of a two-year discretionary will trust, into a will, is often a beneficial solution. This is because a will may be varied within two years after death and the variation backdated for IHT purposes to the date of death, as if written into the will.

The creation of this trust at the time of death, enables the property nominated in the will to go into a trust for the trustees to decide how it will be distributed. Very often in these cases, the testator (person making the will) will leave a letter of wishes, detailing their preferences.

Life policies in trust

A life policy that is paid out on an individual's death would usually be part of the estate and included with the other assets. This then increases the total value of the assets on which there could be an inheritance tax charge. Once the IHT threshold has been exceeded, the rate of tax charged at death is 40 per cent and this is a considerable chunk of the estate and can often deplete the value left for the beneficiaries named in a will, or that would benefit on intestacy.

One method of tax planning is to assign (place) the life policy into trust. If this is done, the amount paid out on the insured's death is not included in the value of the estate. The value is diverted away from the estate and passed directly to the named beneficiaries, thus avoiding a potential 40 per cent tax charge.

Another advantage to putting a life policy into trust is that anything paid out on death from the policy will not be included in the estate, and will not therefore be tied up until probate is granted. Therefore the policy can be useful to pay expenses that are necessary at the time of death, to help the probate process be carried out more smoothly, such as paying for a funeral, paying the IHT etc. In addition, this is a useful tool to leave value to individuals without having to share other assets between beneficiaries, which might be impractical, or impossible, to divide.

Discretionary trusts are usually used when writing life policies into trust. They give greater scope of beneficiaries and tend not to be as limiting, depending, of course, on the wishes of the settlor and how the proceeds are intended to be used.

Placing a life policy in trust can be a simple matter and it would entail initially contacting the insurance provider. The policy can then usually be put into trust by the completion of a form that the insurance provider will supply. The form details the name of the policyholder, the name of the insured, details of the beneficiaries etc., and is not usually a complicated process but can gain much benefit.

Example

Life policy in trust

Marion had a life assurance policy in place during her lifetime, into which she paid regular premiums each month. On her death, the policy would pay out £50,000. Marion already owned assets to the tune of £500,000. She has two options:

1   Assign the policy into trust and therefore into the hands of the trustees.

2   Do not assign the policy into trust.

If Marion were to die during 2010–11, the effect of these two options are as follows:

- Under option 1, the insurance proceeds of £50,000 are paid out directly to the trustees and are not included in her estate for IHT purposes. Her IHT liability is therefore £500,000 less £325,000 nil band = £175,000 at 40% = £70,000

- Under option 2, the insurance proceeds of £50,000 are added to Marion's estate and the IHT liability is as follows: £500,000 + £50,000 = £550,000 less £325,000 nil rate band = £225,000 at 40% = £90,000.

Therefore, it can be beneficial from a tax point of view to write life policies into trust.

Pension policies and trusts

As with life assurance policies, the value of pension policies can also be placed into trust, as detailed above. Again, discretionary trusts are usually used in this situation. The effect of this is that the value paid out on death also has the potential of escaping an inheritance tax liability on the death of the policyholder. It should be noted that if a settlor has transferred a pension contribution, fund or policy into trust within two years of their death, anti-avoidance rules may apply and so specialist advice would always be recommended when dealing with pension policies.

Seeking professional advice

It is advisable to seek professional advice if an individual is thinking about setting up a trust and is unsure of the effects of completely giving away their property either during their lifetime or at the time of their death, via their will. Trusts can be a complex area and the wording of a trust deed at the creation of a trust determines how the trust will be managed, so it is worth seeking specialist advice, especially if a large amount of wealth will be transferred into the trust.

Most medium-to-large accountancy firms will have an experienced adviser who should be able to advise on these matters, as would most firms of solicitors. They would also be able to assist with other compliance issues that need to be dealt with such as completing accounts and tax returns.

Trusts and Scottish law

There are a few differences under Scottish law but these are generally confined to terminology. In Scotland, the settlor is called the granter or truster, and the appointment of new trustees is referred to as 'the assumption of new trustees'.

Life interest trusts

The life tenant of an interest in possession trust is called a life tenant in England and Wales and a life renter/life rentrix in Scotland. The remainderman of the life interest trust, to whom the trust's property is transferred on the death of the life tenant, is called a fiar in Scotland.

Discretionary trusts

Discretionary trusts in Scotland have the same characteristics as those in England and Wales. However, legislation under the Perpetuities and Accumulations Act 2009 that has extended the time that trustees can accumulate income to 125 years, only applies to trusts in England and Wales. The accumulation period for Scottish discretionary trusts remains limited to 21 years.

Investment powers

Over the years, the laws on trustee investment powers have generally become more liberal, to the extent that since 1 February 2001, in England and Wales trustees have been able to make investments *as if* they were the beneficial owners of the trust's assets under the Trustee Act 2000. The same change was made in Northern Ireland, with effect from 29 July 2002.

In Scotland, the Charities and Trustee Investment (Scotland) Act 2005 broadened trustees' investment powers from 2006.

In practice, long before these reforms, most trust deeds gave the trustees the widest possible investment powers, often over-riding the restrictive statutory provisions. It is now mainly statutory trusts (often resulting from intestacy) and very old trusts where the statutory rules are still relevant.

Appendix A

Tax return SA900 relating to the estate administration period and form R185

Form SA900 is the tax return that needs to be completed by the personal representatives during the administration of the estate. You can download a copy of this from:
www.hmrc.gov.uk/forms/sa900.pdf

Figure A1.1 overleaf shows the standard 12-page form. Any of the following types of additional income and gains needs to be given on supplementary pages:

- trade income;
- partnership income;
- property income;
- foreign income;
- capital gains;
- residence of the personal representatives;
- charities;
- pension charges.

These supplementary pages can also be obtained from HMRC.

Form R185: income payments to beneficiaries

A form R185 (Figure A1.2) needs to be completed when an income distribution is made to a beneficiary. An example of when a form R185 would be used is in Chapter 11. This form can be downloaded from the HMRC website:
www.hmrc.gov.uk/pdfs/r185–ie.pdf

 **HM Revenue & Customs**

Trust and Estate Tax Return   for the year ended 5 April **2010**

Tax reference

Date

Issue address

HM Revenue & Customs

For
Reference

Phone

Please read this page first

The green arrows and instructions will guide you through your tax return

*T*his notice *requires you, by law, to send a tax return containing details of your income and capital gains, together with any documents requested, for the year 6 April 2009 to 5 April 2010. We have sent you this paper form to fill in, but you can also file the tax return online using our Internet service (using 3rd party commercial software).*

Make sure the tax return, and any documents we ask for, reach us by:

- **31 October 2010** *if you want* **us** *to calculate the trust or estate's tax or if you file a* **paper** *tax return, or both, or*
- **31 January 2011** *if you file the return* **online***.*

Whichever method you choose, the tax return and any documents asked for must reach us by the relevant deadline or an automatic penalty of £100 will be charged.

If you file online, you have until 31 January to file the tax return and you will receive an instant on-screen acknowledgement telling you that we have received it. You can still file online even if we have sent you a paper tax return. To register and enrol for the online service, go to **www.hmrc.gov.uk** *and from the 'do it online' menu select 'Self Assessment'.*

If this return has been issued to you after 31 July 2010, then you must ensure that you complete and return it by the later of:

- *the relevant dates above, or*
- *three months after the date of issue.*

Make sure your payment of any tax the trust or estate owes reaches us by 31 January 2011. Otherwise you will have to pay interest, and possibly a surcharge.

The Trust and Estate Tax Return may be checked. There are penalties for supplying false or incomplete information.

Calculating the trust or estate's tax

You can choose to calculate the trust or estate's tax. But if you do not want to, and providing we receive the return by 31 October 2010, we will work out the tax for you and let you know if there is tax to pay by 31 January 2011.

However, if you file later than 31 October 2010 or three months after the date this notice was given, see the Trust and Estate Tax Calculation Guide (sent with this return unless we know you have a tax adviser).

The Trust and Estate Tax Return – your responsibilities

We have sent you pages 1 to 12 of the tax return.

You might need other forms - 'supplementary pages' - if the trust or estate had particular income or capital gains. Use page 3 to check.

You are responsible for sending us a complete and correct return, but we are here to help you get it right.

Three ways we can help you:

- *look at the Trust and Estate Tax Return Guide (sent with this tax return, unless we know you have a tax adviser). It should answer most of your questions, or*
- *phone us on the above number, or*
- *go to www.hmrc.gov.uk*

SA900

Figure A1.1 SA900 trust and estate tax return form

INCOME AND CAPITAL GAINS *for the year ended 5 April 2010*

Step 1   You may not have to answer all the questions in this tax return.

Tick if this applies ▼

- see pages 4 and 6 of the Trust and Estate Tax Return Guide

1) **If you are the trustee of a bare trust** (except an unauthorised unit trust), that is, one in which the beneficiary(ies) has/have an immediate and absolute title to both capital and income, you can go straight to Question 19 on page 11. Do not tick the box if you choose to complete the return. ☐

2) **If you are the personal representative of a deceased person** and completing this tax return for a period of administration **and all** the points below apply:

- all the income arose in the UK
- you do not want to claim relief (Questions 10A and 10B)
- no annual payments have been made out of capital (Question 11)
- all income has had tax deducted before you received it (or is UK dividends with tax credits)
- there are no accrued income profits or losses, no income from deeply discounted securities, gilt strips, company share buy-backs, offshore income gains, or gains on life insurance policies, life annuities or capital redemption policies where no tax is treated as having been paid on the gain
- no capital payments or benefits have been received from a non-resident, dual resident or immigrating trust (see the note on page 10 of the Trust and Estate Tax Return Guide)

then, **if you have made no chargeable disposals**, go straight to Question 19 on page 11. ☐

If you have made chargeable disposals, answer Questions 5 and 6 at Step 2 and then Questions 17 to 22. ☐

3) **If you are the trustee of an interest in possession trust** (one which is exclusively an interest in possession trust), and:

- no income arose to the trust, **or** ☐
- you have mandated all the trust income to the beneficiary(ies), **or** ☐
- all the income arose in the UK and has had tax deducted before you receive it (or is UK dividends with tax credits), **or** ☐
- you have mandated part of the income to the beneficiary(ies) where the part you have not mandated comprises only income arising in the UK which has had tax deducted before you received it ☐

and all of the following points apply

- the answer will be 'No' in boxes 8.11 and 8.13 of Question 8
- there are no accrued income profits or losses, no income from deeply discounted securities, gilt strips, company share buy-backs, offshore income gains, or gains on life insurance policies, life annuities or capital redemption policies
- you do not wish to claim reliefs (Questions 10A and 10B)
- no annual payments have been made out of capital (Question 11)
- no further capital has been added to the settlement (Question 12)
- no capital payments have been made to, or for the benefit of, relevant children (see the note on page 6 of the Trust and Estate Tax Return Guide) of the settlor during their lifetime (Question 15)
- the trust has never been non-resident and has never received any capital from another trust which is, or at any time has been, non-resident (Question 16)

then, **if you have made no chargeable disposals**, go straight to Question 19 on page 11. ☐

If you have made chargeable disposals, answer Questions 5 and 6 at Step 2 and then Questions 17 to 22. ☐

4) **If you are the trustee of a charitable trust you must complete the charity supplementary pages as well as this form.**

- If you are claiming exemption from tax on all your income and gains, you can go straight to Question 7. You should answer Questions 10 and 11, if appropriate, and complete Questions 19, 20, and 22. ☐
- If you are claiming exemption from tax on only part of your income and gains, you must answer Questions 1 to 9 for any income for which you are not claiming exemption. You should answer Questions 10 and 11, if appropriate, and complete Questions 19, 20 and 22. ☐

5) **In any other cases**, including if you are the trustee of an unauthorised unit trust, you should go to Step 2.

Step 2   Answer Questions 1 to 7 and 23 to check if you need supplementary pages to give details of particular income or gains. Pages 8 and 9 of the Trust and Estate Tax Return Guide will help. (Ask the SA Orderline for a guide if you want one.) If you answer 'Yes', ask the orderline for the appropriate supplementary pages and Notes. When you have answered Questions 1 to 7 and Question 23, answer Question 8.

Phone the SA Orderline on **0845 9000 404** (textphone available) or fax on **0845 9000 604** for any supplementary pages you need (closed Christmas Day, Boxing Day and New Year's Day). Make sure you ask for the supplementary pages for the Trust and Estate Tax Return. Or you can download from www.hmrc.gov.uk

INCOME AND CAPITAL GAINS *for the year ended 5 April 2010 continued*

Make sure you have the supplementary pages you need; tick the box below when you have got them

Q1 Did the trust or estate make any profit or loss from a sole trade? *(Read page 8 of the Trust and Estate Tax Return Guide if you are the personal representative of a deceased Name at Lloyd's.)* **Yes** ☐ **Trust and estate trade** ☐

Q2 Did the trust or estate make any profit or loss or have any other income from a partnership? **Yes** ☐ **Trust and estate partnership** ☐

Q3 Did the trust or estate receive any UK property income? **Yes** ☐ **Trust and estate UK property** ☐

Q4 Did the trust or estate receive any income from foreign companies or savings institutions, offshore funds or trusts abroad, land and property abroad, or make gains on foreign life insurance policies? **Yes** ☐

Is the trust or estate claiming relief for foreign tax paid on foreign income or gains, or relief from UK tax under a Double Taxation Agreement? **Yes** ☐ **Trust and estate foreign** ☐

Q5 Capital gains
Did the trust or estate dispose of chargeable assets worth more than £40,400 in total? **Yes** ☐
Answer 'Yes' if:
- allowable losses are deducted from the chargeable gains made by the trust or estate, and the chargeable gains total more than the annual exempt amount before deduction of losses, **or**
- no allowable losses are deducted from the chargeable gains made by the trust or estate and the chargeable gains total more than the annual exempt amount, **or**
- you want to make a claim or election for the year. **Yes** ☐ **Trust and estate capital gains** ☐
Read page 9 of the guide.

Q6 Is the trust claiming to be not resident in the UK, or dual resident in the UK and another country for all or part of the year? **Yes** ☐ **Trust and estate non-residence etc.** ☐

Q7 Is the trust claiming total or partial exemption from tax because of its charitable status? **Yes** ☐ **Trust and estate charities** ☐

Q23 Pensions - in the case of an estate, are there any tax charges and/or taxable lump sums? *Read page 9 of the guide, tick 'Yes' if applicable.* **Yes** ☐ **Estate pension charges etc.** ☐

Q8 *Read pages 10 to 12 of the guide. Answer all the questions.*
Are you completing this tax return:

	No	Yes
- for a period of administration	8.1 ☐	8.2 ☐
- as the trustee of an unauthorised unit trust	8.3 ☐	8.4 ☐
- as the trustee of an employment related trust	8.5 ☐	8.6 ☐
- as the trustee of a Heritage Maintenance Fund	8.7 ☐	8.8 ☐
- as the trustee of an Employer Financed Retirement Benefit Scheme (EFRBS)? If this happened during the return year please enter the date the EFRBS first became operative in box 21.11 on page 12. *Read note on page 11 of the guide.*	8.9 ☐	8.10 ☐

If you are a trustee:

	No	Yes
- can any settlor (or living settlor's spouse or civil partner) benefit from the capital or income	8.11 ☐	8.12 ☐
- are you a participator in an underlying non-resident company (a company that would be a close company if it were resident in the UK)	8.13 ☐	8.14 ☐
- is the trust liable to Income Tax at the special trust rates (the trust rate of 40% or the dividend trust rate of 32.5%) on any part of the income or would it be on any income above the standard rate band (for example, it is a discretionary trust)	8.15 ☐	8.16 ☐
- has a valid vulnerable beneficiary election been made?	8.17 ☐	8.18 ☐

Step 3 Now fill in any supplementary pages BEFORE answering Questions 9 to 22, as directed.
Please use blue or black ink to fill in the Trust and Estate Tax Return.
Please do not include pence. Round down income and gains. Round up tax credits and tax deductions. Round to the nearest pound.

HMRC 12/09 ■ TRUST AND ESTATE TAX RETURN: PAGE 3 *Please turn over*

INCOME for the year ended 5 April 2010 continued

Q9 Did the trust or estate receive any other income not already included on the supplementary pages?   **YES** ☐   If yes, fill in boxes 9.1 to 9.40 as appropriate.

If you wish, you may in the following circumstances leave blank some of boxes 9.1 to 9.40:

a) **if you are the trustee of an interest in possession trust (one which is exclusively an interest in possession trust),** you may exclude income which has had tax deducted before you received it (or is UK dividends with tax credit) unless

 (i) that income has not been mandated to the beneficiary and there are accrued income scheme losses to set against the interest or you are claiming losses against general income, **or**

 (ii) its exclusion would make you liable to make a payment on account which would not be due if you included it - see page 13 of the Trust and Estate Tax Calculation Guide concerning payments on account **before** following this guidance.

b) **if you are the personal representative of a deceased person** you may exclude income which has had tax deducted before you received it (or is UK dividends with tax credit) unless there are accrued income scheme losses to set against the interest. If the reliefs claimed at Question 10A on page 6 exceed untaxed income, you will need to include estate income that has had tax deducted to ensure a repayment can be calculated.

Have you received any taxed income (or UK dividends with tax credit) which you are not including in this Trust and Estate Tax Return because (a) or (b) above apply?   **YES** ☐

■ *Interest and alternative finance receipts*

• Interest and alternative finance receipts from UK banks and building societies (including UK Internet accounts) – *if you have more than one bank or building society etc. account enter* **totals** *in the boxes.*

Taxable amount
 - where **no tax** has been taken off   **9.1** £ _____

	Amount after tax taken off	Tax taken off	Gross amount before tax
- where **tax has** been taken off – the *Working Sheet on page 13 of the guide will help you to fill in boxes 9.2 to 9.4.*	**9.2** £	**9.3** £	**9.4** £

	Amount after tax taken off	Tax taken off	Gross amount before tax
• Other taxed UK interest distributions – *see page 14 of the guide (do not include Property Income Distributions)*	**9.5** £	**9.6** £	**9.7** £

Taxable amount
• National Savings & Investments (other than First Option Bonds and Fixed Rate Savings Bonds)   **9.8** £ _____

	Amount after tax taken off	Tax taken off	Gross amount before tax
• National Savings & Investments First Option Bonds and Fixed Rate Savings Bonds	**9.9** £	**9.10** £	**9.11** £

	Amount after tax taken off	Tax taken off	Gross amount before tax
• Other income from UK savings and investments (except dividends)	**9.12** £	**9.13** £	**9.14** £

INCOME *for the year ended 5 April 2010 continued*

■ *Dividends*

- Dividends and other qualifying distributions from UK companies (but excluding Property Income Distributions from UK Real Estate Investment Trusts or Property Authorised Investment Funds)

Dividend/distribution	Tax credit	Dividend/distribution plus credit
9.15 £	**9.16** £	**9.17** £

- Dividend distributions from UK authorised unit trusts and open-ended investment companies

Dividend/distribution	Tax credit	Dividend/distribution plus credit
9.18 £	**9.19** £	**9.20** £

- Stock dividends from UK companies

Dividend	Notional tax	Dividend plus notional tax
9.21 £	**9.22** £	**9.23** £

- Dividends and other qualifying distributions received by unauthorised unit trusts

Amount of dividend only
9.24 £

- Stock dividends received by unauthorised unit trusts

Amount of dividend only
9.25 £

- Non-qualifying distributions and loans written off

Distribution/loan	Notional tax	Taxable amount
9.26 £	**9.27** £	**9.28** £

■ *Gains on UK life insurance policies, life annuities and capital redemption policies*

- on which **no tax** is treated as paid

	Amount of gain
	9.29 £

- on which **tax is** treated as paid

Tax treated as paid	Amount of gain
9.30 £	**9.31** £

■ *Other income*

- Other income (including Property Income Distributions from UK Real Estate Investment Trusts or Property Authorised Investment Funds)

Amount after tax taken off	Tax taken off	Gross amount before tax
9.32 £	**9.33** £	**9.34** £

Losses brought forward	Losses used in 2009–10
9.35 £	**9.36** £

2009–10 losses carried forward
9.37 £

■ *Deemed income - see page 19 of the guide*

- Accrued Income Scheme profits and deeply discounted securities

	Taxable amount
	9.37A £

- Other deemed income etc.

	Taxable amount
	9.38 £

- Company purchase of its own shares

Tax credit	Taxable amount
9.39 £	**9.40** £

Q9A   Standard rate band

- Amount of standard rate band - *see page 21 of the guide*

9A.1 £

HMRC 12/09   ■ TRUST AND ESTATE TAX RETURN: PAGE 5   *Please turn over* ➤

OTHER INFORMATION *for the year ended 5 April 2010*

Q10A Do you want to claim any reliefs or have you made any annual payments? **YES** ☐

If yes, fill in boxes 10.1A to 10.4A and/or 10.1B as appropriate. If not applicable, go to question 11.

■ *Interest and alternative finance payments eligible for relief on qualifying loans and arrangements*

● Personal representatives: interest on loans and payments made under alternative finance arrangements to pay Inheritance Tax

Amount of payment
10.1A £ ☐

■ *Other charges*

● Trustees: annual payments and patent royalties

Amount of payment	Tax taken off	Gross amount
10.2A £	**10.3A** £	**10.4A** £

Q10B Do you want to claim special Income Tax treatment where a valid vulnerable beneficiary election has effect? **YES** ☐

If yes, fill in box 10.1B. If not applicable, go to question 11.

● Amount of relief claimed

10.1B £ ☐

Q11 Were any annual payments made out of capital or out of income not brought into charge to Income Tax? **YES** ☐

If yes, fill in boxes 11.1 to 11.3 as appropriate. If not applicable, go to question 12.

● Annual payments

Amount of payment	Tax taken off	Gross amount
11.1 £	**11.2** £	**11.3** £

▶ *If you are a personal representative, go to Question 17. Do not fill in Questions 12 to 16.*

Q12 Have any assets or funds been put into the trust in year 2009–10? **YES** ☐

If yes, fill in boxes 12.1 to 12.9 as appropriate. If not applicable, go to question 13.

Settlor's name and address
12.1 ☐
Postcode

Description of asset
12.2 ☐

Value of asset
12.3 £

Settlor's name and address
12.4 ☐
Postcode

Description of asset
12.5 ☐

Value of asset
12.6 £

Settlor's name and address
12.7 ☐
Postcode

Description of asset
12.8 ☐

Value of asset
12.9 £

OTHER INFORMATION *for the year ended 5 April 2010 continued*

If you ticked box 8.15 in Question 8, on page 3, do not complete this page - please go to Question 16 on page 9 and carry on filling in the tax return.

If you have ticked box 8.16 in Question 8, on page 3, complete Questions 13 to 16A. Otherwise, go to Question 16

Q13 | **Is any part of the trust income not liable to tax at the special trust rates?** | **YES** ☐ | If yes, fill in boxes 13.7 to 13.21 below. **Otherwise**, fill in boxes 13.19 to 13.21 only.

Boxes 13.1 to 13.6, 13.9, 13.10, 13.15 and 13.16 are not being used

■ *Income to beneficiaries whose entitlement is not subject to the trustees' (or any other person's) discretion*

- Amount of income chargeable at the **10%** rate — **13.7** £ _____

- Trust management expenses applicable to the income in box 13.7 — **13.8** £ _____

- Amount of income chargeable at the **basic** rate — **13.11** £ _____

- Trust management expenses applicable to the income in box 13.11 — **13.12** £ _____

■ *Income allocated to specific purposes*

- Amount of income chargeable at the **10%** rate — **13.13** £ _____

- Trust management expenses applicable to the income in box 13.13 — **13.14** £ _____

- Amount of income chargeable at the **basic** rate — **13.17** £ _____

- Trust management expenses applicable to the income in box 13.17 — **13.18** £ _____

■ *Trust management expenses*

- Total amount of deductible trust management expenses – *see notes on pages 22 and 23 of the guide* — **13.19** £ _____

- Expenses set against income not liable at the special trust rates — total of column above **13.20** £ _____

- Total income not liable to UK Income Tax and not included elsewhere on this Trust and Estate Tax Return (non-resident trusts only) — **13.21** £ _____

Q13A | **Is this a settlor-interested trust where part of the income is not settlor-interested?** | **YES** ☐ | If yes, complete box 13A.1. If not applicable, go to question 14.

Complete box 13A.1 only if you have ticked both boxes 8.12 and 8.16 and part of the trust income, which is liable at the special trust rates, is not settlor-interested.

- Amount of tax pool applicable to income that is not settlor-interested – *see notes on pages 23 of the guide* — **13A.1** £ _____

OTHER INFORMATION *for the year ended 5 April 2010 continued*

If you ticked box 8.15 in Question 8, on page 3, do not complete this page - please go to Question 16 on page 9 and carry on filling in the tax return.
If you have ticked box 8.16 in Question 8, on page 3, complete Questions 13 to 15A. Otherwise, go to Question 16.

Q14 **Have discretionary payments of income been made to beneficiaries?** *Trustees of Heritage Maintenance Funds: do not complete these boxes for expenditure on heritage property. See notes on page 25 of the guide before filling in these boxes.*   **YES**

If yes, fill in boxes 14.1 to 14.15 as appropriate. **Otherwise,** fill in box 14.15 only.

Name of beneficiary	Net payment	Tick the box if the beneficiary was a relevant child of the settlor and the settlor was alive when payment was made.
14.1	14.2 £	☐
14.3	14.4 £	☐
14.5	14.6 £	☐
14.7	14.8 £	☐
14.9	14.10 £	☐
14.11	14.12 £	☐
14.13	14.14 £	☐

- Amount, if any, of unused tax pool brought forward from last year (enter '0' if appropriate)   **14.15** £

Q15 **Have the trustees made any capital payments to, or for the benefit of, relevant children of the settlor during the settlor's lifetime?**   **YES**

If yes, fill in box 15.1. If not applicable, go to question 15A.

- Total capital payments to relevant children   Amount paid **15.1** £

Q15A **Were there capital transactions between the trustees and the settlors?**   **YES**

If yes, fill in boxes 15A.1 to 15A.12 as appropriate. If not applicable, go to question 16.

■ *Capital transactions between the trustees and settlors* - read page 25 of the guide.

Date	Amount	Name of company (if appropriate)
15A.1 / /	15A.2 £	15A.3

Registered office
15A.4

Postcode

Date	Amount	Name of company (if appropriate)
15A.5 / /	15A.6 £	15A.7

Registered office
15A.8

Postcode

Date	Amount	Name of company (if appropriate)
15A.9 / /	15A.10 £	15A.11

Registered office
15A.12

Postcode

OTHER INFORMATION *for the year ended 5 April 2010 continued*

Q16 Has the trust at any time been non-resident or received any capital from another trust which is, or at any time has been, non-resident?

YES [ ]

If yes, read pages 25 and 26 of the Trust and Estate Tax Return Guide and, if appropriate, fill in box 16.1. If not applicable, go to question 17.

If YES, have the trustees made any capital payments to, or provided any benefits for, the beneficiaries?

YES [ ]

- Total capital payments or value of benefits provided

16.1 £ [ ]

Please give details of the payments in box 16.1 in the boxes below. If there are insufficient boxes please provide the additional details on a separate sheet.

Name of beneficiary

16.2 [ ]

Address of beneficiary

16.4 [ ]

Postcode

Amount/value of payment/benefit

16.6 £ [ ]

Name of beneficiary

16.3 [ ]

Address of beneficiary

16.5 [ ]

Postcode

Amount/value of payment/benefit

16.7 £ [ ]

Name of beneficiary

16.8 [ ]

Address of beneficiary

16.10 [ ]

Postcode

Amount/value of payment/benefit

16.12 £ [ ]

Name of beneficiary

16.9 [ ]

Address of beneficiary

16.11 [ ]

Postcode

Amount/value of payment/benefit

16.13 £ [ ]

Name of beneficiary

16.14 [ ]

Address of beneficiary

16.16 [ ]

Postcode

Amount/value of payment/benefit

16.18 £ [ ]

Name of beneficiary

16.15 [ ]

Address of beneficiary

16.17 [ ]

Postcode

Amount/value of payment/benefit

16.19 £ [ ]

If you have received capital from any other trust which is, or at any time has been, non-resident please provide the following details.

Name of trust

16.20 [ ]

Address of trustee

16.22 [ ]

Postcode

Date trust set up

16.21 [/ /]

Amount of value received

16.23 £ [ ]

OTHER INFORMATION *for the year ended 5 April 2010 continued*

Q17 **Do you want to calculate the tax?** | **YES** | *If yes, do it now and then fill in boxes 17.1 to 17.10 below. The Trust and Estate Tax Calculation guide will help you.*

- Total tax due for 2009–10 **before** you made any payments on account *(put the amount in brackets if an overpayment)* | **17.1** £ |

- Tax due for earlier years | **17.2** £ |

- Tick box 17.3 if you have calculated tax overpaid for earlier years and enter the amount in box 17.4 | **17.3** | | **17.4** £ |

- Tick box 17.5 if you are making a claim to reduce your payments on account. Enter your **reduced** payment in box 17.7 and say why in the 'Additional information' box, box 21.11, on page 12 | **17.5** | Tick box 17.6 if you do not need to make payments on account | **17.6** |

- Your first payment on account for 2010–11 *(include the pence)* | **17.7** £ |

- Tick box 17.8 if you are claiming a repayment of 2010–11 tax now and enter the amount in box 17.9 | **17.8** | | **17.9** £ |

- Pension charges due - *enter the amount from box 22 of the Working Sheet in the Notes on Estate pension charges etc.* | **17.10** £ |

Q18 **If the trust or estate has paid too much tax do you want to claim a repayment?** | **YES** | *If yes, fill in boxes 18.1 to 18.12 as appropriate. If not applicable, go to question 19.*
(If you do not tick 'Yes', or the tax overpaid is below £10, we will use the amount you are owed to reduce the next tax bill.)

Repayments will be sent direct to your bank or building society account. This is the safest and quickest method of payment. If you do not have an account, tick box 18.8A. If you would like repayment to your nominee, tick box 18.2 or 18.8B.

Should the repayment (or payment) be sent:

- to your bank or building society account? Tick box 18.1 and fill in boxes 18.3 to 18.7 | **18.1** |

or

- to your nominee's bank or building society account? Tick box 18.2 and fill in boxes 18.3 to 18.7 and boxes 18.9A to 18.12 as required | **18.2** |

- If you do not have a bank or building society account, read the notes on page 26 of the guide, tick box 18.8A | **18.8A** |

- If you would like a cheque to be sent to your nominee, tick box 18.8B and fill in boxes 18.9A to 18.12 as required | **18.8B** |

- If your nominee is your adviser, tick box 18.9A | **18.9A** |

Name of bank or building society
| **18.3** |

Name of account holder
| **18.4** |

Branch sort code
| **18.5** |

Account number
| **18.6** |

Building society reference
| **18.7** |

Adviser's reference for you (if your nominee is your adviser)
| **18.9B** |

I authorise

Name of your nominee/adviser
| **18.10** |

Address of nominee/adviser
| **18.11** |

Postcode

to receive on my behalf the amount due

| **18.12** | *This authority must be signed by you. A photocopy of your signature will not do.*

Signature

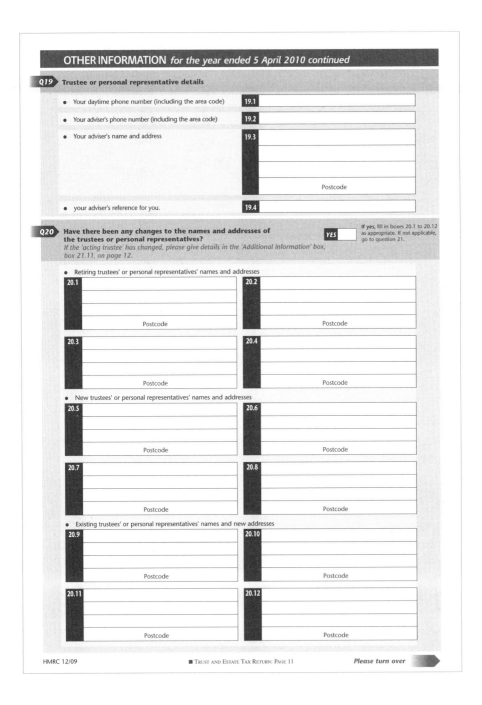

OTHER INFORMATION *for the year ended 5 April 2010 continued*

Q19 **Trustee or personal representative details**

- Your daytime phone number (including the area code) | **19.1**
- Your adviser's phone number (including the area code) | **19.2**
- Your adviser's name and address | **19.3**

  Postcode

- your adviser's reference for you. | **19.4**

Q20 **Have there been any changes to the names and addresses of the trustees or personal representatives?**
If the 'acting trustee' has changed, please give details in the 'Additional information' box, box 21.11, on page 12.

YES

If yes, fill in boxes 20.1 to 20.12 as appropriate. If not applicable, go to question 21.

- Retiring trustees' or personal representatives' names and addresses

20.1

Postcode

20.2

Postcode

20.3

Postcode

20.4

Postcode

- New trustees' or personal representatives' names and addresses

20.5

Postcode

20.6

Postcode

20.7

Postcode

20.8

Postcode

- Existing trustees' or personal representatives' names and new addresses

20.9

Postcode

20.10

Postcode

20.11

Postcode

20.12

Postcode

OTHER INFORMATION for the year ended 5 April 2010 continued

Q21 Other Information

- If you are completing this Trust and Estate Tax Return as a personal representative, please enter in box 21.1 the date of death of the deceased.

  21.1 Date / /

- If the administration period ceased in the year to 5 April 2010, please enter in box 21.2 the date of cessation.

  21.2 Date / /

- If the administration period ceased in the year to 5 April 2010 and there is a continuing trust, tick box 21.3.

  21.3

- If you are a trustee and the trust was terminated in the year to 5 April 2010 please enter in box 21.4 the date of termination and, in the 'Additional information' box, box 21.11 below, the reason for termination.

  21.4 Date / /

- If this Trust and Estate Tax Return contains any figures that are provisional because you do not yet have final figures, please tick box 21.5 - *Read page 26 of the guide.*

  21.5

- If any 2009–10 tax was refunded directly by the HM Revenue & Customs office, or (personal representatives only) by the Jobcentre Plus (in Northern Ireland, the Social Security Agency), please enter the amount in box 21.6. Do **not** include any refunds of excessive payments on account or any Gift Aid repayments claimed on form R68 Claim.

  21.6 Amount £

- **Disclosure of tax avoidance schemes** – if the trust or estate is a party to one or more disclosable tax avoidance schemes you must complete boxes 21.7 and 21.8. Give details of each scheme (up to three) on a separate line. If the trust or estate is a party to more than three schemes, details of the additional schemes must be reported on form AAG4.

Scheme reference number

21.7

Tax year in which the expected advantage arises – year ended 5 April

21.8

- **Business Premises Renovation Allowance (BPRA)** - *Read page 27 of the Trust and Estate Tax Return Guide before you fill in these boxes.*

  Capital allowance **21.9** £   Balancing charge **21.10** £

- If you have used an HMRC Toolkit for managing risks, tick box 21.10A

  21.10A

21.11 *Additional information*

Q22 Declaration

I have filled in and am sending back to you the following Trust and Estate Tax Return pages:

1 to 12 of this form	Trust and estate UK property	Trust and estate non-residence etc.
Trust and estate trade	Trust and estate foreign	Trust and estate charities
Trust and estate partnership	Trust and estate capital gains	Estate pension charges etc.

Before you send the completed tax return back you must sign the statement below.

If you give false information or conceal any part of trust or estate income or chargeable gains, you may be liable to financial penalties and/or you may be prosecuted.

22.1 The information I have given in this tax return is correct and complete to the best of my knowledge and belief.

Signature   Date

- Please print your name in box 22.2

  22.2

- Enter the capacity in which you are signing in box 22.3

  22.3

 **HM Revenue & Customs**

Statement of income from estates

Personal representatives (who can be either executors or administrators) may use this form to advise beneficiaries about income from the residue (see note below) of the estate of a deceased person:
- for each year during the administration of the estate if a 'sum' (see note below) is paid to the beneficiary in that year, and
- for the year in which the administration of the estate is completed.

The beneficiary's estate income for the year ended 5 April `2` `0` `  ` `  ` is the deemed income shown on page 2 of this form.

The beneficiary	The deceased person
Full name of beneficiary	Full name of deceased person
Address	Date of death *DD MM YYYY*
Postcode	

Notes for personal representatives

Personal representatives may complete the relevant boxes on page 2 and give the form to the beneficiary.

For the purpose of this form, a '**sum**' includes cash, assets transferred or appropriated, and debts set off or released. The **residue** is what is left in the estate after you have paid all debts, legacies and taxes.

If the administration period has been ongoing for more than a year, the following example shows how to work out the income which each beneficiary should show in their tax return/repayment form.

Step 1
Add the net amount (the amount **after tax taken off**) of the beneficiary's share of the income from the residue for the tax year to any net amount brought forward.

Step 2
Compare the figure in Step 1 with the sum paid to the beneficiary in the tax year.
- If the sum paid is greater than or equal to the result of Step 1, the beneficiary's share of the income from the residue for the tax year is the amount at Step 1.
- If the sum paid is less than the result of Step 1, the beneficiary's share is the sum actually paid in the tax year. The balance of the beneficiary's entitlement is carried forward to the next tax year, and will then be their income entitlement in the next year if no distributions are made.

For the final tax year of the administration period, the beneficiary's share of the income from the residue will be treated as having been fully paid.

Notes for beneficiaries

Keep this form and refer to it if making a tax return or claiming a tax repayment.

If you need to complete a tax return the box numbers on page 2 match those on the SA107 *Trusts etc.* pages of the tax return. Transfer the amounts of income after tax taken off from those boxes to the corresponding boxes on the SA107 (for more information see SA107 Notes *Trusts etc. notes* - go to **www.hmrc.gov.uk**).

If you need to claim a tax repayment transfer the figures to the relevant boxes in the R40 *Claim for repayment of tax deducted from savings and investments*, as follows:
- income and tax paid or tax credit at box 16 to boxes 4.3 and 4.4 on the R40
- income and tax paid or tax credit at box 17 to boxes 4.5 and 4.6 on the R40
- income and tax paid or tax credit at box 18 to boxes 6.1 to 6.4 (as appropriate) on the R40
- income at box 20 to box 4.10 on the R40
- income and tax paid or tax credit at box 21 to boxes 4.7 and 4.8 on the R40
(for more information see R40 Notes *Notes for completing form R40* - go to **www.hmrc.gov.uk**).

Please note that the tax described as 'non-repayable' or 'non-payable' cannot be repaid.

R185(Estate Income)   Page 1   HMRC 03/10

Figure A1.2 Form R185 for statement of income from estates

Income from the estates of deceased persons

Income from United Kingdom (UK) estates

If the beneficiary was in receipt of income from a UK estate only, enter the net income and tax paid or tax credit in boxes 16 to 21.

16 Non-savings income - **after tax taken off**
This includes rental income and profits from a trade

£ [   ] . [   ]

Tax paid or tax credit on box 16 income

£ [   ] . [   ]

17 Savings income - **after tax taken off**
This includes bank or building society interest

£ [   ] . [   ]

Tax paid or tax credit on box 17 income

£ [   ] . [   ]

18 Dividend income - **after tax taken off**
This includes dividends from foreign companies that do not qualify for UK tax credit

£ [   ] . [   ]

Tax paid or tax credit on box 18 income

£ [   ] . [   ]

19 Non-savings income taxed at non-repayable basic rate -
after tax taken off. *This includes gains realised on certain life insurance policies, and any undistributed estate income carried forward from 1998-99 or earlier years*

£ [   ] . [   ]

Tax paid or tax credit on box 19 income

£ [   ] . [   ]

20 Income taxed at 22% - **after tax taken off**
This includes any income that has had tax taken off at 22% when this was the basic rate of tax, but is not passed over to the beneficiaries until after the reduction in the basic rate to 20%

£ [   ] . [   ]

Tax paid or tax credit on box 20 income

£ [   ] . [   ]

21 Dividend income taxed at non-payable dividend rate -
after tax taken off. *This includes dividends from UK companies and dividends from foreign companies that qualify for UK tax credit*

£ [   ] . [   ]

Tax paid or tax credit on box 21 income

£ [   ] . [   ]

Income from foreign estates

If the beneficiary was in receipt of income from a foreign estate, do not complete boxes 16 to 21.
Instead, enter the income in box 22 and any relief for UK tax already accounted for in box 23.

22 Foreign estate income

£ [   ] . [   ]

23 Relief for UK tax already accounted for

£ [   ] . [   ]

Foreign tax paid on estate income

Complete box 24 if any foreign tax credit relief is claimable but has **not** been claimed on foreign income arising to a UK estate or a foreign estate.

24 Foreign tax for which foreign tax credit relief has not been claimed

£ [   ] . [   ]

Signature and date

I confirm that the information given on this form is correct.

Signature of the personal representative

[   ]

Date *DD MM YYYY*

[ ] [ ] [   ]

Appendix B

Inheritance tax return forms

This appendix contains some examples of the inheritance tax forms that need to be completed by the personal representatives during the administration of the estate:

- form IHT400: inheritance tax return;
- form IHT400: calculation;
- form IHT402: claim to transfer unused nil rate band.

Form IHT 400: inheritance tax return

The main tax return form IHT400 consists of a 16-page return form which consists mainly of the following:

- The personal details of the person that has died.
- The details of the persons acting as personal representatives and dealing with the estate.
- Details of the will, if one was left.
- Details of the assets and liabilities of the deceased.
- Claims for any exemptions or reliefs.
- Details of any additional schedules that are relevant and enclosed with the return.
- Declarations.
- A checklist.

An example of the form is shown in Chapter 12. You can download a copy of this form from:
www.hmrc.gov.uk/inheritancetax/iht400.pdf

The return applies to most estates, and any additional information is reported to HMRC on a supporting schedule that would be enclosed with the main tax return. Only the supporting schedules that are relevant to the person that has died will require completion and submission with the tax return form IHT400.

A list of the supporting schedules is as follows:

IHT401	Domicile outside the United Kingdom
IHT402	Claim to transfer unused inheritance tax nil rate band
IHT403	Gifts and other transfers of value
IHT404	Jointly owned assets
IHT405	Houses, land, buildings and interests in land
IHT406	Bank and building society accounts
IHT407	Household and personal goods
IHT408	Household and personal goods given to charity
IHT409	Pensions
IHT410	Life assurance and annuities
IHT411	Listed stocks and shares
IHT412	Unlisted stocks and shares and control holdings
IHT413	Business or partnership interests and assets
IHT414	Agricultural relief
IHT415	Interest in another estate
IHT416	Debts due to the deceased
IHT417	Foreign assets
IHT418	Assets held in trust
IHT419	Debts owed by the deceased
IHT420	National heritage assets, conditional exemption and offers in lieu of tax
IHT421	Probate summary
IHT422	Application for an inheritance tax reference
IHT423	Direct payment scheme bank or building society account

Any of the above additional schedules can be downloaded from the HMRC website:
search2.hmrc.gov.uk/kbroker/hmrc/forms/viewform.jsp?formId=3309

Form IHT 400: calculation

Whether the personal representatives will have to pay over any inheritance tax will depend on how much the estate is valued at, and whether this is fully covered by exemptions or business reliefs. The calculation of the inheritance tax liability is covered in Chapter 16. Form IHT400 (Figure B1.1) can assist with the calculation of the inheritance tax liability. You can download a copy of this form from:
www.hmrc.gov.uk/inheritancetax/iht400-calc.pdf

Form IHT 402: claim to transfer unused nil rate band

As we have seen in Chapter 16, everyone's estate is exempt from inheritance tax up to a certain threshold. This threshold is also known as the nil rate band. The amounts are:

2008–09	£312,000
2009–10	£325,000
2010–11	£325,000

Married couples and registered civil partners are also allowed to pass assets from one spouse or civil partner to the other during their lifetime or when they die without having to pay inheritance tax as long as the person receiving the assets has their permanent home in the UK. This is known as spouse or civil partner exemption.

If someone leaves everything they own to their surviving spouse or civil partner in this way, it's not only exempt from inheritance tax but it used to mean they didn't use any of their own nil rate band. However, from 9 October 2007, it is possible to increase the nil rate band of the second spouse or civil partner by any unused nil band, when they die, even if they have re-married. It doesn't matter when the first spouse or civil partner died. The amount available for transfer is the percentage unused (see example in Chapter 16).

You can download a copy of claim form IHT402 (Figure B1.2) from:
www.hmrc.gov.uk/inheritancetax/iht402.pdf

HM Revenue & Customs

Inheritance Tax account
IHT400 Calculation

When to use this form

Fill in this form if you have already filled in the form IHT400 up to and including box 109, the simple calculation is not suitable and you now wish to work out the Inheritance Tax yourself.

Help

For more information or help:
- go to **www.hmrc.gov.uk/inheritancetax/**
- phone our helpline on **0845 30 20 900**
  - if calling from outside the UK, phone **+44 115 974 3009**.

Gifts and other transfers of value

If the deceased made any gifts or other transfers of value in the seven years before they died, the chargeable value of these gifts and transfers will reduce the amount of the Inheritance Tax nil rate band available to the estate on death.
Fill in the boxes below to find out the amount of the nil rate band available on death.

1	Inheritance Tax nil rate band at the date of death See *IHT400 Rates and tables*	£
2	Transferable nil rate band (form IHT402, box 20)	£
3	Total nil rate band at the date of death (box 1 + box 2)	£
4	Total chargeable value of gifts and other transfers of value made by the deceased within the seven years before their death (form IHT403, box 7). *Do not include gifts with reservation here, include them on the IHT400, box 104 instead.*	£
5	Balance of Inheritance Tax nil rate band available (box 3 *minus* box 4) (if this figure is a minus, enter '0' in box 5)	£

Calculation of Inheritance Tax

6	Total chargeable estate (copy from form IHT400, box 108)	£
7	Inheritance Tax nil rate band available (copy from box 5)	£
8	Value chargeable to tax (box 6 *minus* box 7). If the result is a minus amount enter '0'. If the figure is '0' do not fill in any more of this form, go to form IHT400, box 119.	£
9	Inheritance Tax (box 8 x 40%)	£ .

Successive charges relief

If in the five years before they died, the deceased inherited money or assets from another person's estate on which Inheritance Tax was paid, you may deduct successive charges relief to stop that legacy being taxed twice in a short period of time.

10	Is successive charges relief due?	

No ☐   *Enter '0' in box 17 and go to box 18*

Yes ☐   *Follow the instructions below for working out successive charges relief*

- You will need to find out the value of the estate of the first person to die and the amount of Inheritance Tax paid in order to work out the relief due.
- You will also need to know what the deceased was entitled to receive from the estate. You can find this out by asking the executor of the estate of the first person to die for this information.
- If you are deducting successive charges relief enter:
  - the IHT reference of the first person to die
  - their full name, and
  - their date of death
  in the 'Additional information' boxes on pages 15 and 16 of form IHT400.

Figure B1.1 IHT400 calculation form

| 11 | How much Inheritance Tax was paid on the estate of the first person to die? | £ | . | |

| 12 | What was the net value of the estate of the first person to die, after deducting liabilities and exemptions? | £ | . | |

| 13 | Box 11 ÷ box 12 | | . | |

| 14 | What was the deceased's entitlement from the estate of the first person to die? | £ | . | |

| 15 | Box 13 x box 14 | £ | . | |

The amount of relief available depends on the number of years between the first and second deaths and is shown in the table.

Years between the two deaths	Percentage reduction
One year or less	100%
One to two years	80%
Two to three years	60%
Three to four years	40%
Four to five years	20%
Over five years	0%

For example, if the second death was on 3 March 2007 and the first death was on 17 August 2005, there is more than one year between the two deaths, but less than two years, so the percentage reduction would be 80%.

| 16 | Enter the percentage reduction | | % |

| 17 | The amount of successive charges relief due: box 15 x box 16. | £ | . | |

| 18 | Inheritance Tax on the chargeable estate (box 9 *minus* box 17) | £ | . | |

Successive charges relief – Example 1

| 11 | How much Inheritance Tax was paid on the estate of the first person to die? | £ 10,000 | . 0 0 |

| 12 | What was the net value of the estate of the first person to die, after deducting liabilities and exemptions? | £ 340,000 | . 0 0 |

| 13 | Box 11 ÷ box 12 | 0 . 0 2 9 4 |

£10,000 ÷ £340,000 = 0.0294

| 14 | What was the deceased's entitlement from the estate of the first person to die? | £ 200,000 | . 0 0 |

| 15 | Box 13 x box 14 | £ 5,880 | . 0 0 |

£200,000 x 0.0294 = £5,880
This is the amount of Inheritance Tax paid on the deceased's share of the estate of the first person to die. You now need to look at how much relief is due on that amount of tax.

The amount of relief available depends on the number of years between the first and second deaths and is shown in the table.

Years between the two deaths	Percentage reduction
One year or less	100%
One to two years	80%
Two to three years	60%
Three to four years	40%
Four to five years	20%
Over five years	0%

For example, if the second death was on 3 March 2007 and the first death was on 17 August 2005, there is more than one year between the two deaths, but less than two years, so the percentage reduction would be 80%.

If there were between one and two years between the two deaths, then the table shows that the percentage reduction would be 80%

| 16 | Enter the percentage reduction | 80 % |

| 17 | The amount of successive charges relief due: box 15 x box 16. | £ 4,704 | . 0 0 |

£5,880 x 80 ÷ 100 = £4,704.
This amount of successive changes relief that is due.

IHT400 Calculation   Page 2

Tax that may be paid by instalments

The tax on some types of unsold property and assets may be paid in 10 annual instalments, that is, one instalment per year for ten years. The property and assets on which tax may be paid in this way are unsold houses, land, buildings, some types of shares and the net value of a business or an interest in a business after deduction of business relief. These assets and properties are listed on pages 6 and 7 on form IHT400 in *column B*. The total value of the assets on which you may pay the tax by instalments is on form IHT400, box 95, plus box 97 + box 99 (if any) .

As soon as any of the property or assets are sold you will have to pay all the remaining tax. If you choose to pay tax by instalments on these assets you will have to pay interest on the outstanding tax.

19	Property and assets on which instalments of tax may be available (form IHT400, box 95 + box 103).	£

20	Value of property and assets shown in **column B** of form IHT400 which have been sold or on which you wish to pay the tax now and not pay by instalments (these may be assets at boxes 49, 51, 66, 67, 68, 69, 70 or 71). Enter the total of these assets which may have been sold and which you wish to pay the tax on now.	£

21	Value of property and assets shown in **column B** of form IHT400 on which the tax is being paid by instalments (box 19 *minus* box 20). If the answer is '0', enter '0' in box 26 and go to box 39)	£

Instalments due now

You only need to work out the tax that is being paid by instalments if the due date for the first instalment has passed or is less than 30 days away. Otherwise you can miss out boxes 22 to 38 and go straight to box 39. The first instalment of tax is due on the last day of the sixth month after the date of death. For example, the deceased died on 17 July 2007, the due date for the payment of the first instalment is 31 January 2008. The table of due dates below will help you to work out the due date.

Month of death	Due date
January	31 July
February	31 August
March	30 September
April	31 October
May	30 November
June	31 December
July	31 January
August	28/29 February
September	31 March
October	30 April
November	31 May
December	30 June

22	What is the instalment due date? *DD MM YYYY*

23	Has the instalment due date passed or is it less than 30 days away?

No   Write '0' in box 24 and then go to box 39

Yes   Go to box 24

24	How many of the 10 instalments are due now?

25	Box 21 ÷ box 6

26	Box 25 x box 18. This is the tax that may be paid by instalments before any double taxation relief is deducted.	£

27	Did the form IHT400 include any unsold foreign houses, land, businesses or control holdings? (form IHT400, box 97)

No   Copy the figure from box 26 into box 36. Continue from box 37

Yes   Read the information about double taxation relief on the next page

Double taxation relief

If foreign tax equivalent to Inheritance Tax was paid on the value of foreign assets, double taxation relief may be due if there is a double taxation convention between the UK and the other country. If there is no convention, we may still be able to give 'unilateral relief'. You can find out more in our customer guide, go to **www.hmrc.gov.uk/inheritancetax/**

If you wish to claim double taxation or unilateral relief, enclose with form IHT400 a 'certificate of tax paid' from the overseas tax authority, showing the amount of foreign tax paid. We may ask further questions about the claim after the Grant is issued. You must also fill in schedule IHT417 *Foreign assets* detailing the assets outside the UK.

28 Is double taxation relief due on the unsold foreign houses, land, businesses and control holdings of shares?

No ☐   *Copy the figure from box 26 into box 36. Continue from box 37*

Yes ☐   *Go to box 29*

29 Value of **unsold** foreign houses, land, businesses and control holdings on which foreign tax has been paid (form IHT400, box 97, £ sterling)   £ _____

30 Inheritance Tax on the chargeable estate (copy from box 18)   £ _____ . ☐☐

31 Total chargeable estate (copy from box 6)   £ _____

32 Box 30 ÷ box 31   ☐ . ☐☐☐☐

33 Box 29 x box 32   £ _____ . ☐☐

34 Foreign tax paid on the unsold foreign houses, land, businesses and control holdings (£ sterling)   £ _____ . ☐☐

35 The relief is the **lower** of boxes 33 and 34. Write the lower amount in here.   £ _____ . ☐☐

36 Net tax to be paid by instalments (box 26 *minus* box 35). If no double taxation relief is being deducted, copy the value from box 26 into here   £ _____ . ☐☐

37 Divide the amount in box 36 by 10 to work out how much each of the 10 instalments of tax should be. Enter the answer here.   £ _____ . ☐☐

38 Tax that may be paid by instalments that is being paid now Multiply the amount in box 37 by the number of instalments that are due now (box 24). Enter the answer here. Go to box 39.   £ _____ . ☐☐

Double taxation relief – Example 2

29 Value of **unsold** foreign houses, land, businesses and control holdings on which foreign tax has been paid (form IHT400, box 97, £ sterling)   £ 20,000

£12,000 ÷ £330,000 = 0.0364

30 Inheritance Tax on the chargeable estate (copy from box 18)   £ 12,000 . 0 0

0.0364 x £20,000 = £728

31 Total chargeable estate (copy from box 6)   £ 330,000

32 Box 30 ÷ box 31   0 . 0 3 6 4

The foreign tax paid was £2,000 so enter that figure in box 34.

33 Box 29 x box 32   £ 728 . 0 0

34 Foreign tax paid on the unsold foreign houses, land, businesses and control holdings (£ sterling)   £ 2,000 . 0 0

35 The relief is the **lower** of boxes 33 and 34. Write the lower amount in here.   £ 728 . 0 0

Compare the two figures in boxes 33 and 34. The double taxation relief due is the lower of the figures in boxes 33 and 34. £728 is lower than £2,000 so £728 is the double taxation relief on the unsold foreign houses, land and buildings. Enter that figure in box 35.

Tax that is not being paid by instalments

Inheritance Tax may only be paid by instalments on unsold houses, land, businesses and on certain types of shares. The Inheritance Tax on all sold houses, land, businesses, shares and all other types of assets, such as bank accounts and household and personal goods must be paid when you send in this form. You can also choose to pay all of the tax now.

39 Property and assets on which instalments are not available (IHT400, box 94 + IHT400, box 102 + IHT400 Calculation, box 20). If the answer is 0, write '0' in box 41 and go to box 53.
£

40 Box 39 ÷ box 6

41 Box 40 x box 18. This is the tax that may not be paid by instalments before any double taxation relief is deducted.
£

42 Did the form IHT400 include any sold foreign houses, land, businesses and control holdings (form IHT400, box 97) or other foreign assets (form IHT400, box 98)?

No   *Copy the figure from box 41 into box 53, then continue from box 54*

Yes   *Read the information about double taxation relief on page 4 then go to box 43*

Double taxation relief

See the note about double taxation relief at the top of page 4.

43 Is double taxation relief due on the sold foreign houses, land, businesses and control holdings, and other foreign assets?

No   *Copy the figure from box 41 into box 53, then continue from box 54.*

Yes   *Go to box 44.*

For an example of how to work out double taxation relief, see Example 2 on page 4

44 Value of any **sold** foreign houses, land, businesses and control holdings (form IHT400, box 97) on which foreign tax has been paid. (£ sterling)
£

45 Value of other foreign assets on which foreign tax has been paid (form IHT400, box 98, £ sterling)
£

46 Total foreign property on which the tax is not being paid by instalments (box 44 + box 45, £ sterling)
£

47 Inheritance Tax on the chargeable estate (copy from box 18)
£

48 Total chargeable estate (copy from box 6)
£

49 Box 47 ÷ box 48

50 Box 49 x box 46
£

51 Foreign tax paid on the foreign property and assets on which the tax is **not** being paid by instalments (£ sterling)
£

52 The relief is the **lower** of boxes 50 and 51. Write the lower amount in here.
£

53 Net tax that is not being paid by instalments
- Box 41 minus box 52
- If no double taxation relief is being deducted, copy the value from box 41 into box 53. (If box 41 was 0, enter '0' in here)
£

Interest

Inheritance Tax is due to be paid on the last day of the sixth month after the date of death. Interest will be due even if you have not got a Grant by then. Interest will also be due even if we have not contacted you or anybody else (for example, the trustees of a trust or someone who received a gift from the deceased). The law says that interest will be added to any unpaid tax after this date. Interest is not a penalty, it compensates the Exchequer for the delay in receiving the money due to it. If you pay too much tax, we pay interest on the repayment to you.

Interest starts on the first day of the seventh month after the date of death. For example, if the deceased died on 17 July 2007, interest will be due from 1 February 2008 on all unpaid tax whatever the reason the tax has not been paid. The table below will tell you the date that interest starts.

Month of death	Interest starts from
January	1 August
February	1 September
March	1 October
April	1 November
May	1 December
June	1 January
July	1 February
August	1 March
September	1 April
October	1 May
November	1 June
December	1 July

54 What is the date interest starts? *01 MM YYYY*

> `0` `1` ☐ ☐ ☐ ☐ ☐ ☐ ☐ ☐

If the tax is being paid after this date you must add interest to the tax being paid.

55 Has the date at box 54 passed, or is it likely to pass before you pay the tax?

No ☐   *Enter '0' in boxes 57, 58, 60 and 61 then go to box 62*

Yes ☐   *Go to box 56 to work out the interest due*

Working out interest using the online interest calculator

56 The easiest way to work out the interest due is to use the interest calculator which you can find on our website, go to **www.hmrc.gov.uk/tools/inheritancetax/interest-rate-calculator.htm**

If you use the interest calculator you should work out the interest on the tax that is being paid by instalments (box 38) and the tax that is not being paid by instalments (box 53).

Do you wish to use the interest calculator to work out the interest due?

No ☐   *Go to the IHT400 Helpsheet 'Working out the interest on Inheritance Tax payments' and follow the instructions there*

Yes ☐   *Go to box 57*

57 Interest on tax that is *not* being paid by instalments

You only need to do this calculation if the figure in box 53 is greater than 0.

- For the interest calculator, go to **www.hmrc.gov.uk/tools/inheritancetax/interest-rate-calculator.htm**
- In the 'start date for interest' box on the calculator enter the date from box 54.
- In the 'end date for interest' box on the calculator enter the date you expect to be sending in the IHT400.
- In the 'Inheritance Tax owed' box enter the amount of tax not being paid by instalments from box 53.
- Use the 'calculate' button to find out how much interest is due.

- Enter the amount of interest in here.   £ [   ] · [ ][ ]

58 Interest on tax that is being paid by instalments

You only need to do this calculation if the figure in box 38 is greater than 0.

- For the interest calculator, go to **www.hmrc.gov.uk/tools/inheritancetax/interest-rate-calculator.htm**
- In the 'start date for interest' box on the calculator enter the day after the date the most recent instalment fell due.
  If there is only one instalment due (the figure in box 24 is '1'), this date will be the date in box 54.
  If two instalments are due, the start date will be one year on from the date in box 54 and so on.
- In the 'end date for interest' box on the calculator enter the date you expect to be sending in the form IHT400.
- In the 'Inheritance Tax owed' box enter the amount of tax being paid by instalments from box 38.
- Use the 'Calculate' button to find out how much interest is due.

- Enter the amount of interest in here.   £ [   ] · [ ][ ]

59 Is '1' the number in box 24?

No [ ]   *Go to box 60*

Yes [ ]   *Enter '0' in box 60 and go to box 61*

60 Additional interest on tax that is being paid by instalments when more than one instalment is due

When more than one instalment of tax is due, you will have to work out an additional amount of interest unless the instalments of tax are interest-free.

Interest-free instalments

Instalments of tax are interest-free for certain types of assets as long as the instalments are paid on time.
The assets on which the instalments are interest-free are:
- shares or securities, except shares in an investment or property company, which will only qualify if the company is
  - a holding company of companies, which are not investment or property companies
  - a market maker or discount house in the UK
- a business or interest in a business carried on for gain
- land which qualifies for agricultural relief
- timber.

It would be a very unusual situation if you need to work out the interest on these types of assets where the instalments are being paid late. The IHT400 Helpsheet 'Working out the interest on Inheritance Tax payments' will explain what to do.

- If the instalments are not interest-free (and most will not be). For the interest calculator,
  go to **www.hmrc.gov.uk/tools/inheritancetax/interest-rate-calculator.htm**
- In the 'start date for interest' box on the calculator enter the date from box 54.
- In the 'end date for interest' box on the calculator enter the date the most recent instalment became due.
- In the 'Inheritance Tax owed' box enter the total amount of tax being paid by instalments from box 36.
- Use the 'Calculate' button to find out how much interest is due.

Enter the amount of interest here. (This is the figure for box 60.)   £ [   ] · [ ][ ]

For example, the deceased died on 6 July 2005. The date tax is due is 31 January 2006. The tax being paid by instalments is £10,000. The first instalment of £1,000 is due on 31 January 2006, the second instalment on 31 January 2007 and so on. The application for a Grant was made on 18 June 2007, so that two instalments had to be paid at that time. The 'end' date in this example would be 31 January 2007.

In the 'Inheritance Tax owed' box enter the total amount of tax being paid by instalments (from box 36). In this example this will be £10,000.

61	Total interest on tax being paid by instalments (box 58 + box 60)	£
62	Total tax and interest payable now where the tax is being paid by instalments (box 38 + box 61)	£
63	Total tax and interest which is not being paid by instalments (box 53 + box 57)	£
64	**Total Inheritance Tax and interest on the estate being paid now** (box 62 + box 63)	£

Tax payable on gifts and lifetime transfers

The tax and interest shown at box 64 is the tax and interest which is payable now in order for you to be able to obtain a grant of representation. Depending on the circumstances of the estate, there may be more tax and interest to pay by the person(s) who received lifetime gifts from the deceased. We may also ask the person(s) who received the gifts for more details of the gifts on a separate account.

If the deceased made lifetime gifts which were over the Inheritance Tax nil rate band or gifts with reservation, further tax will be payable and we will send calculations of the tax when you have sent this form to us. If you want to work this out for yourself, you can find out how lifetime gifts are taxed on death in our customer guide, go to **www.hmrc.gov.uk/inheritancetax/**

Taper relief

If there is additional tax to pay on lifetime gifts, taper relief may be available. This will apply in the following circumstances:
- the total value of gifts must be more than the Inheritance Tax nil rate band
- the gifts must have been made between three and seven years before the deceased died.

The relief reduces the amount of tax payable on a gift, not the value of the gift itself.

You can find more information on taper relief in our customer guide, go to **www.hmrc.gov.uk/inheritancetax/**

Trusts

If the deceased benefited from any assets held in trust shown on form IHT418 and the trustees have not paid the tax with this account, further tax will be due. We will send a calculation of the tax to the trustees named on the form IHT418.

If there are amendments made to the value of the trust assets or the value of the deceased's estate this will affect both the tax due on the trust assets and the tax due on the deceased's estate. If this is the case, we will send you further calculations of tax.

What to do when you have filled in this form

If you are filling in this form without the help of a solicitor or other adviser, send the form in with your form IHT400 so that we can see how you have worked out the tax. Continue filling in the form IHT400 from box 118.

If you are a solicitor or other professional adviser, you do not need to send in this form if you do not want to, but if you have included an amount of successive charges relief in box 17 or double taxation relief in boxes 35 or 52, send this form to us with the form IHT400 so that we can see how these reliefs were worked out.

Claim to transfer unused nil rate band

Schedule IHT402

When to use this form

Fill in this form if:
- the deceased died on or after 9 October 2007, and
- their spouse or civil partner died before them, and
- when the spouse or civil partner died their estate did not use up all of the nil rate band available to it, and
- you want to transfer the unused amount to the deceased's estate.

Filling in this form

You will need to find out who was the executor or administrator of the spouse or civil partner's estate as you will need information from them to complete this form.

Make full enquiries so that the figures you give and the statements you make are correct.

Information you will need

You will need to know:
- who benefited under the Will or intestacy of the spouse or civil partner and what the beneficiaries were entitled to receive
- whether any assets, such as jointly owned assets or assets in trust were part of the estate of the spouse or civil partner, and
- whether the spouse or civil partner had made any gifts or other transfers within seven years before the date of their death that were chargeable on their death (see note 5 on page 4).

The executor or administrator of the spouse or civil partner should be able to help you find out this information.

You should obtain copies of the documents listed aside and use them alongside any records that exist about the spouse or civil partner's estate.

If there are no records, you should try and find out the information about the spouse or civil partner's estate from others who might know, for example, the solicitor who acted for the estate, the executors or administrators, other family members, close friends.

Name of deceased (person who has died now)

Date of death DD MM YYYY

IHT reference number (if known)

Documents to be sent with this form

You must send photocopies of the following documents with this form:
- copy of the grant of representation (Confirmation in Scotland) to the estate of the spouse or civil partner (if no grant has been taken out, please provide a copy of the death certificate – see the note on page 4 about obtaining copies of certificates)
- if the spouse or civil partner left a Will, a copy of it
- if a Deed of Variation or other similar document was executed to change the people who inherited the estate of the spouse or civil partner, a copy of it.

Deadline

You must send this form to us no later than 24 months after the end of the month in which the deceased died.
For example, if the spouse or civil partner died on 15 May 2006, and the deceased died on 10 October 2007, you would need to send this form to us by 31 October 2009.

Help

For more information or help:
- go to www.hmrc.gov.uk/inheritancetax/
- phone our Helpline on 0845 30 20 900
  – if calling from outside the UK, phone +44 115 974 3009).

Spouse or civil partner's details

Fill in this section with details of the spouse or civil partner who died first.

1 Spouse or civil partner's name

Title - enter MR, MRS, MISS, MS or other title

Surname or family name

First name(s)

2 Date of death DD MM YYYY

3 Last known permanent address

Postcode

4 Date of marriage or civil partnership DD MM YYYY

5 Place of marriage or civil partnership (see note 6, page 4)

IHT402   Page 1   HMRC 09/08

Figure B1.2 IHT402 claim form

Spouse or civil partner's details continued

6 Did the spouse or civil partner who died first leave a Will?

Yes ☐ *enclose a copy of the Will and any codicils, instruments of variation or disclaimers*

No ☐

7 What was the value of the spouse or civil partner's estate?
(see note 1 on page 4)

£ [   ]

8 Was a grant of representation (Confirmation in Scotland) obtained for the estate of the spouse or civil partner who died first?

Yes ☐ *enclose a copy of the grant*

No ☐ *enclose a copy of the death certificate*

Spouse or civil partner's nil rate band

Fill in this section to work out the available nil rate band for the estate of the spouse or civil partner who died first.

9 Inheritance Tax, Capital Transfer Tax or Estate Duty nil rate band in force at the date of death *(see note 2 on page 4)*

£ [   ]

10 Total chargeable value of gifts and other transfers of value made in the seven years before the date of death *(see notes 3 and 5 on page 4)*

£ [   ]

11 Nil rate band available against the estate of the spouse or civil partner who died first (box 9 *minus* box 10)

£ [   ]

Spouse or civil partner's estate

Fill in this section with details of the estate of the spouse or civil partner who died first. Enter the value of the assets at their date of death after deduction of exemptions or reliefs.

12 Legacies and assets passing under Will or intestacy of the spouse or civil partner who died first. Do not include legacies and assets that passed to the deceased who has died now *(see note 3 on page 4)*

Legacy/asset	Value £
Continue on a separate sheet if necessary	£

13 Share of assets jointly owned by the spouse or civil partner who died first, excluding assets that passed to the deceased who has died now *(see note 3 on page 4)*

£ [   ]

14 Assets held in trust to which the spouse or civil partner who died first was entitled to benefit *(see note 3 on page 4)*

£ [   ]

15 Gifts with reservation made by the spouse or civil partner who died first *(see note 3 on page 4)*

£ [   ]

16 Total chargeable estate of the spouse or civil partner (box 12 + box 13 + box 14 + box 15)

£ [   ]

Transferable nil rate band

17	Nil rate band available for transfer (box 11 *minus* box 16)	£
18	Percentage by which to increase the nil rate band available on the deceased's death (box 17 *divided by* box 9 and *multiplied by* 100). *Use four decimal places,* **do not** *round up*	☐☐☐ . ☐☐☐☐ %
19	Nil rate band at the date of the deceased's death (the person who has died now) - *see IHT400 Rates and tables*	£
20	Transferable nil rate band (box 19 *multiplied by* the box 18 percentage) *Round up to the nearest £*	£

Example

- If the percentage in box 18 is 66.6666%, and
- the nil rate band in box 19 is £300,000
- then the figure to enter in box 20 would be £300,000 x 66.6666%

  (or £300,000 x 66.6666 ÷ 100) = £200,000 rounded up to the nearest £

Exemptions and reliefs

21	List any exemptions or reliefs, other than spouse or civil partner exemption, taken into account in arriving at the values in boxes 10, 12, 13, 14 or 15 *(see note 4 on page 4)*

Box number	Exemptions or relief taken into account – *state amount and type* (*For example, box 14 Charity exemption £3,000*)

Pensions

Only answer question 22 where the spouse or civil partner who died first died on or after 6 April 2006.

22	Was the spouse or civil partner in receipt of a pension from:

- an Alternatively Secured Pension, or
- a pension scheme or annuity from which unauthorised payments were made after their death? No ☐   Yes ☐

If you have answered Yes, the calculation of the percentage to increase the deceased's nil rate band is complex. You may use the figure you worked out in box 20 provisionally. We will recalculate the percentage once you have sent us the form IHT400 for the deceased's estate.

If the spouse or civil partner was domiciled in Scotland at the date of death

Only answer question 23 where the spouse or civil partner who died first was domiciled in Scotland.

23	Was there anyone who was entitled to claim the legitim fund? No ☐ Yes ☐

If you have answered Yes, the calculation of the percentage to increase the deceased's nil rate band will depend on whether a claim for legitim is made. You may use the figure you worked out in box 20 provisionally. We will discuss the percentage once you have sent us the form IHT400 for the deceased's estate.

Notes

Your claim to transfer unused inheritance tax nil rate band

Where most or all of an estate passes to someone's surviving spouse or civil partner, those assets are generally exempt from Inheritance Tax. This means that most or all of the nil rate band available on the first death is not used.

The amount of the unused nil rate band can be transferred to the survivor of the marriage or civil partnership to increase the value of the nil rate band available on their death.

Since the transfer does not happen automatically, you must fill in this form and make a claim to transfer it. The claim must be made when the second spouse or civil partner dies.

These notes explain how the transfer works and where you can find information to help with filling in this form.

How the transfer works

On the deceased's death, the nil rate band that is available to their estate is increased by the percentage of the nil rate band that was unused when their spouse or civil partner died.

For example:

- A spouse or civil partner died and the nil rate band was £250,000.
- They left legacies totalling £125,000 to their children with the remainder to the surviving spouse or civil partner. The legacies to the children would use up one-half of the nil rate band, leaving the other half (50%) unused.
- In our example, on the deceased's death, the nil rate band is £300,000. So, their nil rate band would be increased by 50% to £450,000.
- If the deceased's estate did not exceed £450,000 there would be no Inheritance Tax to pay on their death. If it did, there would be Inheritance Tax to pay on the value above that figure.

Obtaining copies of grants of representation and Wills

- England and Wales:
  Phone **020 7947 7000**, or
  go to **www.hmcourts-service.gov.uk**
- Scotland:
  Phone **0131 247 2850**
- Northern Ireland:
  Phone **028 9023 5111**

Copies of death, marriage and or civil partnership certificates are available from the General Register Office

- in England and Wales:
  go to **www.gro.gov.uk**
- in Scotland:
  go to **www.gro-scotland.gov.uk**
- in Northern Ireland:
  go to **www.groni.gov.uk**

Spouse or civil partner's estate – notes to help you fill in this form

1 You can find the net value of the estate on the copy of the grant of representation (if one was taken out) or by adding together all the assets in the estate and deducting any liabilities.

2 For the IHT nil rate band in force at the date the spouse or civil partner died, please refer to form IHT400 Rates and tables. If it does not go back far enough, the rates for earlier years are available from:
   - **www.hmrc.gov.uk/inheritancetax/** or
   - the Probate and Inheritance Tax Helpline on **0845 30 20 900**.
     – If calling from outside the UK,
       phone **+44 115 974 3009**.

3 When filling in box 10 and boxes 12 to 15, you should include the value that was chargeable to tax. That is, the value after the deduction of exemptions and reliefs.

Spouse exemption where the first spouse died before 22 March 1972

Under Estate Duty there was no spouse exemption. All legacies, irrespective of the recipient and value should be included in box 12.

Spouse exemption where the first spouse died between 22 March 1972 and 12 November 1974 inclusive

During this period spouse exemption was limited to £15,000 so all legacies that passed to the deceased in excess of £15,000 should be included in box 12.

Spouse exemption after 12 November 1974

After that date there is no limit to spouse exemption unless the deceased was domiciled in the UK and the surviving spouse was not domiciled in the UK, when it is limited to £55,000. If that is the case, legacies that passed to the deceased in excess of £55,000 should be included in box 12.

4 List any exemptions or reliefs (other than spouse or civil partner exemption) you have taken into account in box 21. If you have been unable to find out whether or not any exemptions or relief applied when the spouse or civil partner died, leave this box blank.

   For more information about the exemptions and reliefs that apply to Inheritance Tax, refer to IHT400 Notes.

   If you are including assets which might qualify for an exemption or relief on this form, but are not sure whether the exemption or relief would have applied, tell us. We will discuss with you whether or not the exemption or relief might have applied.

5 For deaths between 27 July 1981 and 17 March 1986 you will need to know whether the spouse or civil partner had made any gifts or other transfers within **ten** years before the date of their death that were chargeable on their death.

6 Name of building, church or register office and locality.

Appendix C

Estate accounts

This appendix contains an example of a set of estate accounts as a guide to what is in such accounts. This is not a statutory requirement of how estate accounts should be laid out, but a suggestion of what might be included. The administration of each estate can vary depending on the content of a person's will and the type of assets held in the estate, and so the accounts will be constructed accordingly to make sure that they are as clear, concise and correct as possible.

Estate accounts would usually include the following:

- A schedule of the capital assets and liabilities at the date of death. This would account for the total value of the estate at death.

- An income account. This would give details of all income such as interest, dividends, rents and so on, received on assets since the date of death, together with deductions for any income tax due on income received gross.

- A capital account. This would also include any inheritance tax, administration expenses and pecuniary legacies that have been deducted from the value of the estate before any residuary distributions can be made.

- A distribution account. This would show how the net estate has passed to the various beneficiaries.

The Estate of

Patsy Wood (deceased)

who died on 1 January 2010

The Estate of Patsy Wood (deceased)

Report to the Executors

We have prepared the accounts from 1 January 2010 for the period of administration from the records and information supplied to us by the Executors.

We have not carried out an audit of the records and information.

Accounts approved:

....

Date   ....

....

Date   ....

Executors

The Estate of Patsy Wood (deceased)

Synopsis of the Will

Testator	Patsy Wood	
Date of death	Friday, January 01, 2010	
Date of probate	Monday, May 03, 2010	
Executors	Gillian Veneto	
	Briony Calabria	

Specific Gifts	Gillian Veneto	Jewel box and jewellery
	Briony Calabria	Antique furniture

Pecuniary Legacies **(free of all taxes)**	Gillian Veneto	£500
	Briony Calabria	£500
	Nicholas Apulia	£500
	The Chapel of St Peter and Paul in Marche	£1,000
	NSPCC	£1,000
	RSPB	£1,000
	RNLI	£1,000
	RSPCA	£1,000

Residue **(after expenses and IHT)**	Gillian Veneto	)
	Briony Calabria	)
	Nicholas Apulia	) In equal shares, absolutely
	Amy Basilicata	)
	Simon Lazio	)
	Abigail Piedmont	)
	Hana Lombardy	)

The Estate of Patsy Wood (deceased)

Schedule of assets at the date of death

			£	£
Assets				
	Property:			
		House		368,000.00
	Personal possessions:			
		Jewellery box and jewellery	2,950.00	
		Antique furniture	650.00	
		Clothes	100.00	3,700.00
	Shares and unit trusts:			
	100	Palermo Ltd shares	6,500.00	
	300	Rome Ltd shares	4,900.00	
	7246	Turin Ltd shares	3,920.00	
	1610.33	Naples Fund Management units	9,630.00	
	678.11	Bologna portfolio management units	8,900.00	
		Verona Ltd shares	3,850.00	
				37,700.00
		Malthouse Ltd shares (unquoted investment company shares)		1,000.00
		Binks Ltd shares		350.00
	Bank and building society accounts:			
		Lloyds TSB current account	6,000.00	
		Barclays bond	60,000.00	
		Santander flexible savings	350.00	
		Barclays bonus savings	1,000.00	
		Barclays tracker	15,000.00	
		Britannia	90.00	
		Alliance and Leicester	2,500.00	
				84,940.00
	ISA			
		ISA	4,080.82	
	National Savings:			
		Guaranteed income bonds	35,100.00	
		Income bond, pensioners	10,000.00	
		Investment account	6,000.00	
		NS income bond	3,000.00	
				58,180.82
	Other			
		Refund due on insurance	50.00	
		Refund due on Sky TV	25.00	
		State pension owing to Patsy	210.00	
		HMRC tax refund	900.00	
		Oxfordshire County Council	170.00	
		British Gas refund	40.00	
		Electricity refund	40.00	
		Thames Water refund	25.00	
				1,460.00
Gross Estate				555,330.82
Less:				
Liabilities				
		Funeral expenses	3,184.00	
		Gardener's wages	250.00	
		Cleaner's wages	120.00	
		Professional fees	2,250.00	
		Local newspaper	60.00	
		London Gazette	75.00	
				-5,939.00
Net estate				549,391.82

The Estate of Patsy Wood (deceased)

Inheritance Tax (IHT)

	£
<u>Net estate</u>	549,391.82
Less legacies to charity	-5000
Less nil band for 2009/10	-325,000
	219,391.82
Tax due at 40% £ <u>87,756.73</u>	

The Estate of Patsy Wood (deceased)

Income Account

			£	£
Assets				
	Property:			
		House		0.00
	Personal possessions:			
		Antique furniture		0.00
	Shares and unit trusts:			
	100	Palermo Ltd shares	202.00	
	300	Rome Ltd shares	0.00	
	7246	Turin Ltd shares	609.00	
				811.00
	1610.33	Naples Fund Management units	30.00	
	678.11	Bologna portfolio management units	77.00	
		Verona Ltd shares	105.00	
				212.00
		Malthouse Ltd shares (unquoted investment company shares)		0.00
		Binks Ltd shares		0.00
	Bank and building society accounts:			
		Lloyds TSB current account	0.00	
		Barclays bond	0.00	
		Santander flexible savings	0.00	
		Barclays bonus savings	0.00	
		Barclays tracker	0.00	
		Britannia	0.00	
		Alliance and Leicester	40.00	
		ISA	0.00	
		Natwest account for the executors (net)	200.00	
				240.00
	National Savings:			
		Guaranteed income bonds	0.00	
		Income bond, pensioners	0.00	
		Investment account interest	250.00	
		NS income bond	0.00	
				250.00
Total income received				1,513.00
	Income tax due on the dividends - deducted at source and tax neutral		0.00	
	Income tax on the bank and building society accounts (received net of tax)		0.00	
	Income tax due on National savings investment interest, (received gross)		50.00	
				-50.00
Net income				1,463.00

The Estate of Patsy Wood (deceased)

Capital Account

	£	£
Net estate		549,391.82
Add:		
Gains on the sale of assets (per capital gains tax computations)	27,367.00	
Income received since death (per income account)	1,513.00	
		28,880.00
Less:		
Inheritance tax	87,756.73	
Capital gains tax (per capital gains tax computations)	2,950.38	
Income tax payable to HMRC	50.00	
Jewellery box and jewellery to Gillian	2,950.00	
Furniture to Briony	650.00	
Clothes to Oxfam	100.00	
Cash Legacies (according to the will)	6,500.00	
		-100,957.11
Net capital		477,314.71
Represented by:		
Distribution account		477,314.71

The Estate of Patsy Wood (deceased)

Distribution Account

	£
Net capital	477,314.71

<u>Available for distribution as residue</u>	477,314.71

	Total share of residue	Malthouse Ltd shares - distributed to the beneficiaries rather than sold	**Still to receive**
	£		£
Gillian Veneto	68,187.82	142.86	68,044.96
Briony Calabria	68,187.82	142.86	68,044.96
Nicholas Apulia	68,187.82	142.86	68,044.96
Amy Basilicata	68,187.82	142.86	68,044.96
Simon Lazio	68,187.82	142.86	68,044.96
Abigail Piedmont	68,187.82	142.86	68,044.96
Hana Lombardy	68,187.82	142.86	68,044.96
	477,314.71	1,000.00	476,314.71

Appendix D

Further help

There are many sources of information for people who are dealing with an estate or coping with the death of an individual.

Direct.gov.uk Use the link to the government website, www.direct.gov.uk to access a vast source of information surrounding estates and probate.

Community Legal Service Direct Provides free information direct to the public on legal problems. Call 0845 345 4 345. If you qualify for legal aid, you can also get free advice from a legal adviser about benefits and tax credits, debt, education, employment and housing. You can also find a local legal adviser or solicitor. Go to www.clsdirect.org.uk to find out more.

Cruse Bereavement Care The national telephone helpline 0844 477 9400 is answered by trained volunteers. They should be able to advise you about benefits available to bereaved people, as well as offering support to those greatly affected by someone's death. Email: helpline@cruse.org.uk or visit the website www.crusebereavementcare.org.uk

Probate registries There are probate registries in cities and larger towns, where the application for probate will need to be made. There is a list of probate registries on the Courts Service website: www.hmcourts-service.gov.uk/infoabout/civil/probate/registries.htm

The Probate and Inheritance Tax Helpline The helpline will tell you where your nearest registry is, and can also answer questions and send you information about applying for probate or letters of administration. Telephone: 0845 302 0900

The Society of Trust and Estate Practitioners (STEP) Members of this organisation are knowledgeable in the area of estates and trusts and it is possible to locate a member using the STEP website (www.step.org)

HM Revenue and Customs for England and Wales

HM Revenue & Customs
Ferrers House, PO Box 38
Castle Meadow Road
Nottingham
NG2 1BB
Tel: 0845 302 0900

Website: www.hmrc.gov.uk

Law Society This is a useful source of information if you wish to find a solicitor. Phone: 020 7242 1222 or go to www.lawsociety.org.uk

The London Gazette Tel: 0870 600 3322 or website: www.gazettes-online.co.uk

Citizens Advice Bureau (England and Wales) Your local Citizens Advice Bureau is listed in the phone book. Website: www.citizensadvice.org.uk

The Community Legal Service Set up to help you find the right legal information and advice to solve your problems. You can get help through a national network of organisations including Citizens Advice Bureaux, law centres, independent advice centres and thousands of high street solicitors. All of these services meet quality standards set by the Legal Services Commission. Many of the organisations offer some or all of their services for free. If you cannot afford to pay for advice you may be eligible for financial support through the Community Legal Service Fund (Legal Aid). You can order leaflets about funding from the LSC Leaflet line on 0845 3000 343. You can use the directory on the Community Legal Advice website www.communitylegaladvice.org.uk to find details of quality assured advice providers.

Legal Services Commission (LSC) The Community Legal Service and the Community Legal Service Fund are managed by the Legal Services Commission. To find out more, go to www.legalservices.gov.uk or look in the phone book.

Natural Death Centre www.naturaldeath.org.uk

Citizens Advice Bureau (Scotland) http://www.cas.org.uk

Scottish government

Civil Law Division
Area 2W, St Andrew's House

Regent Road
EDINBURGH
EH1 3DG
Tel: 0131 244 3581

National Association of Funeral Directors

618 Warwick Road
Solihull
B91 1AA
Tel: 0121 711 1343
Email: info@nafd.org.uk
Website: www.nafd.org.uk

HM Revenue & Customs in Scotland

Meldrum House
15 Drumsheugh Gardens
Edinburgh
EH3 7UG
Tel: 0845 302 0900
Website: www.hmrc.gov.uk/inheritancetax

Law Society of Scotland

26 Drumsheugh Gardens
Edinburgh
EH3 7YR
Tel: 0131 226 7411
Website: www.lawscot.org.uk

Cruse Bereavement Care Scotland

Riverview House
Friarton Road
Perth
PH2 8DF
Tel: 01738 444 178
Email: info@crusescotland.org.uk
Website: www.crusescotland.org.uk

General Register Office for Scotland

New Register House
3 West Register Street
Edinburgh
EH1 3YT
Tel: 0131 334 0380
Website: www.gro-scotland.gov.uk

Northern Ireland Court Service

Communications Group
Laganside House
23–27 Oxford House
Belfast BT1 3LA
Tel: 028 9032 8954
Textphone 028 9041 2920
Email: communicationsgroup@courtsni.gov.uk

Coroners Service for Northern Ireland

May's Chambers
73 May Street
Belfast
BT1 3JL
Tel: 028 9044 6800
Email: coronersoffice@courtsni.gov.uk
Website: www.coronersni.gov.uk

Registrar of Births, Deaths and Marriages: General Register Office (Northern Ireland)

Oxford House
Chichester Street
Belfast
BT1 4HH
Tel: 028 9025 2000

Probate and IHT Helpline (Northern Ireland)

Tel: 0845 302 0900

HM Revenue and Customs in Northern Ireland

HM Revenue & Customs
Level 5
Millennium House
17-25 Great Victoria Street
BT2 7BN
Tel: 0845 302 0900
Website: www.hmrc.gov.uk

Glossary

Abatement describes distributing the legacies of a will in proportion to original legacies, if there is insufficient funds to pay out all of the legacies

Administrator The person who deals with (administers) the estate of a person who has died intestate (without a will)

Assets of the deceased All of the property and possessions belonging to the person that has died, such as bank account funds, land and buildings and furniture

Beneficiary An individual that benefits from the estate of a person that has died. A beneficiary can be a named individual in the will, or from intestacy if no will has been left

Bequest A gift of a particular object (for example, an item of jewellery)

Capital gains tax (CGT) A tax due on the disposal of capital assets

Child In will or intestacy matters, the children of the person who has died include adopted children and illegitimate children (children born to parents who were unmarried), but not their stepchildren (unless they are specifically mentioned)

Civil partner A person who has formed a civil partnership with someone else

Civil partnership The legal relationship existing between two civil partners who have registered their partnership in accordance with the Civil Partnership Act 2004, which came into force on 5 December 2005

Clearance certificate The personal representatives can apply for a clearance certificate using form IHT30 once they have supplied the necessary forms and paid all the inheritance tax and interest due

Codicil An amendment, or an addition to a will, usually in the form of an additional document

Common-law spouse and co-habitee An unmarried partner. This term has no legal force, although a partner who lived with the person who died for two years before their death may be able to claim a share of the estate

Confirmation The process of obtaining a grant of confirmation in Scotland. In England, Wales and Northern Ireland the equivalent is known as probate

Coroner The official from the coroner's office who may need to be consulted if a death is sudden or suspicious, and the coroner decides whether further investigation, an inquest, is necessary

Creditor A person or organisation that is owed value from the estate

Demise A lease of a house or flat

Devise A gift of a house or land

Discretionary trust A trust that is managed by the trustees where income and capital of the trust can be distributed to beneficiaries by the absolute discretion of the trustees only

Domicile The term used to describe the country which an individual believes to be their homeland

Donee A person who receives a gift

Donor A person who makes a gift of some of their assets

Estate All the assets and property of the person who has died, including houses, cars, investments, money and belongings

Excluded property The property of an individual that is not liable to inheritance tax, usually in cases where that individual is, or was, not domiciled in the UK

Executor The person appointed in the will to deal with the estate of a person who has died

Grant of letters of administration The grant that is obtained by the administrators when there is no will left by the deceased

Grant of probate The grant that is obtained by the executors when there is a will left by the deceased

Grant of representation This is a general term which includes grants of probate and grants of letters of administration

GWR and GWROB 'Gift with reservation of benefit'. Describes the fact that benefit is still being received from an asset, or wealth, that has been given away

Heritable property A Scottish term: any interest in land and things affixed to land

HMRC Her Majesty's Revenue and Customs

IHT Inheritance tax

Inheritance The acquisition of property from an estate

Inheritance tax The tax that may have to be paid when the total estate of a person who has died is more than a certain amount (£325,000 in 2010–11).

Interest in possession trust A trust managed by trustees where there is a life tenant who benefits from the income of the trust property

Intestate Where a person dies without having made a will

Intestacy An estate where the person died intestate

Insolvent estate An estate where the value is insufficient to cover the debts of the deceased

Issue All the descendants of a person (children, grandchildren, great-grandchildren and so on)

Legacy A gift, share, or benefit from a person's estate

Legal rights In Scotland, children and spouses have fixed legal rights to a share of a person's estate, even if there is a valid will and despite what their will says. Their legal rights, or 'legitim', are to a fixed share of moveable property, but not of heritable property. They arise on intestacy or as an alternative to any provision in the will. They may be accepted or, as is often the case, renounced

Letters of administration The document issued to the administrators by the Probate Registry to authorise them to deal with the estate

Liabilities All of the debts and amounts owed by the person who has died

Life interest The right to receive the income or benefit from a property or capital sum (but not to get the capital sum itself) for life

Living will A document drawn up which states a person's wishes in relation to treatments they feel they would want or not want in the event that they should lose mental capacity during their lifetime

Minor A person under 18

Moveable property A Scottish term to describe all property that is not heritable property

Nil rate band The value of an estate up to which inheritance tax is not payable

Partial intestacy Where some of the estate is to be distributed according to a will, with the remainder of the estate not being covered by the will and must be distributed according to intestacy

Pecuniary legacy A gift of a sum of money under a will

Personal chattels Belongings, including jewellery, furniture, wine, pictures, books and cars (but not money, investments, property or business assets)

Personal estate (personalty) All the investments and belongings of a person apart from land and buildings

Personal representative A general term for administrators and executors

Post mortem A medical examination of a deceased's body to find out the cause of death

Probate The term used when talking about applying for the right to deal with a deceased person's affairs. It is sometimes called 'administering the estate'

Probate of the will The document issued to executors by the probate registry to authorise them to deal with the estate

Probate registry A court within the Family Division of the High Court which deals with probate and administration matters. The principal registry is in London and there are district registries in other cities and some large towns

Prior rights Under intestacy in Scotland, a spouse has certain prior rights to benefit from the deceased's estate, including elements of both heritable and moveable property. These rights do not arise if there is a valid will

Real estate (realty) Land and buildings owned by a person

Remainderman The person who gets the property or capital sum after the death of the person holding a 'life interest'

Residue What is left to share out after all the debts, inheritance tax and specific bequests and legacies have been paid

Specific bequests Specific, particular items gifted by the will. They may be called 'specific legacies'

Testator A person who makes a will. Testatrix is sometimes used to mean a female will-maker

Will The legal document in which you say what will happen to your money and your possessions on your death

Index

Page numbers in *italics* denotes a figure/table

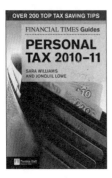

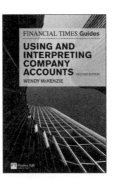

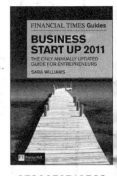
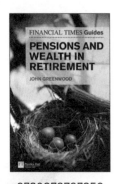
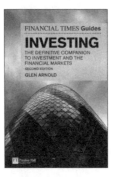

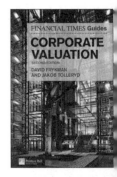